TANKS IN HELL

TANKS
IN HELL

A MARINE CORPS
TANK COMPANY
ON TARAWA

Oscar E. Gilbert & Romain Cansiere

CASEMATE
Philadelphia & Oxford

Published in the United States of America and Great Britain in 2015 by
CASEMATE PUBLISHERS
908 Darby Road, Havertown, PA 19083
and
10 Hythe Bridge Street, Oxford, OX1 2EW

ISBN 978-1-61200-303-0
Digital Edition: ISBN 978-1-61200-304-7

Cataloging-in-publication data is available from the Library of Congress and
the British Library.

10 9 8 7 6 5 4 3 2 1

Printed and bound in the United States of America.

For a complete list of Casemate titles please contact:

CASEMATE PUBLISHERS (US)
Telephone (610) 853-9131, Fax (610) 853-9146
E-mail: casemate@casematepublishing.com

CASEMATE PUBLISHERS (UK)
Telephone (01865) 241249, Fax (01865) 794449
E-mail: casemate-uk@casematepublishing.co.uk

CONTENTS

DEDICATION

To the officers and men of Charlie Company, First Corps Medium Tank Battalion and their families, and to Christiane.

ACKNOWLEDGMENTS

The effort to reconstruct the story of Charlie Company spanned nearly two decades.

Most of all we would like to acknowledge the help of the surviving veterans; they are listed individually in the "Later Life" section at the end of the book. Colonel Ed Bale (USMC, ret.) has been particularly patient with Ed Gilbert's innumerable questions over the course of a quarter-century or so. Dan Josefson shared photographs from his father's wartime album, and Ken Engstrom Sr. provided referrals to several veterans. John Oberg freely shared the results of his correspondence with veterans conducted over the course of many years. Hans Zeiger (http://generouspeople.blogspot.com/) provided family background information on Lieutenant Sloat, and additional contact information.

As usual, Annette Amerman and Kara Newcomer of the United States Marine Corps History Division at MCB Quantico provided immense help in locating documents and photographs, as did the staff of the National Archives II at College Park Maryland, particularly Molly Reed.

As always, Lieutenant Colonel Ken Estes (USMC, ret.) provided the authors with a trove of documents unearthed from many sources. Reagan Grau of the National Museum of the Pacific War (Fredericksburg, Texas) provided information and a behind-the-scenes tour of the museum and its relevant artifacts. Akira Takizawa (http://www3.plala.or.jp/takihome/) provided information on the Japanese tanks and weapons used at Tarawa.

General Daniel Postec, Colonel Jean-Francois Nicloux, Lieutenant Colonel Jean Louis Dubois, and Capitaine Philippe Dion made available the resources of the Musée du Général Estienne (Musée des Blindés tank museum) at Saumur, France—particularly their operational M4A2 tank MONTMIRAIL. Yvan Chollet advised on operating a damaged tank on one engine.

Major David Vickers (USMC, ret.) shared the preliminary results of his work using period photos to place the wreck sites of the individual medium tanks. Barbara Nevala and Kim Harrison provided additional photographs, and thanks to Bill Bartsch for his help in locating and photographing the remaining tank wreck on Betio.

Philip Wright sponsored the website tanksontarawa.com, the basis for much of Romain Cansiere's early research. Jonathan Stevens (http://tarawa ontheweb.org/) provided interviews with veterans, photographs, and contact information. Pierre-Olivier Buan, Webmaster at (http://the.shadock. free.fr/sherman_minutia/), provided technical data on the M4A2 tank. Larry Martin (lmww2.com) and David Brown (Second Marine Division Association) provided additional information. Michael Hanz (aafradio.org) freely shared his knowledge of World War II radios, and helped Ed to plow through the complexities of 1940s radio communication systems. Jody Hewitt of the University of Florida Library System provided information from World War II era technical manuals.

Thanks to Bobby Horton of Bobby Horton Music (bobbyhorton.com) for providing the source of the lyrics for the song "Long Ago."

Catherine Gilbert and Oscar E. "Bill" Gilbert III edited the first version of the manuscript. In her usual fashion Catherine also assisted Ed with his research at Quantico and College Park, and in tracking down information on the veterans' later lives.

Romain gratefully acknowledges his mother, Christiane, who tolerated her son's peculiar interest in Marine Corps history, and who enabled him to travel to the United States for research. And thanks to Caroline for her extraordinary patience in the face of a novice author's behavior and Marine Corps passion.

Long ago we were boys in the ranks comrades,
Our hearts light and happy as the day,
Cheeks were ruddy, eyes bright, locks dark, comrades,
As we marched from our homes far away.

But now we are aged and gray comrades,
The trials of life are nearly done,
But to us life's as dear as it was comrades,
When you and I were young.

—*Long Ago,* VERSE ONE AND CHORUS
   BY J. M. CARMICHAEL, 1902
   (recorded by Bobby Horton Music)

A NOTE ABOUT THE PHOTOS IN THIS BOOK: *The wrecked medium tanks on Tarawa were extensively photographed; most of those photos are available in a number of sources so only those specifically related to the text are reproduced here. Similarly, only selected aerial photos used in analysis are reproduced here for space reasons. Some period snapshots are not reproduced because resolution is inadequate for printing. Many of these photos—particularly personal snapshots showing the personnel of Charlie Company—can be seen at* tanksontarawa.com, *and* tarawaontheweb.org. *Other photos exist but resolution is too poor for publication, or the copyright provenance is unclear.*

PREFACE

Romain Cansiere

TARAWA, IWO JIMA, ENIWETOK, and PELELIU are names unfamiliar to the French ear.

I knew very little about the Pacific war before starting this project. Although a couple of battles occurred between the Siamese (Thai) forces allied to Japan and the French colonial army, for the French our history sticks to what happened in Europe. We are more familiar with names such as Caen, Bastogne, Saint Lô, and Carentan, Allied victories near the end of the war.

The Pacific, for the French a forgotten theatre of operations, was interesting to me. Since my English was not of the best (I was then a teenager), I started to read French magazines or website articles. I quickly focused on the battle of Tarawa and the few medium tanks (fourteen) involved in it. Maybe the originality of the unit symbol and the limited number of tanks led me to that choice. I quickly realized that versions of what happened to the "Shermans" on Tarawa were contradictory.

When I was able to read and write better English, I bought US books and began to go through US websites on the subject. I found even more versions of the story of the tanks involved on Betio. In March 2012, I decided to investigate what really happened to that company. At that time, I contacted the United States National Archives for photos and official documents regarding Charlie Company, First Corps Medium Tank Battalion. I made some interesting discoveries including the Battalion after action report. That was the beginning of an adventure.

I got in touch with MIA relative Philip Wright. Phil is the nephew of Raymond Barker, the driver of CONDOR, a Third Platoon M4A2 disabled behind enemy lines in the first few hours of the battle. Phil told me the background story of his uncle, and the tragedy it represented for the family. I realized that something had to be done for those men and their families. They need to be remembered for what they sacrificed for their country. Phil quickly convinced me to create a website where we could gather specific information on the medium tanks on Tarawa, and that's how www.tanksontarawa.com was born.

The most important research was to interview the last survivors. I contacted Ed Gilbert, who was interested in what I was trying to do. He helped me, and we developed a good friendship. He interviewed veterans and edited the text for the website (English is not my first language) among other things.

The idea to write a book came in the winter of 2012–2013 when Ed suggested we permanently preserve the history of Charlie Company. The plan became concrete by July 2013, when I visited the U.S. and met Ed.

I carried out more research in the National Archives, at the Marine Corps History Division, and at The National Museum of the Pacific War. I met with Dave Vickers who had carried out research on the tanks. He generously shared results of his work, and took me to the National Museum of the Marine Corps for a private guided tour.

Ed and I compared what we had. It took us many hours to check and re-check what information we had, and decide what more we needed. We wanted to use as much original material as possible from the archives. Together we also interviewed two veterans in person: Joe Woolum and Ed Bale. Those were the most memorable moments of my life. I was becoming aware that this book was taking on more importance not only to me, but to the veterans as well.

Back in France, research took another year, keeping in touch with people I've met during my travel and especially Annette Amerman from the Marine Corps History Division. Writing went quickly since Ed is an experienced author and because we had already spent countless hours doing research.

This story was in one sense becoming ours. The more I looked at the company roster, the closer I felt to these men. It's like I knew them, their story. I felt very honored when Ed Bale wrote on the Tarawa Talk forum: "I was astonished at how much Romain knew about the battle for Betio and the operation of the medium tank company, which I had the good fortune to command. I found him to be one of the most personable and polite young men I have met in a long time. He is a real asset to this forum."

Isle sur la Sorgue, Vaucluse, France, December 2014.

PREFACE

Ed Gilbert

Contrary to common belief, history is not a fixed thing. It begins to metamorphose almost as soon as events occur. After a few decades the historical record can become distorted almost beyond the recognition of those who lived it. The history of the battle for Tarawa in November 1943 was a victim of this peculiar process.

Despite initial defeats and government efforts to convince them that America was in for a long struggle, as in all wars too many Americans somehow convinced themselves it would be a short and relatively painless struggle. Sanitization of the war by Hollywood did little to help.

Civilian and military correspondents had accompanied troops into battle from the beginning of the war, but at Tarawa they would accompany the very first assault waves to record what was destined to be one of the most brutal battles of World War II. Yet from the very first minutes this plan began to disintegrate. By chance most of the reporters and cameramen ended up on a small, relatively isolated area of the precarious beachhead. And as always, critical events—along with countless acts of heroism and self-sacrifice—went unrecorded.

Still, from the correspondents and cameramen would emerge some of the finest war reporting of any conflict, classics like Robert Sherrod's book *Tarawa: The Story of a Battle*, and the Academy-award winning short documentary *With The Marines at Tarawa*. Unfortunately they were long in coming. Both Sherrod's book and the film were not released until the following year. For most of the public, perceptions of the battle were shaped by the relentless propaganda machinery of the government and news media.

Still photographs and news film shot on Tarawa were released in newsreels and published in newspapers and magazines, and the results were graphic and truly disturbing to American audiences accustomed to Hollywood's pap. But then people who were not there began to "improve" the reporting for propaganda purposes. Following the usual practices of the time, for "morale purposes," the accounts were rendered into exercises in cheerleading. One radio program—with voice-over actors representing Lieutenant Ed Bale (the commander of the medium tank company) and correspondent Master Technical Sergeant Sam Schaffer, both veterans of Tarawa—was truly cringe-worthy by the standards of today.

Then the *real* embellishment began. Writers began to "improve" upon the stories. Like the game Telephone, where children stand in a circle and relay a whispered message, the original stories of Tarawa morphed into strange—and often fantastic—tales as they were repeatedly rewritten over the ensuing decades. In the year 2000, Colonel Ed Bale told me that the only accurate account of the encounter between his tank and a Japanese tank on Tarawa had once appeared in the old newspaper column *Ripley's Believe It Or Not*. Despite his repeated efforts to clarify actual events, reputable historians and popular writers alike propagated some very peculiar versions of the event into the twenty-first century. Countless other events in the battle underwent similar metamorphoses.

In 2012 Romain Cansiere embarked upon his own effort to record the story of the Charlie Company medium tanks on Tarawa. He contacted me, and a lengthy and fruitful collaboration followed. Along the way Romain underscored some old truths, and his dogged persistence in archival research taught me some new things.

One of the most irritating practices of both historians and authors is the tendency to present only a single linear narrative, the "absolute truth" if you will. In reality, as General George Patton (among many others) noted, "Battle is an orgy of disorder." Senior officers may set events into motion, but battles must be understood from the bottom up. The outcome of any battle is the end result of the millions of tiny random incidents—Clausewitz's famous "friction of war"—that disrupt the tidy plans of the most careful general.

Tarawa was this, in spades, as units were fragmented and communications collapsed. The end result was an even more exaggerated version of the already colossal ambiguity of battle.

We have approached the story of a single company on Tarawa from three lines of evidence. The first and most valuable are the written memoirs of, and recorded interviews with, surviving veterans. Second are the official records of the period—unit diaries, reports, and other documents. Third is an analysis of photographic evidence, still photos and films taken on the ground by the combat cameramen, and aerial photos taken by naval aircraft as real-time reconnaissance to document the course of the battle.

In most cases we have been able to reconcile and integrate all three lines of evidence. However, each of these must be viewed judiciously. Colonel S.L.A. Marshall, founder of the US Army's field history program in World War II, found that frequently soldiers in the same squad offered significantly different accounts of the same action. In battle each man develops an astonishing tunnel vision, concentrating on events that immediately impact personal survival.

Even in a tank crew, with five men working as a team in a confined space, the phenomenon persists. Each man views his portion of the outside world through the tiny field of view of a periscope, and single-mindedly concentrates on his assigned role. Each man experienced a subtly different version of the battle from another man an arm's length away. Marshall found that differences could usually be reconciled by discussing the action as a group. Decades after the fact, many men who participated in veteran's groups and reunions have for the most part sorted through these discrepancies on their own. But disagreements persist, and it is critical to record even disparate remembrances, since the surviving participants are now all in their nineties.

Period records are often regarded as the holy grail of historians, but must also be viewed skeptically. After action reports were naturally based on still-incomplete information, and prepared by exhausted, psychologically numbed officers. Analyses of the efficacy of both American and enemy weapons was often colored by personal passions rather than cold fact: the partisan struggle between advocates of the M4A2 versus the M4A3 tank persisted until the end of the war, and the psychological impact of some Japanese suicide weapons far outweighed their physical effects. Clashes of personalities and self-serving selective memory too often colored reports by senior officers; it's not only politicians who have egos.

As Colonel Ed Bale recently pointed out, it's pretty hard to argue with a photo, although over many years I have encountered an alarming number of people who will quite happily do so. But you can argue with the *interpretation* of a photo, so even photo analysis has its problems. Combat photographers on the ground understandably did not record the precise times and locations where their photos were taken. Aerial photo sets, though usually better annotated, are maddeningly incomplete, with individual photos and entire sets missing from the archives.

For all these reasons we have recorded the instances where different lines of evidence disagree. This is our analysis of a battle, and we do not pretend it is the absolute truth.

Katy, Texas, December 2014

FOREWORD

Edward L. Bale, Jr.,
Colonel, U.S. Marine Corps, Retired

This book deals with the employment of a green United States Marine Corps Medium Tank Company in the first amphibious assault on a heavily defended beach. I was fortunate to command this company as a young first lieutenant.

For a number of years, I have had the privilege of knowing and providing information to the authors of this book. They have endeavored to clear the fog surrounding the employment of this tank company. In so doing, they have tapped the memory of known survivors as well as historical records and reports. Historical records, in this instance, are not what one would expect. The official records of the Marine Corps do not accurately reflect the role this company played during those seventy-six hours. Those records were compiled for the most part by commanders of infantry units. The Marine Corps was, and is today, an infantry oriented service. This is as it must be if the Corps is to serve the nation.

A detailed report of the operation of this company was prepared aboard the USS *Ashland*, LSD-1, en route from Tarawa to Hawaii and delivered to the commanding officer, Second Tank Battalion. Extracts from that report were included in the after action report of the Second Tank Battalion. Much of the detail was not included in the final report.

It is safe to say that the experience of this company had a profound effect on the Marine Corps. All Marine Corps Tank Battalions were converted from light to medium tanks. Tank-infantry communications and tactics were developed and joint training was accelerated. Deep water fording kits for installation on tanks were developed and provided for subsequent operations. The Marine Corps converted some light tanks from gun to flame throwing vehicles.

The assistance I have provided to the furtherance of this project is done so in memory of the Marines of this company I had the privilege of commanding.

Houston, Texas, December 2014

CHAPTER ONE

A NEW DOCTRINE FOR A NEW WAR

*In preparing for battle I have always found that
plans are useless, but planning is indispensable.*
—General Dwight D. Eisenhower

I
n the hours after midnight on 20 November, 1943 the officers and men
of the Second Marine Division aboard ships and boats lying in the darkness off Betio had studied and trained for a new type of warfare. Amphibious operations dated back to ancient Greece, when ships first transported
and disembarked armies for land battles with the enemy. But this was
something new, an amphibious assault, a full-scale frontal attack from the
open ocean against powerful fixed defenses.

In the eyes of many military theorists, the British debacle at Gallipoli
in the Great War had conclusively discredited the amphibious campaign.
That operation, a pet project of First Sea Lord Winston Churchill, was
intended to secure the Dardanelles Straits and knock Turkey—a German
ally—out of the war. The first attempt failed disastrously when Allied
battleships ran afoul of mines and shore batteries. Seeking to open the
straits by a land campaign, on 25 April 1915, a British and Commonwealth
force began to land at two remote locations on the Dardanelles Peninsula
overlooked by high hills, at Cape Hellas on the southern tip, and at "Anzac
Cove," south of Suvla Bay on the west coast.

British commanders, faced with minimal opposition but absent any
direct orders to advance, simply sat on the beach. Quick reinforcement by
the Turks penned the huge Allied force into the two shallow beachheads.
A force that eventually numbered nearly 490,000 British and Common-

wealth and 49,000 French and French Colonial troops piled up in the small beachheads. A horrific struggle against Turkish defenses, climate, disease, and day-to-day extremes of weather continued until the last position was finally evacuated on 8 January 1916.

For many military and naval theorists the lesson was clear—shore batteries and machine guns had rendered amphibious operations a thing of the past.

For the US Navy this new "common wisdom" presented a conundrum. Ever since the 1904–1905 Russo-Japanese War, the Navy's planners had foreseen a potential naval war with expansionist Japan. During the aftermath of the Great War, in 1918, Japan was granted a protectorate over the former German colonies in the Pacific and East Asia. By the 1920s the Japanese Empire sprawled into the Central and Southwestern Pacific, and American planning for a naval war took on new urgency. Increasing Japanese militarism, and particularly expansionism in China throughout the 1920s and 1930s, left little doubt that despite any diplomatic efforts, Japan and the Western powers would eventually clash.

Following the long-established naval doctrines of Alfred Thayer Mahan, the Navy planned for a drive across the Central Pacific, culminating in a climactic naval battle with the Imperial Navy. Landing forces would be needed to seize islands in the Marshalls, Marianas, and other island chains to serve as supply and fueling bases. These could only be secured by amphibious operations.

For its part, the US Army had no interest in risky amphibious operations; their future war plans centered on Europe and to a lesser degree the large land masses of the Asian periphery. The assumption was that in Europe the Army could land at friendly ports as it had in the Great War. In other regions, Sir Basil H. Lidell-Hart's "strategy of the indirect approach"—in vogue as a way to avoid bloody stalemates like that on the Western Front—decreed landing at some unopposed site, quickly seizing a port, and marching overland to battle.

The Navy leaders, grappling with how to prosecute a naval war in the vast reaches and small islands of the Central Pacific, found itself without the means to capture the forward bases required by such a war.

The Marine Corps, smarting under the accusation that it had become a "second Army" and struggling to find a role in the gutted post-war defense establishment, would be the ideal service to serve as the Navy's Advanced Base Force to both capture and defend forward naval bases. The Marine Corps eagerly seized upon the role. By the late 1930s the Marines had developed a detailed doctrine for amphibious assault, and trained for years. But they had never actually conducted such an assault against an enemy.

The fall of France in 1940 and the stunning advance of the Japanese in early 1942 had, of course, thrown all the Army's careful war plans out the window. In all theaters of war, amphibious assaults would be necessary prerequisites to any attack upon the Axis Powers. The first Allied offensives came in the southwestern Pacific, but did not test the new Marine Corps doctrine of amphibious assault.

At Guadalcanal the Japanese fled into the jungle rather than oppose the landings, and on the smaller islands nearby, small landing operations had been met by disorganized defenders. It was fortunate. The first assault landings conducted by the Marines were chaotic, with units landing in the wrong positions, wandering about, and critical supplies just piling up on the beach.

On New Georgia, the Marine Corps units were under the operational control of the Army in a test of Lidell-Hart's much-advocated "strategy of the indirect approach"; the soldiers and Marines landed at an undefended spot and attacked overland. The offensive bogged down in horrific jungle warfare, and the cherished strategy was soundly discredited. Learning from the experience, on Bougainville the Marines had again landed in a relatively remote—and lightly-defended—location, but constructed airfields and let the Japanese endure a grueling struggle with the jungle, as they marched overland to counterattack the American lodgment.

All these battles had been fought in a theatre of war where the Marines and Navy had never intended to fight, and had been fought to secure the vital sea lanes to Australia. By late 1943, Japanese southward expansion had been blunted, and the Navy returned to its pre-war plan for a Central Pacific naval offensive.

Inherent in the plans for any amphibious assault was the risk of an enemy naval counterattack, to catch the vulnerable transport ships as they stood off the invasion beachheads. For their part, the Marines accepted that assault landings under threat of a naval counterattack would need to be hastily mounted, prone to confusion, and probably excessively violent. They had attempted to train accordingly.

Mahan had published his seminal work *The Influence of Sea Power Upon History, 1660–1805* in 1890, in the days when airplanes were the stuff of science fiction. Even the Navy's fundamental plan for war in the Pacific—War Plan ORANGE, the case for a naval war against Japan—was a 1920s concept based upon the needs of a battleship navy. Pearl Harbor, the Coral Sea, and Midway suddenly changed everything.

By late 1943, islands were even more important than in Mahan's plan, but now had a new significance as sites for air and submarine bases. The Gilbert Islands, tiny coral specks never before considered particularly important to anyone, now had immense strategic value. They could provide air bases from which land-based bombers could "soften up" the more valuable islands of the Marshall Island chain to the northwest. Aircraft based in the Marshalls would in turn help neutralize the main Japanese naval base at Truk, the linchpin of Japanese power in the southwestern Pacific. Elimination or isolation of Truk would pave the way for *two* Pacific offensives—a naval drive through the Central Pacific, and Douglas MacArthur's second drive through Melanesia to the Philippines. The two campaigns, planned to converge on Formosa, would utilize America's numerical and material superiority to neutralize any advantage the Japanese might have gained from interior lines of communication.

The capture of Betio would be the vital first step in the new "second front." It would also be the first real-world test of the doctrine of amphibious assault to capture advanced island bases.

The Japanese had not intended to fight for the Gilbert Islands. Occupied almost as an afterthought, bases in the Gilberts were merely part of a screen, positions from which patrol planes could search the emptiness of the Central Pacific and give warning of American threats to more significant positions in the Marshall Islands. The Japanese were so confident, that following their initial seizure, they actually reduced the size of the garrison at their main base on Butaritari Island (Makin Atoll) to about 70 men.[1]

Then on 17–18 August 1942, the Second Marine Raider Battalion fell upon the floatplane base and long-range communications facility on Butaritari, destroying the facilities and annihilating the small garrison. Though intended only as a diversion to support the Guadalcanal campaign, like many things in war, the raid had unintended consequences. Alarmed, the Japanese launched a crash program to expand the defenses of their outlying bases from the Aleutians to the Bismarcks, and particularly in the Gilberts.

For the Americans, speed was now of the utmost importance. After the victories at Midway and the Coral Sea, the US Navy seized the initiative. It was important to apply immediate and unrelenting pressure upon the Japanese. Delays simply gave the enemy time to dig deeper and more formidable defenses. Lost time now would later be paid for in American blood.

In the revised Japanese defensive scheme, their primary base in the Gilberts would not be Butaritari, but the tiny island of Bititu (Americanized as Betio) on Tarawa Atoll. The natives were exiled to smaller islands. Elite *rikusentai* (naval infantry) and sailors of the Imperial Japanese Navy would garrison the new base, and Japanese and Korean laborers were assigned to build an airfield and to construct strong defenses on the small (291 acres/about 1.2 square kilometer) and much more defensible island.

The purpose of the defenses was not necessarily to repel an attack. As anticipated by the Americans, the Japanese strategy was that of a *yogaki*, or waylaying attack, code-named *Z Operation*. The defenses were only required to slow an attack and pin the vulnerable amphibious shipping in place long enough for a naval counterstroke. Aircraft would be staged through nearby islands, and submarines and surface vessels would converge from bases like Truk.

Today it is difficult for many Americans to understand the concerns of Navy admirals over such a threat, but for all the Allied navies, and throughout the war, the global shortage of amphibious shipping was an overarching concern. (The Chairman of the Joint Chiefs of Staff, General of the Army George C. Marshall, famously remarked that he thought of little else). In 1943, many of the US Navy's amphibious troop transports were ancient converted ocean liners, and only a handful of specialized seagoing landing craft, like the Landing Ship, Tank (LST), had as yet entered service. The really critical class was the Landing Ship Dock (LSD) used to transport and land heavy equipment such as medium tanks.*

The LSD was the brainchild of Sir Roland Baker of England, the designer of the LST. His original designs were the Landing Ship Stern Chute, a modified ferryboat that slid loaded landing craft off a ramp from the vehicle deck, and the Landing Ship Gantry, a modified oil tanker that lowered loaded landing craft over the side with a huge crane. Neither proved very satisfactory. The LSD was a large specially designed ship that could carry pre-loaded tank landing craft internally. The ship could flood the internal cargo bay (called the well deck), and open the entire stern like a huge ramp, allowing the loaded landing craft to emerge ready for action. The design eliminated the dangerous practice of lifting heavy vehicles into landing boats with cranes, and greatly speeded landing operations. Most important, it could carry the new thirty-ton M4 medium tanks, too heavy to lift with existing ships' cranes. All LSDs for the US and British navies would be built in American shipyards.[2]

In late 1943, only three of these priceless vessels existed in the world. Despite the Allied "Germany first" policy, the irascible American chief of naval operations, Fleet Admiral Ernest J. King, had allocated all three to the Central Pacific campaign. The LSD-1, USS *Ashland,* would transport Marine Corps medium tanks to Betio. The LSD-2, USS *Belle Grove,* would transport Army M3 medium tanks for landings on Butaritari. The LSD-3, USS *Carter Hall,* was still en route from California. The shortage of LSDs would be a limiting factor in amphibious operations as late as the invasion of Peleliu in September 1944.

In 1943, the admirals were painfully aware that the loss of even a few key transport ships would prolong the war, and play to the Japanese overall strategy—a war of attrition in which America would lose hope and accept the new boundaries of an expanded Japanese Empire.

If the Japanese could fall upon the vulnerable shipping standing off a beachhead and destroy even a few precious transports, it would be a major coup. Many armchair admirals have criticized the Navy's seeming timidity,

---

* The LSTs were used primarily as "mother ships" for amphibious tractors. The LSD, carrying pre-loaded LCMs (Landing Craft, Mechanized) internally, remained the primary transport for tanks until 1945. In more modern form the class is still a fundamental part of the US amphibious fleet.

but the American Navy had already proven itself far from timid in the brutal slugfests in the dark waters around the Solomon Islands. The Navy was "... far from reluctant to risk its carrier planes against Japan's island fortresses," and by extension the aircraft carriers that launched the planes. Beginning on 17–18 September the fast carriers pounded Betio and other targets in the Gilberts, and moved on to blast other objectives, leaving the islands to be the target of heavy land-based Army bombers and nocturnal raids by Navy long-range bombers.[3]

Thus the stage was set for a clash of theories. The combatants would stumble blindly into unknown ground, like two fighters in a pitch-black cave. The Americans would face the first real-world test of their new doctrine of amphibious assault. The Japanese would test their new doctrine of defense at the water's edge and the *yogaki*. The Japanese had constructed powerful defenses that would—they hoped—slaughter any attacker before he set foot on dry land. At worst the defense would bog down an attacker until naval forces arrived to inflict terrible carnage on American ships sitting immobile offshore.

Such blind clashes of untested theories inevitably prove chaotic and violent beyond the wildest imaginings of either side.

The personnel of Charlie Company never lived in buildings. PFC Warren S. "Stan" Doherty is standing in front of a typical pyramidal squad tent at Camp Pendleton. He wears the P1941 utility uniform with a dress overseas cap.—Olaf Johnson via Oberg

CHAPTER TWO
SALAD DAYS—FORMATION AND TRAINING

It's not the will to win that matters—everyone has that.
It's the will to prepare to win that matters.
—PAUL "BEAR" BRYANT

In the early period of World War II there was still considerable ambiguity as to the role of the Marine Corps in the nation's military and naval establishment. America had been entirely unprepared for its entry into the Great War, on 6 April 1917. Isolationist sentiment had long been strong in America, and a powerful Navy controlling the Atlantic Ocean moat was perceived as the guarantor of that neutrality. By 1917 the Navy—and its ancillary service, the Marine Corps—had already greatly expanded and was prepared for war, but the War Department scrambled desperately to mobilize an army to send to France. The commandant of the Marine Corps, General George Barnett, correctly perceived that the Corps would have to send troops to fight in France in order to justify the force expansion already begun. In April 1917, Britain and France, their populations demoralized and manpower resources nearing exhaustion, sent a delegation to urge an immediate American commitment on the Western Front.

The War Department balked at sending the fledgling American Expeditionary Force, which would be composed almost entirely of new and untrained volunteers and conscripts, into battle piecemeal and before it could be brought up to strength and adequately trained. Eventually the War Department agreed to send a token division under General John J. Pershing, but given its training commitments, could not form a full division. Secretary of the Navy Josephus Daniels immediately volunteered a Marine

Corps regiment for immediate service, with another soon to follow. Secretary of War Newton Collins and Army Chief of Staff Tasker Bliss informed Pershing that he would accept a Marine Brigade of two regiments for immediate service in France. To his credit, Pershing pledged to treat the Marine Brigade equitably in all matters.[4]

The Marine Brigade served with distinction as part of the Army's Second ("Indianhead") Division, but that distinction would come at a long-term cost. As a result of a censor's violation of policy, the Marine Brigade won considerable fame in the month-long fighting for Belleau Wood in June 1918. Many Army leaders felt that the Corps had functioned as a "second army," and garnered what they believed to be an undue portion of glory at the expense of the Army units fighting alongside them.

The ever-reserved Pershing held himself aloof from the controversy, and famously said that "The deadliest weapon in the world is a Marine and his rifle." But the controversy aroused the enmity of many future US Army leaders who also felt that Pershing had been pressured to accept Marines into the American Expeditionary Force. Many of these future generals, including George C. Marshall, Dwight Eisenhower, and Omar Bradley, revered Pershing as a father figure, and in 1942 would brook no inclusion of the Marines in Europe.

However, the circumstances of 1942—primarily another desperate shortage of combat-ready Army units—resulted in the limited use of Marines in the Atlantic region. Following the fall of France to the Nazi juggernaut in July 1940, the Corps prepared an operation to seize the Caribbean island of French Martinique, when planners feared that the Vichy French government would allow German occupation of the island as a base for disrupting the flow of American supplies and equipment to embattled Britain, and threaten the approaches to the Panama Canal. The operation was aborted when Free French Forces seized control of the Caribbean colonies. In the summer of 1941, a Marine brigade temporarily augmented the British garrison on the critical island of Iceland. The joint service planning staffs eventually decreed that Europe would be an "Army only" theatre, and the Navy was perfectly happy to have its amphibious specialists devote their attentions entirely to the naval war against Japan.

Despite the long-standing focus on potential support of naval operations, primarily in the Pacific, the Corps was, to some extent, temporarily distracted by emulating the successful German *blitzkrieg* mechanized warfare model. The original D-Series Tables of Organization and Equipment specified a very large (and probably unwieldy) light tank battalion for each division, to be equipped with 72 light tanks, organized into four companies of eighteen tanks each, plus a mechanized Scout Company with fourteen M3 Scout Cars.

Actual combat experience quickly disabused the Marine Corps of the notion of mechanized warfare in the Pacific. The mechanized Scout Companies were converted to rubber boat and foot or jeep reconnaissance companies, and reassigned to direct Division control. In practice, no tank battalion ever had so many tanks, and the light tank battalion was quickly reduced to 54 with a further three fitted out as recovery vehicles.[5]

The situation was further complicated because the Corps was forced to accept an assortment of light tank types—M2A4s, and several models of the M3. All were armed with the basic 37mm cannon and a varying number of machine guns, but were otherwise significantly different: some were diesel-powered, others gasoline-powered; some had turret floor cages while others did not; some had gyrostabilized main guns and others did not, and so on. Altogether the Corps had six types of light tanks in service and six more types in the acquisition stream, creating logistical and maintenance nightmares. This count did not include several models of the hopelessly obsolete Marmon-Herrington light tanks, organized into separate companies.[6]

The 37mm cannon of all the light tank models proved woefully inadequate as early as Guadalcanal, but the global shortage of newer medium tanks faced by the Allies hampered Marine Corps tank acquisitions. The ramp-up of the American armaments industry resulted in several models of the new M4 medium tank entering production, including the diesel-powered M4A2. The US Army had decreed that diesel-powered tanks would not be used overseas, citing fuel logistics and maintenance issues. Other Allied armies were not so picky, and the Corps still had to wait for the urgent requirements of those Allies to be met before they could acquire adequate numbers of medium tanks even for training.

Given its global commitments, the Army was reluctant to part with any medium tanks. Eventually new medium tanks of the M4 series were acquired, but in limited numbers, so two new medium tank battalions were to be formed to utilize the new tanks. In practice only one was activated, but benefitted from a double quota of tanks.[7] The concept was that companies of medium tanks would be "loaned" to support divisions for specific operations. (Other types of equipment, notably amphibian tractors and 155mm artillery, would later be used as similar corps assets.) The concept was to use the divisional tank battalion's more easily transported light tanks in the landing phase, with the medium tanks landed as reinforcements for prolonged land operations.

The original light tank companies had been raised as individual companies attached to rifle regiments. The personnel in medium tank companies that would make up the I Corps Medium Tank Battalion would be among the first to benefit from at least some degree of formal training before being shipped overseas to combat.

On 18 January 1943, the I Corps Medium Tank Battalion was formed at Jacques Farm, the primitive training site of the 2nd Marine Raider Battalion, on an old ranch on what is now Camp Pendleton, north of San Diego. The landscape was perfect for tank training, with vast areas of grassland in which tanks could easily maneuver

The first commanding officer was Lieutenant Colonel Bennet G. Powers, the son of a prominent retired senior staff officer. Powers had previously commanded the Second Scout Company, equipped with obsolete Marmon-Herrington CTL-3M light tanks and wheeled M3 Scout Cars, and served as the executive officer of the partially-formed Third Tank Battalion. Powers brought many of his officers from the Third Tank Battalion.[8]

Powers had attended the basic tank school at Jacques Farm (an unusual assignment for a major), but for whatever reason seemed not to have been highly regarded in the miniscule Marine Corps tank community. Captain Bob Neiman, who had known Powers at the tank school, was offered the billet of executive officer for the new battalion, but "...wanted no part of that."[9]

The battalion executive officer was Arthur "Jeb" Stuart, who would go on to become one of the Corps' pre-eminent tank authorities.

Standing up a new unit is always a difficult, and in some ways risky, proposition. The officers and senior NCOs are generally unknown to each other. Many junior men are fresh from specialist schools or even straight out of boot camp. It is not unusual for commanders in other units to fill a transfer quota by dumping inept men or disciplinary problems.

In the usual way, some of these men would continue to be problems. In late 1943, a report concluded that "The discipline of the 1st Corps Medium Tank Battalion was not of the best...." The loose discipline was a source of complaint by a civilian employee of the Army Ordnance Department, who noted that "Both officers and men were a friendly crowd and made my stay very pleasant...." but complained that "I was annoyed by the looseness of control and lack of authority exercised over the soldiers [sic] by the officers who were very seldom with the troops at all. A large number of the officers and men were on leave, which may have made the situation appear worse than it really was."[10]

First Lieutenant Ed Bale, who would later assume command of C Company, thought that among the enlisted men "We had one or two bad apples." Weighing disciplinary decisions is one of the most difficult of a commander's duties, because one of the paradoxes of the military is that some of the men who are disciplinary problems in training achieve their finest moment only in combat. In Charlie Company, Edwin H. Vancil was reduced from Corporal to PFC, then from PFC to Private while still at Pendleton.[11]

A typical outdoor wash rack at Camp Pendleton; washing, shaving, toothbrushing, and laundry were all done here with cold water. PFC Jack Trent is on the left.—Bill Eads

Charlie Company's first commanding officer was Second Lieutenant Richard O. Sloat, a high school speech and drama teacher from Puyallup Washington nicknamed the "red dog fox" by the men for his bright red hair. Ed Gazel thought Sloat was "The finest young man I ever met in my life." Bill Eads was the loader/radio operator for the lieutenant, and thought Sloat "Was a real nice guy. We all liked him a lot."

Ed Gazel recalled that during the time Sloat was company commander, "One guy reported his wallet was gone. Somebody stole his wallet. Dick Sloat fell the company out, we all lined up. He marched up and down the company and he said 'I'll have no thieves in my company. Anybody caught stealing'—we weren't allowed to use live ammunition. He said 'You catch a thief in my company, you can bring his body and leave it in front of the first sergeant's desk. That very next morning the thief had took off. We never saw him again."

"He knew people," remembered Joe Woolum.[12] Sloat was later promoted to first lieutenant and became the Second Platoon leader. Bale thought that "The best lieutenant I had in that company was Sloat.... But you never hear anything about him."

Lieutenant William I. Sheedy, from Bloomington, Indiana, was simply "a nice guy" and "a good lieutenant" remembers Ed Bale, who thought Sheedy had joined the Corps to keep from being drafted. The eternal problem for military leaders is that of maintaining an emotional distance from the men they might have to send to their deaths. Bale thought that Sheedy "was too much one of the boys" but still, "I have nothing but respect for him." When he landed on Tarawa, Sheedy was a first lieutenant and the First Platoon leader.

The executive officer was First Lieutenant Orrell F. Kent, a rarity in the Corps: a non-smoking, non-cursing teetotaler. Kent simply "...was a nice guy from Mississippi..." He eventually became a company commander late in the war.

Second Lieutenant Louis R. "Lou" Largey was a mustang, formerly a sergeant aboard the USS *Texas*. "He was as tough as they make them," said Bale, "and he'd fight at the drop of a hat, and I never saw him lose one." Ed Gazel recalled Largey as "The picture-boy of the Marine Corps. Young, tough, good-looking." Largey was the platoon leader for Third Platoon.

As usual, the enlisted men came from wildly different backgrounds.

Bill Eads's father was operating Army laundries, and was transferred to Fort Ord California to construct a new base laundry. When Eads tried to enlist in the Army Air Corps, his blood pressure was too high "So I walked across the hall and joined the Marine Corps." After boot camp, "I spent a month or so in radio school." Upon completing the school "I was transferred up to Camp Elliott on the way to the I Corps Medium Tank Battalion."

Ed Gazel, from Michigan, was twenty-one years old and one of the original members of the company. He was "about to get drafted," so he and his wife's cousin decided to join the Marines. His friend failed the eye test, but "They put a big Mercurochrome number on my chest, and I'm in!" the next morning he began a three-day train ride to boot camp in San Diego.

After boot camp "They sent us to tank school—light tanks—and at the end of December [1942] the Marine Corps decided to activate a medium tank battalion. So they got a bunch of guys together and shipped us to Pendleton. About eighty guys formed a company of a tank battalion." The company remained at Pendleton from January to the end of May 1943.

Though still without tanks, Ed Gazel said, "The Marine Corps was shipping us guns, thirty calibers and fifty calibers, brand new, shipped in Cosmoline, that we had to clean. We used hundred octane gas to clean all these weapons." The shipments also included "ammunition, though we weren't allowed to use live ammunition.

"They said 'What'd you do before?' I said 'Well, I worked in a grocery store.' [They said] 'Okay, you'll be a good guy to be our supply sergeant.' The other guys became mechanics. Anybody that didn't know any better, they became reconnaissance men. If they could drive a car or a truck, they became truck drivers. That's how they formed our company."

Charles D. Mason was a farm boy who had worked for ten months as a welder for the Oregon Shipbuilding Company. With a skilled trade he could have enlisted in the Navy, but instead joined the Marine Corps because he had a brother in the Corps. He thought it was "Hard training, but it didn't bother me. I was an old farm boy. It was tough, it was hard, but being from the farm I was hard too." The long hours were nothing new, but "We noticed very distinctly who the city boys were. They couldn't take it."[13]

He applied for aviation and wanted to be a gunner, but only much later found out that "I blacked out in a dive. I wouldn't have been worth a darn as a gunner in a plane. After I got into the tanks, I liked it." He thought the medium tank battalion was "...a bastard outfit.... But we were the best-supplied organization around. They had put every thief in the country in there." Mason was made the gunner in Sergeant Robert E. Baker's tank CLIPPER in the Second Platoon.

Oklahoman Joe D. Woolum was assigned to Robert F. Shook's crew in the tank CONDOR, in the Third Platoon. Woolum grew up outside Oklahoma City, one of five children of a union painter. His senior year he dropped out of high school and joined the Marine Corps because "You had to join something." Older boys who he had grown up with had entered the Marines before the war, and one wrote letters to Woolum's older brother about Guadalcanal. Woolum enlisted "...because of him, mainly." Then, "You hit boot camp, about five minutes I done seen I'd made a mistake! I don't know how they think of all the bad stuff to do to you." In the final stage of boot camp the recruits were given a choice, "And I picked the tanks. I don't remember why."

Woolum vividly recalled the light tanks used in training at the tank school. "To start that thing you had a shotgun shell.... You put that in a chamber and fired it, and the blast 'Vrooom—room—room room!' starts this engine. No starter." Woolum found the tank school "Dirty. You come out of spit-and-polish boot camp, and you go to Jacques Farm and everything out there is sand dust that deep [several inches] on tents, everything. Tanks running around stirring it up.... You get used to that."

In the dirt and grime the new tank crews at least benefited from the newly-adopted, and easier to launder, Marine Corps P1941 "utility" uniforms.

Gazel recalled that "We slept in tents. C Company never slept in barracks. The only barracks we ever slept in was in boot camp for the rifle range. Because we were in tanks we had to sleep along the highway. They wouldn't let us into camp. They wouldn't let our tanks into camp, because they'd tear up the roads."

When the company moved onto the main Pendleton area, Woolum said, "You drove out across this dry wash...Lieutenant Kent had the company fall out and says 'If you want to sleep in a tent, you better get busy and get 'em up. Otherwise you sleep out under the stars.' We'd never touched a tent before. None of us. We tried to get these up." The big pyramidal squad tents were never easy to erect. "We tried to get these tents up, and sure enough it started raining. It rained for two weeks. That dry wash was a raging river. Nobody could get in or out. We were stuck there, with what little they took in with us.... That was our start at Pendleton."

The unending cycle of cold rain and mud alternating with hot wind and dust was not the only hazard of the California hills. William R. "Scot" Kinsman was a Scottish immigrant who had enlisted from West Peoria Illinois:

> At the end of the day we bivouacked our tanks under a tree, and put a camouflage net over them. As I was giving signals to the driver to do this, to maneuver the tank into position, I was walking backward with my two hands held up. Then I signaled him to come forward as I was walking backward, but he stopped and yelled and kept pointing toward me. Each tank had twin diesel engines and they were very noisy. I could not hear what he was saying but did turn to see what he was pointing to. What I saw sent a cold chill up and down my spine. Four feet away was a huge diamond back rattlesnake ready to strike on my next backward step. PTL! [Praise The Lord] I picked up a large rock and hit it in the head. As he was twisting I held his head with a stick, took my knife and cut his head and rattles off, nine in all.[14]

Other men filled out a questionnaire that asked what type of duty they would prefer. In boot camp, Melvin Swango "... received a questionnaire from the Marine Corps and they asked what would be your first choice of service, and your second choice. I never thought it would amount to anything, but I said I might like to be a radio operator or a member of a tank crew." Swango was assigned as a radio operator/loader in the new medium tank unit. Then "While we were in training in California we formed this new Reconnaissance Platoon. I liked that because we had halftracks and jeeps, so I was a radio man with reconnaissance." Swango was transferred to the Reconnaissance Section of the medium tank company.[15]

John R. Marn was more experienced; he had enlisted from Belt Montana in 1940 "Because there was a war on." He was assigned as a tank commander in the Third Platoon.

Michael "Mike" Shivetts was working in a steel mill and enlisted in June 1942, because he felt "It was my duty to do it. I was twenty-one years old at the time." Like most, there was no particular reason he was assigned to tanks. "I was a radio man. I didn't know a tank from a Volkswagen car. I paid very little attention to what they were doing mechanically or whatever."

Clifford Quine was assigned to the Second Platoon. He had been working in a factory, and "I signed up in Peoria, Illinois on November the tenth, nineteen forty-two. . . . I was a young guy, eighteen years old." After Pearl Harbor "I kept my job. I had a car and a real good time. . . . We could get gas for twenty-five cents a gallon, when you was lucky if you had twenty-five cents." Then gas rationing and tire rationing were implemented, and they began to draft eighteen- and nineteen-year-olds. "So I just sold my car and joined the Marines." Like so many, he had seen a movie—he does not recall which one—and "The Marines just got stuck in my head." He sold the car for fifty dollars, and ". . . took off for California."

At boot camp "On the last day you could go over and sign up for whatever you wanted. . . . They said if you don't have any particular thing, you could sack out the whole afternoon. So I went over and I was gonna join up with cooks. I went over and there was a big long line, and I said 'I'm not waiting in that line.'" Quine went back to his tent and slept. Men were needed for the new medium tank battalion "So I was put in that. That's how I got into the tanks."

After about a month the new company got its first tanks. "The first tanks were Chryslers [M4A4s]," according to Gazel. "Gasoline. And they were having trouble. After about two months, the Marine Corps changed to GMs."

The M4A4 tank's A57 engine consisted of five Chrysler engines powering a single drive shaft—with thirty cylinders. Historian Ken Estes noted that it had ". . . five carburetors, five water pumps (later reduced to one), five sets of pulleys, and so forth." It was a maintenance nightmare ". . . requiring careful synchronization of carburetion, clutch, and ignition components." The Marine Corps received only 22 of these tanks before they were phased out, replaced by the diesel-powered General Motors M4A2.[16]

The first batch of M4A2 tanks such as CHERRY used in training were fitted with the early T-49 track, quickly abandoned by the Marines. Note the dust covers over machine guns and the recovery cable kept fitted. Barely visible is a set of crosshairs for boresighting the cannon. The small sign at far right indicates the designated parking site for CHERRY, and a temporary workshop building is in the background.—Ed Gazel

Another shot of CHERRY. Note the early spoked wheels, also quickly abandoned, and the lighter patches where the damaged paint has been touched up.—Ed Gazel

More succinctly, Charles Mason said of the M4A4s "They were a *miserable* thing." When the ignition systems were out of synchronization, "You couldn't shift that thing. Why it affected the transmission I don't know. Never could figure it out.... It was a powerful engine when they was synchronized, but it took a lot of upkeep on those."

Most of the training was in basic skills. Marn thought that in contrast, the diesel tank was "Easy to drive, actually. Easy to operate . . . Just like a big truck."

Training was also hampered by unforeseen events. Gazel: "We would start [brush] fires with the ammunition. Then we had to fight the fires."

After about six months a new officer senior to Sloat arrived to assume command of C Company. First Lieutenant Edward L. Bale was an "old timer" who had enlisted on 14 June 1939. Bale attended Texas A&M University and was commissioned through the Marine Corps Platoon Leader's Class program in lieu of two years of Reserve Officer Training Corps classes then required of all students at the land-grant college. Bale's was the last Platoon Leader's Class to be taught at the old Philadelphia Naval Yard, with field training conducted at the Army's field training center at Indiantown Gap, Pennsylvania. Bale, at least, had some formal training in tanks, having attended an Army tank maintenance course at Fort Knox, Kentucky. He had then been the platoon leader of the light tank platoon in the 51st Composite Defense Battalion.[17]

The so-called fifty-series defense battalions were racially segregated units with black enlisted men and white officers. In the segregationist views that dominated all of American society in that era, it was thought that white officers from the South were more suitable to lead these units. Unlike the traditional Defense Battalions, the Composite Defense Battalions included an over-strength infantry company, and an over-strength platoon of light tanks.

Bale: "It was there [Fort Knox] that I met other Marine students, including then-Major A. J. "Jeb" Stuart, who was the executive officer of this First Corps Medium [Tank Battalion]. When I got back to Lejeune after the course was over, had been back there maybe a month, they disestablished this tank platoon, disestablished the infantry company, and just called the thing the 51st Defense Battalion. At that point in time was when I asked for a transfer to the west coast, to this medium tank battalion.

"I reported in out there in May of forty-three to Camp Elliott, which was the area command.... I was a really young, green, ignorant lieutenant." The area command chief of staff, Colonel Graves B. Erskine, told Bale "We can send you up to Pendleton, to this tank battalion, but you'll probably be leaving the States in sixty days. I said 'Send me.'

"I was the senior first lieutenant in the battalion, so I took over C Company."

Bale was the most junior company commander in the battalion, but he still found it "...the strangest battalion I have ever in my life seen. When I look back on it, I'm absolutely horrified." The battalion commander had no hands-on experience with tanks and paid little attention to administrative detail so that "...every company did absolutely its own thing. You developed your own training schedule, did what you wanted to all week long."

In truth, the Corps was stumbling up a steep learning curve, basing many assumptions on inexperience, such as Powers's recommendation that tank crews be increased to seven men, so as to have familiar replacements for crew casualties. The proposal was rejected by the acting commandant, and the decision stood despite Powers's repeated appeals.[18]

The battalion as a whole was slow to come up to full strength and capability, and shortages of key parts and equipment typical of the era were common complaints. There were hundreds of fire extinguishers but no carbon dioxide gas or gas handling equipment to fill them. There were no suitable welding units, engine lifting slings, and the lack of field glasses was a continuing source of complaint. Heavy trucks were dead-lined for months for want of inexpensive bearings that could be easily purchased on the civilian market.[19]

Despite the problems, Ed Bale (who went on to become a tank battalion commander) thought, "That was the best pure tank training I ever went through. I was criticized by some others because we would work five days a week and take two days off. We'd come in on Monday morning and I would take my company and . . . we had all the ranges and everything at Pendleton. I would take my company and go to the field on Monday morning, come back Friday about noon, do the maintenance, and then liberty call went.

"We spent four nights out in the field, and we usually did some kind of training at night. Looking back I don't know how I knew to do this, and those people—I say people, most of them were kids, some of them still seventeen years old, less than six months in the Marine Corps.

"I had a first sergeant [William H. Atkinson Jr.] who knew absolutely nothing about a tank. In fact, when I joined that company he was a staff sergeant. I had a master gunnery sergeant* who had been with the First Tank Battalion on Guadalcanal, and gotten malaria and was on old-timer . . . by the name of Duke [Alphonse] Dumais.

"You had corporals and sergeants with maybe eight, nine months in the Marine Corps as platoon sergeants when we started out. You had lieutenants who had even less experience than I did. Largey was a lieutenant who three months earlier had been a buck sergeant. . . .

"I didn't have a single individual that I wasn't proud of."

At Pendleton the company was organized into platoons; the fourteen tanks were organized as three gun platoons of four tanks each, and a headquarters section with the commanding officer's and executive officer's tanks plus the company's M32B2 VTR recovery vehicle.

During the six-month training period, each man was trained on all positions in the tank, to see where he was the best. Also, more than half of the men in the company would be potential replacement personnel for casualties.

Joe Woolum remembered being initially assigned as a driver before becoming a gunner. "Each night coming in, a different person would drive in. Each one got to do some driving. And it was my first day of driving a tank, a medium tank. Only thing I've done was in Jacques Farm, a little bit on the light tanks. That particular day I had took some whiskey up, what you shouldn't do, but I did." Woolum had taken a few drinks, and ". . . just before you get to our camp, you come upon a real steep hill, about thirty feet down. . . . When you get there, you're driving in fifth gear—thirty miles an hour—and before you get to that hill, you have to shift down. . . .

"Me not being a good driver, not being experienced . . . I didn't start shifting down . . . I try to shift down, I put it in neutral [gear] and off this [hill] we go [hand gesture] . . ." The thirty-ton tank briefly became airborne,

---

* A rank equivalent to sergeant major, the "Master Gunny's" duties are primarily technical as opposed to administrative.

Most units were equipped with a mixture of tank sub-models. The first tanks used by Charlie Company were an assortment of models like this unidentified very early production tank with cast armored hoods and direct vision blocks for the driver and assistant driver, but late-model tracks.

The men are left to right: Seward, Sooter, and Josefson.—Dan Josefson

The crew of COUNT at Camp Pendleton, dressed in P1941 utilities and the early white skivvy shirt. From left to right: PFC Bruce J. Seward, PFC Donald J. McConville, CPL Olaf G. Johnson, and PVT John E. Irvine. At far right is Platoon Sergeant Charlie Sooter. Note the dress shoes worn by McConville, and the overseas cap worn by Sooter.—Olaf Johnson via Oberg

The crew of CECILIA at Camp Pendleton. Standing left to right: Zeibak (assistant driver), Keller (tank commander), Shivetts (loader/radio operator). Kneeling is Chavez (driver). Photo probably taken by Martin (gunner).—Mike Shivetts

The somewhat disheveled crew of CONDOR at Camp Pendleton; left to right: SGT Robert F. Shook, SGT Cecil J. Sherman, PFC Eugene M. Josefson, and PVT Joe D. Woolum. Note the Rawlings tank crew helmets. The War Production Board serial number in light blue indicates a vehicle built at the Fisher plant.—Joe Woolum

and "...it hit down 'BLAMM!' Nobody got hurt. It just banged us up."

The tank commanders were selected by Bale, based on the platoon leaders' recommendations, but he moved some men between platoons to pick the men he thought best for the tank commander positions. Otherwise, all crew assignments were made by the platoon leaders, based on demonstrated skills.

Factors that figured into the choices of crew position were many; the loaders had to be trained radiomen. It took considerable upper body strength to be a driver or loader, and gunnery was an art. Loader/radio-operator Mike Shivetts described his duties: "I was up in the turret, I loaded the seventy-five millimeter. It was an SOB. Those seventy-five millimeters [shells] weren't light, and then you had to reach wherever you could find them. . . . You had to reach down into the basket surrounding the turret, pick one out, pull it up, shove it in. I've got the radio going; I'm running radio operations because we were the lead tank. . . ."

One result of this selection process was that rank did not always correlate with crew position. Later in the war the loader would usually be the most junior—and hardest-working—crewman. But in these early days the loader had to be a trained radio-operator, a technical specialty that usually resulted in rapid promotion. As a result, the loader/radio-operator was often senior in rank to other crewmen. Similarly, a few men were considered best suited to be tank commanders, though they might actually be lower in rank than other crewmen.[20]

Tanks belonging to officers typically had an NCO assigned as the lead crewman to supervise operations and maintenance whenever the officer was not present, which was much of the time. The officer could choose to "bump" the NCO and take over as tank commander. In combat, platoon leaders typically commanded their own tank. In later campaigns it was common for the company commander to direct his company from a radio jeep, with the command tank serving as a reserve vehicle in case of need. At Tarawa, Bale elected to go ashore in his tank. The company's executive officer usually operated with the company command group to better direct vital functions like supply and communications, with his tank commanded by the designated NCO. This was the case at Tarawa, where Lieutenant Kent was with the company command group on foot.

The Corps had not settled upon any standardized form of tactical markings, so each battalion designed its own system. The tactical marking system for the company at Tarawa was a name beginning with the company designator—C in the case of Charlie Company—painted onto the sides of the tank just outboard of the driver's and assistant driver's positions.

The tanks did follow the usual Marine Corps system of designation in which each tank was identified by a tactical number, but these were not painted onto the exterior of the tanks or used as radio call signs at Tarawa. Under this system, the four-tank platoons were numbered so that the platoon leader's tank was number one, the platoon sergeant's tank was number four. Clifford Quine is one of the few who recalled the actual tactical number of his tank CLIPPER, C-22. The number indicated C Company, Second Platoon, tank number two. The two tanks of the Headquarters Section would have been numbered C-41 (Bale's command tank) and C-42 (Kent's tank).

Few men recalled the tactical numbers because each tank's radio call sign was the name, not the tactical number. Each crew was responsible for selecting its own tank's name, a process which in some cases led to considerable argument. The reasoning behind each name has largely been lost, although CECILIA (Bale's command tank) was named after the wife or infant daughter of driver Al [Alfonzo] Chavez. (There is some disagreement

PFC Hank Trauernicht and CPL Bill Eads relaxing on COBRA at Camp Pendleton. Note the M1 carbine, helmet liner worn without the steel helmet, and the limited-issue blue enameled steel canteen on the fender.—Bill Eads

among those who recall the highly-regarded Chavez). CONDOR's name was selected by the driver, Corporal Raymond A. Barker, according to Joe Woolum. "The condor's a huge bird, and that's why he named it." For John Marn's tank, "It was named COLORADO in honor of my radio man [PFC William F. Schwenn], who was from Colorado." When one crew could not agree upon a name, the final compromise was to name the tank CHINA GAL, the stage name of a stripper in San Diego (she was not Chinese).[21] Bill Eads recalled that Lieutenant Sloat's tank was dubbed COBRA because "Probably that was the only name we could think of." In fact most of tank names had no particular significance "it just had to start with a C" remembered Quine, who was the driver in CLIPPER. CONGA came from the Cuban dance music "which was very popular in Southern California in those days and times," said Bale.[22]

The names of the tanks and their assigned platoons, reconstructed from photos, documents, and interviews with crewmen, is presented in Table 1.

TABLE 1: TANK NAMES AND ASSIGNED PLATOONS

HQ SECTION	1ST PLATOON	2ND PLATOON	3RD PLATOON
CECILIA[1]	CHICAGO[3]	COBRA[3]	CANNONBALL[3]
COMMANDO[2]	CHINA GAL	CLIPPER	CONDOR
	COUNT	CUDDLES	CHARLIE
	CHERRY	CONGA	COLORADO

One name, not shown in this table but often mentioned by veterans is CHEROKEE. Since we were not able to find any photo, report, or direct testimony from a crew member or surviving veteran verifying the existence of the name in a specific platoon, we believe that this was perhaps the name given to the VTR left behind in New Caledonia.

1 Company Commander's tank; 2 Executive Officer's tank; 3 Platoon Leader's tank

The distinctive marking for the tank battalion was the elephant painted onto each side of new tanks just before departure for the combat zone (the symbol was not used during training). John Marn recalled, "That was one of the boys in the company, in the maintenance area." As a former apprentice painter, Woolum recalled stenciling the elephants onto his tank. He remembered the symbol being white, though it shows up as yellow in the color film of the era, and Bale recalls the color as yellow.

The battalion was hastily issued brand new M4A2 tanks to replace those so heavily used in training. The training tanks were worn and in bad condition, many dead-lined for lack of spare parts. Bale acknowledged that the vehicles were ". . . in bad condition and stripped."

The condition of the tanks prompted an investigation by the Judge Advocate General's office. A December 1943 report concluded that the condition of the tanks could be attributed to ". . . inexperienced personnel; mechanical deficiencies inherent in a new product; lack of tools, accessories, parts, and repair facilities; lack of discipline; and finally, to vandalism [which occurred after the tanks were left by the battalion] . . ." The lengthy investigation came to nothing. This would hardly be the last instance of training vehicles being left derelict. In 2002, vehicles left by 2nd Tank Battalion to be used by elements of the 8th Tank Battalion in Iraq prompted almost identical complaints.[23]

In addition to the purely military, there were other distractions that the officers and men had to deal with. World War II caused massive social disruption in America, and considerable internal migration. With so many men leaving civilian jobs to enter the military, for the first time thousands of women traveled across the country to enter heretofore "male" jobs. Others followed husbands and boyfriends to their new bases. Most of the young Marines—officers and enlisted men alike—had no marital entanglements, but spur of the moment marriages were common. Kinsman later recalled his marriage after boot camp, and his limited marital life during the training at Camp Pendleton:

My girlfriend from Peoria, Rosemary Hoffman, surprised me by coming to California on a bus to visit me. My friend, "Josie" Josephson's [sic] fiancé, Joan, came out to marry him. Somehow or other we got together and when we received our first liberty, and boot camp was over, we went out the front gate of the Marine Base (the four of us), walked up five or six blocks, spotted a small Christian Church, and asked the pastor (Pastor Cron) if he would perform a double wedding ceremony. He consented and we were married. We stood up for each other. We had a 72-hour pass and the four of us went to San Diego and went to a movie (some honeymoon). We found a one-night's lodging in San Diego and then returned to Oceanside, to catch the last truck going back to camp, as we had to be back by 6:00 a.m. Monday morning to Jacques Tank Farm. The wives both got a job and stayed in Oceanside at Rosecrusean Lodge, in separate rooms. "Josie" and I were only given five or six 72-hour passes, which added up to about two weeks in all with our new wives.[24]

It was quite common for wives and fiancés to join servicemen, living and working in nearby towns. Joan McClure Josefson, Charlie Sooter,"Josie" Josefson, and Bruce Seward ham it up for the camera in front of the recreation tent.—Dan Josefson

On 1 June "They drove the tanks down to San Diego," said Gazel. The loading process was time consuming, but on 19 July the company sailed out of San Diego aboard the SS *John McLean*. "We were twenty-eight days to New Caledonia, on a Liberty ship, at a top speed of six knots."[25]

One of the time-honored naval traditions of sailors and Marines is the initiation of novice "pollywogs" into the ranks of the "shellbacks"—men who have sailed across the equator. The ceremony can be simple or quite elaborate, depending upon the size of the ships complement, the effort invested by the shellbacks, and of course the sadistic inventiveness of the shellbacks. No one is spared, regardless of rank. Like combat, it is one of those great levelers that everyone remembers in detail, but usually everyone recalls different details.

No photos exist of the initiation of the Charlie Company Marines into King Neptune's Realm, but this photo illustrates typical improvised costumes, the "royal baby" (traditionally the fattest shellback) in the diaper, and the "see lawyer" who holds the "book of regulations."—Grey Research Center, Quantico

Bale thought it was "Kind of like an initiation at a college. . . . Dressing people up in imitation grass skirts. Painting them up with body paint, ink, and that kind of thing. Pouring water on people, and having them do pushups and handstands, and that sort of thing."

Gazel recalled that the senior shellback sat bare-chested on a "throne," wearing a robe. "King Neptune sits on a throne, and you gotta fall in front of him. . . . You reach down to kiss his feet, and he puts a dead fish there. And that's what you kiss."

Scot Kinsman wrote briefly of his experience:

. . . you must be initiated into King Neptune's Realm. It is called a "day to remember." Everyone goes through the gauntlet including officers. It is a time when if you hold a grudge against anyone, you have the freedom to unload. You fall out in "skivvy drawers" (under shorts). There is a long line with men standing on both sides and a high-pressure hose is used on the buttocks of the help-less men. These men on both sides are holding paddles like ping-pong paddles. They drill holes in them so when they make contact, they suck the blood right out. It is worse than taking a trip "to the woodshed." Then you may be called upon to sit in a chair while they shave off all of your hair, or paint it red or green or yellow. Some of the other crazy things they do are enough to make you not want to go through this experience again.[26]

Woolum also vividly recalled the gauntlet of paddles. "The lowest pri-vate, he leads the deal . . . I guess it's the sailors that are giving you a swat on the ass; they've got their paddles and whatever they're gonna hit you

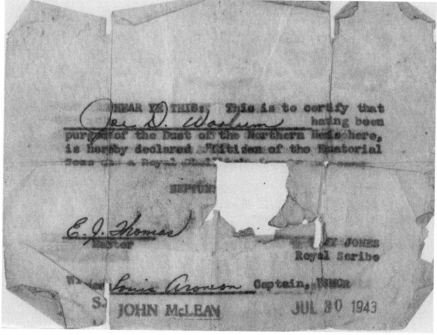

Larger ships issued elaborately printed Shellback Certificates, but Joe Woolum's bedraggled simple typewritten example indicates that the SS John McLean crossed the equator on 30 July 1943. It was prepared by Royal Scribe Davy Jones, certified by the ship's Master, and witnessed by a veteran shellback (a Marine Corps Reserve officer) aboard ship.—Joe Woolum

with. So they whack you. When that [most junior] guy gets through, then he's a shellback, so he can pick up something to hit the rest of them with it. Therefore the captain [*sic*, in this case Lieutenant Bale] is the last one through. All his men get to whup the hell [out of him]. . . . It was kind of a fun day they had."

Arriving in New Caledonia on 13 August, the tankers were held at a transit center near Noumea. When the battalion commander arrived, said Bale, ". . . he called a conference and the first thing he said was 'Where are the nurses?' His next question's 'Where's the bar?' And it went on from there."

"They took us to a camp called Camp Magenta," said Ed Gazel, who later noted that "Camp Magenta was nothing but red mud."[27] The camp was about fifteen miles by bad road from the tank park near the docks, where the tanks remained for three months. "They didn't need tank maintenance every day because we weren't doing anything. So we'd go on hikes." Bale corroborated Gazel's assessment: "It was a miserable situation. There was no place that you could train and when we weren't doing maintenance it was hikes.

"In fact, on one occasion the battalion communications officer and I took a jeep and went *way* up the island looking for areas that maybe some arrangements could be made with the French, and we could train."

The only notable event was the Nickel Dock Fire of 1 November; ammunition being unloaded from merchant ships at a nearby dock caught fire and detonated in a huge explosion. Bale: "I took the two Headquarters tanks and went down on those docks . . . in case they wanted to get behind them and use them as a shield to play fire hoses on those ships. They had high-pressure water down on those docks.

"We took those two tanks down there, and when we got down there they didn't need anything. So we went back. We didn't do anything but make a run down to that dock."

The event remained classified until 1976.[28] "I don't know why we thought that, because thousands of US military on New Caledonia knew about it. You could see the smoke from miles and miles away, and the French and the natives certainly knew about it." Bale estimated their involvement was no more than five minutes. "When it became obvious there was no need for us, I got out of there."

The unit diary recorded that on 11 September the entire battalion moved from Camp Magenta to more permanent quarters at Camp St. Louis. The camp was the old Raider camp—typically primitive—that in the interim had been occupied by a signals battalion. There was at least protected storage for spares and tools. However "No facilities are afforded in this locality for the operation of Medium Tanks."[29]

The condition of the camps caused Gazel to recall New Caledonia as "The asshole of the universe." Some of the men decided to socialize with the local women who gathered firewood in the adjacent forest. "Boy, all of a sudden about ten or twelve came running out of there and a big black guy with a big ol' knife, a machete. He runs them out of the woods." Gunny Dumais "...could speak the language [French].... He went down there and talked to the guy, talked him out of it. So everything was settled peacefully." The camp was also near the new Second Raider Battalion camp, and "Nobody fooled with them guys."

The tank battalion finally located a suitable training site, "...but then in the middle of negotiations," said Bale, "I got orders to take this company and go to New Zealand to join the Second Division.

"We were out hiking one day, and when we came back into camp somebody told me 'The colonel wants to see you.' First thing went through my mind was 'What the hell have I done wrong now?' I went up there and he said 'You're going to New Zealand.'" Thus Bale learned by word of mouth that they had been formally attached to the Second Marine Division as of 16 September. "He said 'I didn't make the decision.' He said 'We drew straws, and in your absence Major Jeb Stuart, the battalion exec, drew for you.'" Twenty-five years later Bale learned that Stuart rigged the drawing "...because I had the best-trained company."

On 27 September, the company (six officers, 151 men, and two Navy medical corpsmen) was detached from the parent battalion. It was "...embarked aboard the SS *Mormacport* for duty in the field with the Second Marine Division."[30]

Note that the unit diary correctly refers to the SS (not USS) *Mormacport*. The *Mormacport* was a Type C-3 bulk cargo ship built in 1940 under the Merchant Marine Act of 1936, so it was well suited for the cargo of tanks. Built for the US–South America trade, it was never intended as a troopship, but had "extensive passenger accommodation" and served as a combination cargo and troopship throughout the war. It was operated under contract by the Moore-McCormack Line, with a Merchant Marine crew.[31]

Bale recalled that the company loaded out of Noumea for a storm-tossed passage to New Zealand. At JERK (the code name for Wellington), Bale first met Major Alexander B. Swenceski, the commander of the Second Tank Battalion to which he would be attached as of 9 October. Overall his brief first impression was favorable:

> Al was a former motor transport officer, having commanded the Motor Transport Company, Fourth Marines in Shanghai, China around 1938–1940. My contact with him was limited to a few days in both New Zealand and New Caledonia, followed by shipboard time sailing to Tarawa. I found him to be professionally knowledgeable and anxious to lead the battalion in combat. At Efate, New Hebrides Islands, he went out of his way to insure that I attended all the Task Force and Division briefings. In addition he introduced me to the regimental and appropriate battalion commanders. When he learned of the presence of an Australian who had lived on Tarawa for several years, he arranged for him to visit the ship and discuss the reef, lagoon and tides.[32]

Bale further recalled: "Swenceski met the ship and took me to DivHQ where we checked in with the adjutant and proceeded to the G-3 shop, where I met Shoup and Tompkins (this was the start of a long time relationship with both). We were told that there would be a delay of a day or so in unloading and that I should give the troops liberty on a daily basis until we unloaded.

"Strange thing. The adjutant did not take even a copy of the movement order and it was very vague as to whom I reported. I was instructed to report daily to Tompkins pending the unloading.

"Ski took me to the Tank Battalion where I met McCoy, and Lt. Spike Henasay, the S-4, a mustang and long time tanker. Following a late lunch in the Officer's Mess I was returned to the ship. That was my last contact with the 2nd Tk Bn in New Zealand.

"On the fourth morning I checked in with Tompkins. Tommy told me that the Div was going on an operation but we were to return to New

Caledonia to await the arrival of a special ship which would transport us. I was told that I was to unload 1 tank and turn it over to McCoy. Upon returning to the ship, I found McCoy there and he explained that as soon as the tank was offloaded we would sail and our berth would be filled by an APA [Navy Personnel Attack Transport] which would load the tank and an infantry battalion going to Hawke's Bay on an exercise. Off-loading was delayed. I will never forget the tank coming out of the hold, the whistle blowing and the civilian dock workers taking time off for 'tea time' leaving the tank suspended in the air over the hold."[33]

During the brief four-day stop many men were given a one-night shore liberty, but "We never unloaded," said Bale, "we turned around and went back to New Caledonia."

The Army had developed fording kits to allow traversing deeper water, but none were available to the Marines. Actually, two tanks and eleven enlisted men under Lieutenant Kent were left behind for a fording test at Hawke's Bay, New Zealand. Bale: "We sent these tanks up there because I was quizzed extensively as to how much water that thing could ford. And I didn't know. All I could do was refer him back to the manual. So these two tanks were sent up to Hawke's Bay to see how much water they could ford. It turned out they could ford forty inches like the manual said." Shivetts, in the contingent left temporarily in New Zealand with Lieutenant Kent, thought liberty in New Zealand was "Rather nice. You had to buy tea, or go to a movie." Following the test, the test vehicles (probably the two Headquarters tanks) were loaded onto the USS *Doyen* and USS *Zeilin*, and shipped out to rejoin the company at Efate, in the French New Hebrides (now the Republic of Vanuatu).[34]

The two transports were typical of the cobbled-together amphibious fleet. *Doyen* (APA-1) was a purpose-built amphibious transport launched in 1942. *Zeilin* (APA-3) was—despite its later number—the former ocean liner SS *President Jackson*, launched in 1921, acquired by the Navy and hastily converted to an amphibious assault transport in 1940. Neither was capable of launching the tank landing craft required for the medium tanks.[35]

A potentially worse problem than fording deep water was communications, the bane of so many military operations. "Liaison with the commanders was bad," wrote Bale. "It was established through assigning the Co. XO, O.F. Kent, to the Command Group of the Second Marines. The platoon sergeants were assigned to each of the assault BLTs [Battalion Landing Teams]. There was no means of communication with the platoon leaders, individual tanks or with me. We had no radios to provide them. No com [communications] plan included the tank company."[36]

With no communications other than runners, or chance encounters, Lieutenant Kent and the platoon sergeants could only advise the infantry commanders.

The unit diary recorded their arrival back at New Caledonia aboard the *Mormacport* on 14 October.[37]

The company was to meet up with the brand new *USS Ashland.* The *Ashland* had sailed from San Diego in August, delivering troops and equipment to the southern Pacific, and shuttled back to Hawaii. From Hawaii she delivered troops and cargo to New Caledonia, and did not have time to reach New Zealand.[38]

On 4 November, the bulk of the company—five officers, 134 men and corpsmen and twelve tanks—left New Caledonia aboard the *Ashland.*[39] Due to lack of space aboard the ship, the M32B2 had to be left back in New Caledonia.

The SS Mormacport *in its wartime configuration. Note the life rafts, numerous anti-aircraft gun tubs, and lookout position on the forward kingposts. Cargo ships like* John MacLean *and* Mormacport *could transport medium tanks between ports, but their cargo booms could not unload them, nor could they launch the LCMs needed to carry tanks ashore.*—Army Signal Corps

The two rehearsal tanks were reunited with the rest of the company embarked aboard the *Ashland* for a hasty division rehearsal at Efate, an island totally unlike the actual objective. At the landing rehearsals on 7 and 9 November, there was little or no actual coordination among units, and Bale recalled that "I had met the regimental commanders and the battalion commanders, but my junior officers had never met any of them. During the rehearsal area, we landed [at Mele Bay] but couldn't move off of the beach because of the jungle. In the meantime the troops that we're going to have to work with in the operation had already moved inland. We backloaded and sailed to Tarawa."[40]

Bale also noted that "The rehearsal really didn't do much for us except give us the chance to move the vehicles out of the landing craft and all." Rather than any meaningful training "We landed and sat on the beach."

At Efate, Swenceski and some of his staff visited aboard the *Ashland*, but despite being officially attached to the Swenceski's command, Bale and his company were functioning more as a separate unit attached to Division Troops. "What was the command relationship? To be very candid about it, I don't know. And I don't know to this day, because it was a strange thing. We were attached to the Second Marines, and the only contact I ever had with the Second Marines was at a briefing and a conference aboard one of the APAs at Efate during this rehearsal period. And of course they were kind of in turmoil because that's where the regimental commander got relieved and Dave Shoup [the Division Operations Officer] took over the regiment.

"I met the three battalion commanders. The platoon leaders of the tank platoons met them and we arranged to have a liaison NCO or somebody to land with them." A plan was worked out that in the absence of any ability to communicate directly with the infantry, an experienced tank NCO would land with each battalion as a sort of advisor. "But there was no training with the infantry. None at all.

"Looking back on it, it was a strange, strange thing. I was getting most of my instruction from a Major Tommy Tompkins, who was the assistant G-3 [operations officer] of the Division. . . . Swenceski was there almost for the ride, that was it. Our orders were simply to land on the three beaches behind the three battalions."

One fateful effect of the confused command structure was that "No provisions were made for resupply of fuel and ammo."[41] Looking back on the preparations for Tarawa seventy years later, Ed Bale thought that "The Marine Corps was naïve. I don't know a better term than naïve, about how to employ these things [tanks and amtracs]. They had not learned a damn thing from Guadalcanal." The Marine Corps had a flawed tank doctrine "And that came from Marine officers going to the armor school at Fort Knox."

Bale thought that "This business of going out front and running around and cruising and all, that all got started with the Army. . . ." At the time, Army tank doctrine emphasized penetrating, freewheeling attacks by armored formations, a misreading of the successful German *blitzkrieg* combined-arms tactics. Jim Carter, a very young light tank driver in B Company, Second Tank Battalion at Tarawa, aptly described it as ". . . operating pretty much with the Army manual, as cavalry, where you dashed here and dashed there."[42]

To avoid potential damage to coconut (copra) trees and the unimproved roads and bridges on New Caledonia, the tanks had never rehearsed with the infantry. They had never even seen the infantrymen they were to support in one of the most vicious battles of World War II.

It was not a very well prepared operation. Bale recalled, "We hadn't fired a gun since we began to move out of Pendleton" 166 days earlier.

Only after leaving Efate did the enlisted men of Charlie Company learn their objective: the tiny atoll of Tarawa.

CHAPTER THREE

THE TANKS OF CHARLIE COMPANY

You should not have any special fondness for a particular
weapon, or anything else, for that matter. Too much is
the same as not enough. Without imitating anyone else,
you should have as much weaponry as suits you.
—MIYAMOTO MUSASHI, The Book of Five Rings

The tanks used in combat by Charlie Company were diesel-powered M4A2s, a model of the famed tank that the Army considered unreliable and hard to maintain. So how did the Marine Corps end up with these diesel tanks? The story of Marine Corps tank procurement was complex, and continues to be misunderstood.*

In the last days before the country was drawn into the global war, America was playing catch-up. Crippled by two decades of isolationism and relentless budget cuts, the Army was small in size ("nineteenth, after Portugal"), and armed with hopelessly obsolete equipment. The design of the first generation of "modern" medium tanks, the M3, harkened back to the Great War, with a turret mounting a 37 millimeter cannon that fired armor-piercing rounds for fighting other tanks, and a hull-mounted medium velocity 75 millimeter cannon for firing high-explosive rounds at other targets. American factories could not yet manufacture the critical race ring, the huge toothed gear and ball-bearing mount that allowed the rota-

---

* The commonly seen name "Sherman" applied to all tanks of the M4 series and was coined by the British. The name was not used by American soldiers and Marines during the war, and most veterans still do not use the name.

tion of a turret large enough to mount the seventy-five millimeter cannon.

The next generation medium tank, the M4, remedied that problem with the 75mm main gun mounted in a turret with 360 degree traverse, but the new tank still suffered from relatively thin armor and a main gun not designed to pierce thick armor. It was not the best tank in the world by far, but it would be more than adequate if produced in mass. One of the major limiting factors would be availability of a suitable power plant. So the War Department elected to simultaneously procure five models of the same basic tank, differing primarily in the engine.

The M4 (welded hull) and M4A1 (cast hull) would utilize proven Wright Whirlwind R-975 radial aircraft engines. The M4A2 would use two General Motors diesels originally designed as boat engines, powering a single transmission through a transfer case (the entire rig was known as the 6046 engine). The M4A3 would utilize a powerful but as-yet unproven Ford GAA gasoline engine, but that tank would not enter common service until late 1943. The M4A4 would utilize a complex Chrysler A57 multi-bank engine. By early 1943 the situation had clarified, but much to the detriment of the Marine Corps. There was considerable debate among senior Marine Corps tank officers as to which tank was best, with each model of the tank having its very passionate advocates.[43]

In the end the determination came from much higher authorities. Given the pressing need for tanks by the enormously expanded US Army and the Allied powers, it was decided to give the Army priority for the preferred M4A1. The Soviets preferred diesel engines and would accept only the M4A2, but the Marine Corps could be allocated some of the production. The M4A3 would be provided first to the British and US Army, and secondarily to other users when it finally became available in large numbers. The only tank nobody wanted was the M4A4, though the British would accept them, and others were foisted upon the Chinese. So in the final analysis the Corps took the tank they could get.

Like all tanks in World War II the M4A2 underwent several changes over the course of production to improve combat capability, reliability, and to simplify and speed construction, although all the basic systems of the tank remained the same. It is important to remember that these design improvements were usually introduced piecemeal rather than as distinctly different sub-models. The great virtue of the M4 series of tanks was that all the basic parts of all sub-models were interchangeable, and it was not uncommon for a unit to be equipped with several sub-models of tank. This was the case with Charlie Company, as indicated by the variety of features on the tanks used in training.

The M4A2s ultimately used by Charlie Company at Tarawa are often referred to as "mid-production" vehicles, although military procurement agencies—and certainly not the tank crews—made no such distinction.

As a very junior lieutenant, Ed Bale was not involved in matters of procurement policy, ". . . but I do know that the battalion commander, Lieutenant Colonel Ben Powers, and the battalion maintenance officer, who was a captain, Charlie Dunmore, who before World War II had been a sergeant driver for a number of Marine Corps generals in San Diego, went back to the Detroit area [in early May 1943]. They had, apparently, almost an open checkbook because they bought tank recovery vehicles, which were the first the Marine Corps had." The first production batches of M32s were converted from gun tanks, so "When they were built, they even shipped the turrets that came off the hulls, and the guns that came out of the turrets. When I left the States I had all that stuff. An extra turret, extra gun. They bought machine shops. Even in a tank company in this battalion we had a full machine shop. All kinds of stuff.

"I didn't know any better then, but now I figure that nobody in the Marine Corps knew what to buy and what not to buy. And they had an open checkbook. They took spare track and all kinds of stuff, in the company. We did all the maintenance in the company."

The main distinguishing characteristic of the new mid-production vehicles issued to Charlie Company was the lower slope to the glacis (called the slope plate by Marine Corps tank crewmen), sloped at 56 degrees from the vertical. This low slope had required raised boxes to accommodate the driver's and assistant driver's vision devices, and to allow adequate space inside the front of the hull. On these mid-production vehicles, the older raised cast hoods were replaced by improved welded hoods with no direct vision blocks. However, the new tanks lacked another significant improvement, the addition of an overhead hatch for the loader/radio operator. Combat experience by the British in North Africa had demonstrated that the loader, who had to duck under the gun breech to escape a burning tank through the tank commander's hatch, was often trapped.[44]

The more detailed technical specifications of the M4A2 are not covered here, as that material is readily available from a number of commonly available books and Internet sources.[45]

The crews eventually came to love the diesel-powered M4A2. Cooped up inside a steel box with tons of fuel and ammunition, one of the tank crewman's greatest fears is fire. Charles Mason: "Number one, if a gasoline engine was hit, you had a darned good chance of fire. We had fuel tanks blown out of ours, and it never caught fire. So yes, the diesels were far superior." The resistance of the diesel tank to fire was probably best illustrated by the experiences of the 1st Tank Battalion on Okinawa. When Japanese anti-tank rounds ruptured the fuel cells on one tank, the vehicle continued to operate with smoking diesel fuel sloshing about on the deck under the crew's feet without catching fire.[46]

Operating the tank in combat was a complex balancing act, said Mason. "The gunner and the driver had to work together. Otherwise the crew would have never made out. If anything was wrong with the tank, and the gunner didn't know about it, he had no way of compensating in a combat situation. Likewise if there's something wrong with the gunning department, the driver could compensate and make up for it."

To rotate the turret "You could operate it manually, there was a little crank, or on automatic, which was electrical. It was a little handle that you just turned." The tank had two gun sights, "You had the telescopic sight, which I never used, and the periscope that had sights in it. It had arms that attached to the gun, and it was all synchronized."

In the 1940s, tank gunnery was still something of an art form. To engage a target the tank commander would typically describe the target to the gunner, and estimate the range to the target. The gunner's periscope sight for the main gun incorporated a simple stadiametric range finder. The gunner estimated the size of the target (for example a man would be approximately six feet tall), and compared the estimated size of the target against the size of the target as seen through his sight. The size as seen through the sight was determined by a reticle—a simple bar scale—built into the sight. The estimated true size of the target as compared to the apparent size in the sight as measured against the reticle gave the estimated range to the target. The system worked well at the close ranges typical of combat in the Pacific. At longer ranges the gunner and tank commander could work together, adjusting the range by observing the impact of the first round.

The gunner operated both the main cannon and the coaxial machine gun. Mason: "... the triggers for that were two little buttons, about three inches apart on the floorboard. My foot was just wide enough to have them both. I could just rock my foot and fire the machine gun and rock it the other way and fire the seventy-five."

The gunner could aim the coaxial machine gun into the general vicinity of the target at short combat ranges. The bow machine gun operated by the assistant driver had no sighting system. Both the coax and the bow machine gun were aimed primarily by observing the path of tracer rounds, or the dust and debris thrown up by the impact of the rounds, and "walking" the machine gun fire onto the target.

It is important to remember that the fighting men of World War II were products of an earlier age—and for most, the deprivations of the Great Depression. They came of age in an era without air conditioning and most of the other creature comforts that so many of us today take for granted. The everyday life of the individual tank crewmen in the Pacific consisted of brutal extremes of heat and humidity, in addition to the dirt and grime associated with the vehicles themselves. This was such an integral part of their daily lives that few former tank crewmen even remark upon the harsh conditions of daily life in a tank.[47]

As part of the research for this book, Cansiere arranged to ride in an M4A2 tank preserved at the Saumur Tank Museum in France, as described in Appendix C.

MODIFICATIONS

American tank crews were incorrigible tinkerers, constantly making changes to their tanks that they hoped would make life easier or help increase their chances of survival in combat. This was particularly true of the Marines in the Pacific and reached its high point on Iwo Jima with the addition of elaborate wood and concrete supplementary armor, protective cages over periscopes, water tanks for the infantry, and many other features. When Charlie Company departed for the Pacific they had no combat experience and little information to guide them, and made few such changes to the tanks.

One feature seen on several Charlie Company tanks, notably CUD-

DLES and CHICAGO, was welding small support brackets to the sponsons and turret sides to support very heavy wire. This was apparently done to facilitate mounting locally-cut vegetation as camouflage, a common practice in Europe and taught during training in the US military. Of course, in an amphibious assault there is no vegetation to cut ahead of time, and the short violent battles usually left no time for the niceties of camouflage.

Another rare modification was to construct a steel rack on the back of the tank to hold standard five-gallon storage cans. The fact that the cans, visible in photos, are the narrow-mouthed "fuel" cans rather than the enamel-lined "water" cans with the larger opening, has led some to argue that these were extra fuel. However, it was not uncommon to use the "fuel" can for water. "We were more afraid of lacking water than fuel," said Bale. Neither the camouflage brackets nor the can racks were seen on all tanks.

All tanks were re-equipped with new steel-faced tracks to replace the less durable rubber-faced track provided at the factory.

Just prior to shipping out from San Diego the company welded on mounts for .50 caliber heavy machine guns to replace the .30 caliber guns on the turret roofs of the new tanks. This big .50 caliber machine gun, intended as an antiaircraft weapon, provided more firepower.[48]

The big machine guns were generally not used, but kept stowed inside the turrets. The heavy machine gun was seldom seen on Marine Corps tanks. It was awkward to use, hard to maintain, and had a slow rate of fire. The tank crews preferred light machine guns and various hand-held weapons for close defense against suicidal Japanese infantry attacks. Tarawa was one of the few battles where the big machine guns were used, to try and suppress enemy fire from positions in The Pocket, a cluster of tenacious Japanese positions between two of the landing beaches.

Surprisingly, the critical modification that was not made was to adequately prepare the tanks for wading ashore in an amphibious operation. The Marine Corps had expended considerable fruitless effort in attempts to develop an amphibious tank, or at least a lightweight "expeditionary tank" that could be readily put ashore in an assault landing. The Army had foreseen no such need, but Army-designed vehicles were built to ford streams and other minor water obstacles. The typical fording depth was specified at forty inches/101cm, but no consideration was given to surf, fast currents, or the particularly pernicious effects of salt water.

The British had first designed deep-wading kits (actually just simple pipes welded onto the air intakes and exhausts) used on the Churchill tanks in the Dieppe Raid of 19 August 1942. The US Army Ordnance Department and the ordnance units in Europe and North Africa had belatedly recognized the need for special equipment that would allow tanks to traverse deeper water. Special kits were quickly designed for extending the exhausts, waterproofing the hull and turret/hull joint to prevent flooding, and to prevent water from entering the air intakes. Even if kits could not be provided, the designs allowed for manufacture from local resources.

Various waterproofing solutions for the M4 tanks had been successfully used as early as the Sicily landings (Operation HUSKY) in June 1943. None of these solutions had as yet made their way to the Pacific. Waterproofing for Marine Corps tanks consisted at best of sealing all possible lower openings on the hull with shaft grease, a particularly heavy lubricant and sealant used on the propeller shaft bearings of naval vessels.

COMMUNICATIONS

Perhaps the greatest weakness of the early Marine Corps tanks was the radio system. The radios in the first Marine Corps tanks, beginning with the ill-fated Marmon-Herrington light tanks, were obsolete US Navy GF/RU aircraft radio systems, first designed in 1934 by the Aircraft Radio Corporation of Boonton, New Jersey. Even the radio operators habitually called these radios the RU/GF, and usually referred to them as "Ruji-Fujis."

Compared to the improved FM (Frequency-Modulated) radios already being installed in US Army and newly-procured Marine Corps tanks by mid-1943, these early "tuned radio frequency" Amplitude-Modulated (AM) systems were plagued by poor sensitivity, significant vulnerability to interference from nearby transmitters, and deliberate enemy jamming (though the latter was never a major problem in the war against Japan). Furthermore, the delicate vacuum tubes, designed almost a decade earlier, did not possess the reliability of newer tubes available by the beginning of the war, a major factor in applications like tanks, where severe jostling, extreme heat and humidity, and possible exposure to water were everyday facts of life.*

---

* Unless otherwise noted, information on the design and functionality of the radio systems is from e-mail correspondence, Gilbert with Michael Hanz, June 2014.

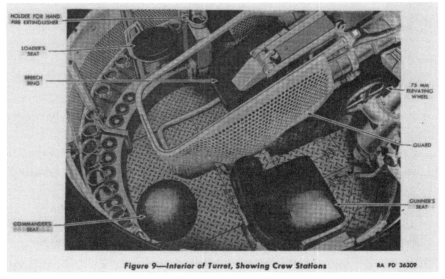

Figure 9—Interior of Turret, Showing Crew Stations   RA PD 36309

Turret crew positions in an M4A2. Rings and clamps at left are 75mm ready-ammunition racks. The loader had to climb under the recoil guard to escape a damaged or burning tank through the commander's hatch.—Army Technical Manual, University of Florida Libraries

Driver's controls. Steering was by manual braking of the left or right track, and required considerable upper body strength.—Army Technical Manual, University of Florida Libraries

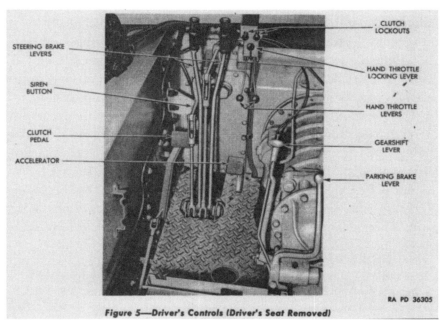

RA PD 36305

Figure 5—Driver's Controls (Driver's Seat Removed)

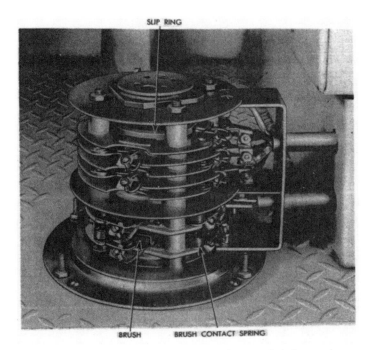

The slip ring (shown with protective cover removed) provided electrical connections between the hull and the rotating turret. If it shorted out, electrical turret and weapons controls failed.—Army Technical Manual, University of Florida Libraries

Critical components that failed at Tarawa. The voltage regulators and slip ring were vulnerable to salt-water intrusion if the tank flooded, and the unreliable radios had to be operated by the already overburdened loader.—Army Technical Manual, University of Florida Libraries

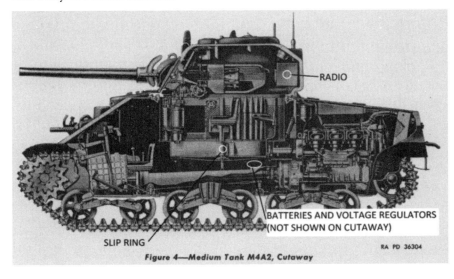

Figure 4—Medium Tank M4A2, Cutaway

Like all AM systems, these radios were also susceptible to static from natural sources like electrical storms, and from the spark plugs of vehicle engine ignition systems. The diesel engines in the M4A2 did not create as significant a problem as gasoline engines, but Marine Corps Tables of Equipment differentiated vehicles with shielded ignition systems suitable for radio installation as "reconnaissance" or "radio-equipped." Interestingly, the 1943 Marine Corps Division Table of Organization specified that trucks were to be equipped with Army Signal Corps SCR-193 and SCR-299 radios, while tanks and amphibian tractors retained the GF/RU radios.[49]

The GF/RU was similar to the Signal Corps Radio 183 (SCR-183) in US Army Air Corps service. Both were considered a low-power "command" set for local communication as opposed to a more powerful and longer-ranged "liaison" radio. By 1941, the GF/RU radios were already obsolete, and most were being replaced by newer "superheterodyne" radios in first-line naval combat aircraft, making these units available in relatively large numbers. The transmitter (GF) and receiver (RU) were separate units and were produced in a number of different models depending upon production period and application. There were at least twenty different RU receiver models and twelve GF transmitter models, but no record is known to exist concerning which specific models were used in tanks.*

The system was band-limited, with operating frequency limits established by coils that plugged into the radio chassis. Each coil set allowed transmission/reception over a small range of frequencies; the communications capabilities of each tank were thereby limited to the frequency band of the installed coils.

A hand-operated dial, not so affectionately known as a "coffee grinder," was used to tune to the limited range of frequencies allowed by the coils installed. This tuning dial was not calibrated by frequency; it was num-

---

* The Army Signal Corps and the Army Air Corps were at the time (1940) engaged in a jurisdictional battle over procurement of aircraft radios. The Signal Corps fought to procure an equally inadequate design for the SCR-183, but the Air Corps succeeded in forcing the Signal Corps to adopt the new Navy radios, rubbing it in a bit with the unusual designation SCR-274-N, where the N indicated their Navy origin. For more detail on the early radios see White, *Tubes, Transistors, and Take-overs,* and Hanz, *SCR-AE-183.*

bered 0 to 100. To tune to one of the available frequencies the radio operator had to refer to a prepared calibration chart for the individual tuning unit, and interpolate the chart to the dial reading. In combat, requiring this extra step was clearly daunting.

Another fundamental problem was that although these radios were in theory functionally compatible with the Navy-designed TBX and TBY tactical radios used by most Marine Corps ground units, there was no practical way for tanks to communicate directly with infantry, artillery, or aircraft radio nets. Compatibility was limited by the coils installed and by the near-impossibility of rapidly switching among several nets using the "coffee grinder." One clue that no one had foreseen the need for compatibility between the infantry and tank radios, was in Ed Bale's statement that "They [the radio operators] had all these coils. The coil covered certain spectrum and you had a box of coils like this [hand gesture], but we didn't have a damn thing that would work with the infantry."

This problem did not lie wholly within the tank and amphibian tractor units. Communications between infantry battalions and their subordinate companies were by field telephone, and below company level by paper message blanks carried by messengers (a duty designated in the Table of Organization). Under the best of circumstances, the tank company commander could have talked only to the infantry battalion headquarters.

The few portable radios that equipped the infantry, artillery, and the air and naval gunfire liaison parties were themselves unreliable. The TBX was a heavy, bulky radio carried in two steel chests and powered by a hand-cranked generator. It was the basic tactical radio. The smaller TBY battery-powered backpack radio was developed as a Navy emergency radio known as the "walky-talky."*

Neither was really suitable for tactical operations. "The TBX lacked the necessary range, and the TBY was not sufficiently waterproof."[50]

The situation was even more complex for supporting arms. In theory a tank company commander could, for example, request artillery support by sending a radio message to the tank battalion command group, where the message would be recorded and crossed-over by paper message blank

---

* The Marines called the later SCR-536 handheld radio, so beloved of Hollywood movies, the "Handy-talky" or "Spam-can" radio.

onto the artillery field telephone net for relay to a firing battery. In practice the system was so limited that control of artillery, naval gunfire, and aircraft support was restricted to special liaison parties, each with their own dedicated radio or telephone network.

The communications capabilities within a tank unit also reflected the inherent limitations of the radios. In a tank unit, the company commander could not easily talk both "up" to battalion and "down" to his platoon leaders. Platoon leaders in turn could talk "up" to the company commander, and "down" to his subordinate tanks only with some difficulty.

To switch to another frequency on the radio net—as example, for a platoon leader to switch from his platoon frequency to the company command frequency—the radio operator had first to refer to his frequency "cheat sheet" or remember the proper dial setting for each sub-unit within his unit. Michael Hanz, who has made a study of these radios, said that "If you had to keep track of your tank to tank frequency and still get your company commander on another frequency, it was difficult in the extreme. Even if they were all on the same coil set, you had to crank that little coffee 'grinder' tuning control back and forth between the two frequencies (lessee, the C.O. is on 38 and the rest of the unit is on 43 . . . or was it the other way around?) Then 'Whang [expletive deleted] a shell just hit my tank!' That does wonders for thoughtful contemplation. And if you added a TBX or TBY tactical network to contact, you might have to swap out the transmitter and receiver coil sets, only to have to swap them back when you needed to be in the tank network. Impossible . . ."

To add to the confusion, the radio doubled as the intercom within the tank. In the more compact light tanks with a four-man crew, the tank commander doubled as gunner. He communicated by shouting and hand signals to his loader. To signal the driver he used his feet. Bill Finley was a light tank crewman: "If he wanted the driver to go forward, he would just kick him in the back of the head. . . . If he wanted to stop, he would mash his foot down on his head. If he wanted to turn right, you mash on the right shoulder, left, mash on the left one . . ."[51]

Clearly this would not work in the larger medium tanks, so each crewman was hooked into the radio that doubled as an intercom. In each tank the tank commander did most of the talking, but in a four-tank platoon there was ample room for confusion in the chaos of battle.

There were no voice-activated microphones, so the tank commander had to manually key his microphone to talk. The induction microphones worked by detecting the vibrations of the speaker's larynx. Strapped tightly to the throat, they chafed and caused skin rashes in hot conditions. In addition, there was yet another switch that controlled whether the tank commander was speaking over the radio or the internal circuit.

The radios were also bulky, with multiple components, and this created problems unique to the tanks. The only readily accessible space for placement of the bulky radios was the bustle, the overhang at the rear of the turret, with the single external antenna mounted on the left rear of the turret roof.[52]

This location of the radio meant that the radio operator—already the busiest man in the tank—doubled as the loader, creating enormous functional problems. The loader not only had to load the main gun with the appropriate round specified by the tank commander, but also: (1) collect empty shell casings as they came out of the cannon breech and dispose of them through the pistol port; (2) rearrange main gun ready ammo storage as rounds were fired; (3) recover main gun ammo from storage racks to replenish ready racks; (4) load the .30 caliber coaxial machine gun, clear any jams or malfunctions, and change overheated barrels as necessary; and (5) empty the shell casing bag from the machine gun to prevent expended brass from spilling out and jamming mechanical components in the turret. In his spare time he operated the radio.

The lack of ability to communicate directly with the infantry was a problem recognized from the experiences of the 1st Tank Battalion on Guadalcanal, and the light tank platoons of the 9th, 10th and 11th Defense Battalions on New Georgia. The 1st Marine Division had reported on their communications problems, and by late 1943 tanks were being equipped with the new SCR-508A and SCR-528A radios. This was not a practical solution for tactical communications, since infantry communications below battalion level were still by field telephone or message carriers. The Defense Battalion Tank Platoons had solved the immediate tactical coordination problem by jury-rigging two sound-powered EE-1 field telephones, one on the rear of the tank and the other in the turret, to allow infantry to communicate directly with the supporting tank. Neither solution was available to the 2nd Tank Battalion or to the supporting C

Company, I Corps Medium Tank Battalion already en route to Tarawa.[53]

In the absence of any practical communication with the infantry, the tank battalions had adopted a system in which each company had a section of reconnaissance scouts in the Headquarters Platoon. Their mission was to advance, on foot, in front of the tanks to locate targets. This system had been successfully used on New Georgia, with native Solomon Islanders acting as guides in the dense jungle. The scout designated a target by laying his rifle on the ground pointing in the direction of the target, and standing in front of the tank to communicate the nature of the target and the range by hand signals. This assignment should have been easily recognized as nearly suicidal in combat.[54]

In summary, the tank units that would go into battle on Tarawa were hamstrung by poor communications at all levels and in all functions. What nobody foresaw was the price to be paid for these shortcomings.

COLORS AND MARKINGS

The color of Marine Corps equipment in World War II is a source of considerable debate among model builders who wish to be as close as possible to the "true" color for their models. But if you ask a veteran what color the tanks were, you get a puzzled look and the answer "green." Tank crewmen had more important things to think about than subtle differences in shades of green. Most do not recall the tactical number of their tank, or details like personal markings that appear in period photographs.

The paint color of tanks, and all other equipment, was determined by the branch of service administering the procurement contract. This led to some interesting peculiarities. For example, early amphibian tractors were procured under a US Navy contract and were considered "naval vessels." Delivered in the standard Navy ship color, many went on to serve in combat wearing this gray paint unless there was some pressing need—such as corrosion control—to warrant repainting.

In the 1920s and 1930s the Marine Corps had experimented with numerous vehicles from both civilian sources (trucks and automobiles) and vehicles purposely designed to Marine Corps specifications (Marmon-Herrington light tanks). In the less restrictive pre-war period, the Marine Corps could and did specify a distinctive color for vehicles procured under their contracts. This Forest Green was probably a tribute to the distinctive color

The first M32B2 retrievers were manufactured by converting gun tanks, and C Company had a complete spare turret left over from the conversion. The mortar was intended to lay protective smoke during recovery operations.—NARA

of the Marine Corps field service uniform worn in the early part of American involvement in the Great War. Industry documentation exists of specifications for this paint in the pre-war period, but the specifications are clearly for "administrative" or non-combat vehicles, as a semi-gloss texture was specified.

In January 1942, the War Production Board (WPB) was established, replacing two pre-existing agencies. The administration of production contracts was streamlined, and the allocation of war material rationalized. The primary impact was on truck procurement. For major truck types, the Army would receive General Motors trucks, and most Studebakers would go to allies like the Soviet Union under the Lend-Lease program. The Navy and Marine Corps would use International trucks, with which the Corps had extensive pre-war experience and design input. Since the Marines would be the primary tactical user, International 1-ton M-2-4 and 2-1/2 ton M-5-6 trucks were produced to Marine Corps specifications—and were painted Forest Green.

After disappointing efforts to develop its own unique light tank for amphibious landings, the Marine Corps had adopted US Army light tanks. Since the Marine Corps requirements for tanks were miniscule compared to the Army, all tanks were procured under Army specifications and painted olive-drab.[55]

The first M4A2 tanks received by Charlie Company were manufactured by Fisher Body Works, and delivered in the usual olive-drab paint. These early-production vehicles were marked with standard War Production Board codes, beginning with the letter W, painted in low-visibility light blue on the sides of the tank. This was strictly a WPB code number; tanks taken into American service were assigned an Army (USA prefix) or Marine Corps (USMC prefix) serial number. A photo of Sergeant Robert F. Shook and his crew taken at Camp Pendleton shows their training tank with a typical WPB code number: W 3.063.673. Other photos indicate that these numbers were never painted over and replaced by USMC serial numbers on the training tanks. The individual tank names/call signs were painted in small block letters onto the forward part of the hull sides.

Most of these new tanks, issued just before departure from San Diego, carried WPB serial numbers such as USA 3.035.025, visible through a thin coat of new paint on CONDOR. This indicates a vehicle pre-allocated to the Army as a training vehicle, but provided to the Marines from Army depot stocks. These numbers were hastily painted over, but in the intense sunlight on Betio, some of the WPB serial numbers remained visible through the thin coat of paint. Another indication that these vehicles were provided from Army depot stocks are the white stars, barely visible through a thin coat of paint, on some vehicles.

New Marine Corps serial numbers were not yet assigned to these vehicles. Ed Bale: "We had no Marine Corps serial numbers on these tanks ... We used the manufacturer's serial number ... There was a plate inside to the left of the driver that had the manufacturer's serial number on that. And that's what we picked up for regular purposes ... Nobody paid attention to property records anyway. Everything was expendable including the tanks."[56]

New markings included the tank names, in much larger script for better visibility, painted onto the hull sides. It was at this time that the very distinctive emblem of the 1st Corps Medium Tank Battalion was added above the name. The symbol was an elephant with one front foot upraised, firing a cannonball with a puff of smoke from his trunk. Draped across the elephant's back is a blanket, painted in red.

Once again, the colors of the markings are to some degree problematical. Color film was shot at Tarawa, but the viewer should be wary. Color film was very sensitive to heat, and the film was exposed to temperatures in excess of 110F/43.3C for a prolonged period before processing. The film was also sensitive to water temperature during the developing process, using cold water from the refrigeration units on ships offshore. Finally, the developed film has been stored for over seventy years, much of that time before the controlled storage conditions now available at the National Archives. The original film at the National Archives is grainy and somewhat gray-tinted.

Some efforts have been made to restore this film, and the results can be seen on the website Critical Past (www.criticalpast.com). However, the viewer should be skeptical, since what assumptions were made to adjust color during the restoration process are unknown.

The authors have concluded that the emblem and tank names were most likely yellow for the following reasons: (A) In black and white the markings show up as a distinctly denser shade of gray than the very light-colored coral sand or light-colored smoke; (B) In the color film of sunken CHICAGO, the markings are a distinctly darker shade than the preserved white star on the turret side, although this might be an effect of shading from the sunlight; and (C) In color film of both CHICAGO and COLORADO (with no shading) the puff of (white?) smoke at the elephant's trunk is markedly lighter than the remainder of the elephant marking.

CHAPTER FOUR

THE CLOTHES ON THEIR BACKS—
CLOTHING AND EQUIPMENT

---

*I was in uniform for four years, and I know that heroism
doesn't occur from taking orders, but rather from people
who through their own willpower and strength are willing
to sacrifice their lives for an idea.*
—THOR HEYERDAHL

B y the time the battalion was raised, the Marine Corps had completed the transition to a new combat uniform, the so-called "utility
uniform." This far more practical uniform replaced the pre-war
battle dress which consisted of the everyday/dress uniform with the addition of canteen, ammunition pouches, Great War vintage "dishpan" helmet,
leggings, and other combat gear.

There is a persistent myth that the Marines usually "made do" with
castoff Army equipment, but in reality much of their gear was made at
Marine Corps supply depots to unique Marine Corps specifications, and
this was particularly true of the utilities. The name derives from the fact
that the baggy jacket and trousers were patterned after the heavy-duty
denim clothing worn by civilian industrial workers. This new uniform was
intended to replace the dark blue denim work clothing issued to spare the
dress uniform when doing particularly dirty or rough work, hence the
name. These first utilities included two types of clothing, the shirt-jacket
combination, and the one-piece mechanics coverall issued only in tank and
other mechanized units. Designed to be less expensive and more durable,
the clothing was quickly adopted as a combat uniform.[57]

The men of Charlie Company were first issued the relatively new Utility Uniform, HBT, Sage Green, P1941. Introduced in late 1941, this uniform was designed and manufactured to unique Marine Corps specifications. The utility jacket and trousers, and the coveralls, were made of rip-resistant cotton HBT (herringbone twill). Herringbone twill was a type of zigzag weave that showed up as a subtle striped appearance when seen from a distance. (The fabric of some civilian clothing, notably tweed, is woven in this herringbone pattern.)

The jacket had three pockets, one over each hip and a third one on the left breast, with the Eagle, Globe and Anchor and USMC stenciled onto the breast pocket with black ink. The front of the jacket closed with bronze—later steel—buttons, but the large pockets were simply open pouches with no closure flaps. The jacket was designed to be worn outside the trousers. Inside the collar was a manufacturer's label on which Marines would write their name. Because of sweating, the labels quickly became lost or faded, so men often wrote their name with a pen or painted a stenciled name inside or outside the jacket, often on the back. By the time of Tarawa, the division symbol—a diamond—was sometimes stenciled onto the back of the jacket, with a numerical code that identified the wearer's unit, rank, and billet. This was apparently not yet a widespread practice in the Second Division.

There were actually two models of trousers, distinguished only by the presence or absence of a small watch-pocket (then common on civilian trousers) on the right front. This feature was hidden by the jacket tails worn loose and hanging over the trouser waist. The trousers were designed with four pockets; two slash pockets on the front, and two pouch-like hip pockets without closure flaps. To accommodate very tall men, the trousers were issued in one standard length ("too long"). Because the trouser legs were designed to be tucked into leggings, individuals would cut the trouser legs to the correct length, and either neatly hem them or leave the ends ragged.

A baseball-style cap made of the same fabric, with a short visor and a stand-up front, was introduced as part of this uniform. It never fully replaced the older soft cloth hat with a narrow, all-around brim, since the hat provided better protection from the sun.

By late 1943, the newer Utility Uniform, HBT, Camouflage, P1942 was common issue, replacing the P1941 clothing. Stocks of new P1942 utilities were issued to Charlie Company and other units while on New Caledonia, and both were worn on Tarawa. In many cases individuals wore a mix of P1941 and P1942 clothing items.

The P1942 uniform was reversible, with a predominantly green and brown "jungle" camouflage pattern on one side and a predominantly brown and tan "beachhead" pattern on the other. The reversible design resulted in unpopular compromises. Each side of the new jacket had only two pockets, on the left breast and right skirt; the corresponding pockets for the reversible side were inside and inaccessible. Many Marines improvised, cutting slashes through the jacket to make the inside pockets useable. The new reversible trousers had a similar problem, with the same solution.

The new uniform also introduced the unique Marine Corps reversible camouflage cloth helmet cover made of the same material. The cloth cover fitted snugly over the standard M1 steel helmet, held in place by six flaps of cloth that were tucked between the helmet and the fiber helmet liner.

The issue skivvies (underwear) were initially white and eventually replaced by khaki ones, but at Tarawa, issue underwear was still white. Many men stenciled their name, rank, and serial number on underclothing. Photos indicate that in some unusual cases the cotton summer service khaki dress shirt was worn as underwear by tankers of C Company during training.

Footwear was the brown rough side out leather low-topped "boondocker" boots. These were designed to be worn with canvas leggings, but tankers usually did not wear leggings.

Each man was issued a pair of identification tags which were, according to the Readiness Report of the 1st Corps Medium Tank Battalion for April 1943, the type used by the Corps since 1917. They were round discs made of Monel metal and were worn on a cord around the neck. Usually one large loop encircled the neck, with a smaller loop attached to the first and holding second tag. If a man was killed, the tag on the smaller loop was removed as a record, the other buried with the body.[58]

The front of the tag contained (from top to the bottom): family name, first name and middle initial, serial number, blood type, month and year of tetanus vaccination, and branch of service (USMC or USMCR). On the backside was the Marine's fingerprint engraved with acid.[59]

All Marines were issued "782 gear," the standard field equipment. This material belonged to the unit and the name originated from the form the Marine signed for receipt. According to the Readiness Report for April 1943, it was composed of the M1941 Marine Corps Pack System. Other gear included items like the M1 steel helmet and liner with the reversible cover, the bayonet and scabbard for men issued a rifle or carbine, and appropriate ammunition pouches for the personal weapon. Some items were to be attached to a wide web belt, including appropriate ammo pouches, a small field dressing pouch, and the M1910 canteen and cup in a cloth carrying pouch. Some men were issued a unique style of Marine Corps canteen pouch with crossed closure flaps.

The belt was supported by a pair of adjustable belt suspender straps. The suspender straps were also designed to help support the haversack, a large pouch-like carrying bag that contained things like the mess kit (two steel pans with a knife, fork, and spoon), spare clothing and socks, toiletry kit, weapons cleaning and repair gear, rations, and any personal items like cigarettes, magazines or mail. For longer trips aboard ship, a second bag, the knapsack, was suspended below the haversack to carry additional clothing or other items.

The canvas shelter half—one half of a two-man tent that fastened together with buttons—was carried rolled into a U-shape and secured to the pack with special straps. Inside were one collapsible pole, a guy rope, and five tent stakes. If needed a blanket could be carried rolled inside the shelter half. A rubberized rain poncho was usually carried in some easily accessible spot.

Strapped to the back of the pack was each man's part of the entrenching tool system, either the M1910 T-handled shovel, and a mattock that consisted of a steel head and wooden handle. Each man was also issued a gas mask and carrying bag, often quickly discarded in combat. Other items unique to the Marines included laced leggings, different from the Army issue, reaching higher on the calf and markedly lighter in color.

Items unique to officers included the M1941 Officer's Field Bag and the Map Case. The Field Bag was patterned after the Army's Musette Bag, and had a long strap to be worn over the shoulder. The Map Case was another shoulder bag, with pouches for folded maps, pencils and pens, acetate map overlays, and printed message blank books.

Of course this mass of material, sixty-five pounds (nearly 30kg) and quite bulky, could not be carried inside a tank, and was subject to destruction by enemy fire if carried outside. Any really critical items were simply stashed in odd nooks and crannies inside the tank, but most was left stowed aboard ship. The only really common items carried in the tank were the steel helmet and the web belt supporting the pistol in its holster. Many did not wear even the web belt in the confined space, fearing that the belt might snag and prevent escape in case of a fire.

Items specific to tank crews included the football-type Rawlings armored force helmet, with hinged plastic earflaps to accommodate the earphones of the tank intercom. William R. "Scot" Kinsman commented about the helmet in training, and the reasons for its use:

> The enemy was a bunch of old cars which we would fire at with 75mm guns. These tanks weighed 35 tons and not knowing the terrain up ahead, when the tank flew off the ground into a ditch, since I was looking through a periscope at the terrain, my head crammed into the periscope, and even with a crash helmet on, I still got a bloody nose. At least the crash helmet protected the rest of my head. This was common in tanks for everyone.[60]

The crewman's helmet was always equipped with the M1938 Resistol™ (commercial Model 1021 early model) goggles with two separate eye lenses. The more modern single-lens tankers goggles were available in limited supply, but not commonly worn. Tankers also carried the M1 steel helmet (part of the 782 gear issue) for wear outside the tank; it was stored inside while the tank was moving. Another common practice was to wear only the liner and cloth cover for protection against the sun.

PERSONAL WEAPONS

The standard issue personal weapon for tank crewmen was the .45 caliber M1911A1 semi-automatic pistol. This weapon is often referred to as the Colt pistol, though that company accounted for only about twenty percent of wartime production. Reliable, and with considerable stopping power for a pistol, it remained in US service for nearly a century. The pistol could be carried in a shoulder holster, but was usually worn in a russet leather M1916 holster attached to the web belt.

Each tank included a Thompson submachine gun as part of the vehicle's parts and equipment (OVM) inventory. This weapon, with sixty-four magazines, was stored in the turret, nominally for the use of the tank commander. There were several versions of the Thompson procured by the military, but photographs indicate that the most common in Marine Corps usage was the older M1928A1, distinguished by the cooling fins on the barrel and the Cutts compensator on the muzzle. This version of the weapon could accept either 50-round drum or 30-round magazines. Although beloved of wartime photographers and Hollywood filmmakers, the Thompson was not particularly popular among tank crews; it was heavy (10.8pounds/5kg), and the magazines were slow to replenish with single rounds. The Thompson fired the same round as the M1911A1 pistol, and though powerful, it did not have the accuracy or penetrating power of the Browning Automatic Rifle (BAR) used by the infantry squad.

Tank crew weapons included the Thompson sub-machine gun (top) included as part of each tank's equipment, and the personal M1911 .45caliber pistol issued to each man. The M1 carbine (bottom) was not authorized, but in practice many men acquired one for personal use. This weapon had replaced the unreliable Reising sub-machine guns (second and third from top).—Marine Corps History Division

In the early days of the war, the Marine Corps had procured large numbers of the Reising Model 50 submachine gun for issue to supporting personnel like communicators and vehicle crewmen. Though an innovative weapon, it proved unreliable in combat. By the time the I Corps Medium Tank Battalion was raised it had been replaced by the new semi-automatic .30 caliber M1 carbine. This weapon arrived in the battalion in May 1943 as a limited issue weapon. Accuracy and penetrating power were generally considered superior to both the Thompson and Reising submachine guns.

The carbine was not intended for issue to tank crewmen, but appears both in photos taken during training and in post-battle photos such as those showing COLORADO's crew. It was common for units to have extra small arms over and above the official allocation of one issue weapon per man.

Fragmentation, smoke, and incendiary grenades (twelve in all) were carried inside the tank for close-combat protection, but none of the tank crewmen mentioned their use.

The Marine Corps began the war with a Great War vintage Mark I trench knife, but it was unsuited to general utility tasks since it was made of materials like brass that were in short supply. Many Marines privately acquired large general-purpose hunting knives. The US military eventually standardized a knife with a seven-inch (18cm) blade which went by several official designations. These fighting knives were used primarily as utility tools for everyday tasks—opening cans, cutting wire, and breaking open ammunition crates. All were generically known as "KA-BAR" knives after the marketing designation of the original designer and manufacturer, Union Cutlery.[61]

CHAPTER FIVE
OBJECTIVE: CODE NAME HELEN

All delays are dangerous in war.
—JOHN DRYDEN

I n his postwar memoir *Coral and Brass,* Holland M. Smith questioned the need for the seizure of the Gilberts, and it has become common in some circles to question the wisdom of the operation. From the vantage point of seventy years later it is easy to criticize the decisions that led to the bloody battle on Betio. As with all history, it is important to know what the planners knew at the time, and what their limitations of resources were, not what we now know (or choose to believe) in hindsight.

Japan had gone to war over access to natural resources to feed her industries, and for potential markets in a captive "Greater East Asia Co-Prosperity Sphere." In this scheme of things the prize was the oil, rubber, tin and other resources of the East Indies. All else was secondary.

The Japanese strategy was to quickly occupy many of the island groups of the Central Pacific as concentric defensive rings that the Americans would have to penetrate. Japan's militarists believed that Americans lacked martial spirit, and that the cost of recapturing these island fortresses would be so high that the dispirited Americans would accept a new *status quo,* leaving Japan in possession of its easily-won prizes. But Japan was too successful in its conquests, and found itself stretched thin in its new empire.

The major Japanese bases in the south were at Truk and Rabaul, in the north at Saipan and Guam—an American Territory seized on 8 December 1941—in the Marianas. The Americans had long foreseen the Marshall Islands as the first prize of real value in a naval counteroffensive. To the

Japanese, their positions in the Gilberts were to be little more than part of a screen, outliers to these major bases.

The Japanese had at first paid scant attention to the Gilberts, seizing only a few atolls in the northern part of the chain. Not until September 1942 did they finally complete the seizure of the southern atolls. Butaritari on Makin Atoll became the site of the main Japanese base in the southern Gilberts, with a radio station and seaplane base hosting long-range Kawanishi H8K "Emily" flying boats.

So why invade the Gilberts? The American plan for war with Japan, first formulated as a contingency in the 1920s, had always envisioned a march across the small islands of the Central Pacific culminating in a climactic naval battle with the Imperial Fleet. Of course, the short-sightedness in this long-range vision was "What then?" The plan envisaged a climactic naval battle with the Japanese Fleet, but there was no plan for the ultimate subjugation of the Japanese state or the invasion of the home islands. Mahan and his students had missed the lessons of the American Civil War and the Great War of 1914–1918. The goal of modern industrial war was not simply the neutralization of the enemy's armed forces, but the complete destruction of his war-making power. Modern war was economic and industrial annihilation.

The unforeseen loss of so many key positions in the Pacific, and the need to blunt Japanese southward expansion and secure Australia, had temporarily derailed Allied strategic planning. With Japan bloodied at Midway and thwarted in the Battle of the Coral Sea and in the Solomons, Allied planners returned to the long-standing and well-conceived plan to defeat Japan.

By 1943, the Chief of Naval Operations, Admiral Ernest J. King, had begun to argue persuasively the advantages of a renewed but altered Central Pacific drive. Geographically two jumping-off points were possible, a recaptured Wake Island or the Gilberts, but the former was a few isolated specks of land, and really too small to support major logistical facilities and airfields.

There was also a well-founded need to implement the new strategy as quickly as possible. With the Americans clearly on the strategic offensive, the Japanese were fortifying the outlying islands of their defensive screen at an alarming rate. The August 1942 raid on the Japanese base on Butaritari Island on Makin Atoll—then the Japanese primary position in the Gilberts—had been a sideshow intended to divert Japanese resources from the invasion of Guadalcanal. The raid was little more than a pinprick, but for the Japanese it highlighted the vulnerability of their outlying positions.

The result was that in September 1942, the Japanese began to reorganize their defenses in the Gilberts. More troops were dispatched to the Gilberts, and the main Japanese base was relocated to more defensible Betio Island. Betio was chosen because, as the former center of British colonial government and commerce, it already possessed a few facilities, notably piers that allowed unloading of heavy cargoes like concrete and construction equipment, and a suitably large airfield site. In addition, the island was small enough so that unlike Butaritari, the entire perimeter could be fortified to repel an amphibious assault.

British and New Zealand citizens were rounded up from throughout the Gilberts, and nineteen of the prisoners were assembled on Betio.

The Japanese quickly constructed an airstrip capable of operating medium bombers like the Mitsubishi G4M "Betty," but it was used only as a temporary forward base. The typical Japanese practice was to stage aviation support personnel into such forward bases by transport aircraft shortly before an operation. Prisoners captured in the battle for Betio revealed that in November, the two aircraft found on the island, Mitsubishi Type A6M "Zero" fighters, were non-operational and that only five aviation support personnel were present. The same prisoners reported that the Japanese were anticipating an attack, but the precise target and strength of the attack were unknown to them.

The defenders included the *rikusentai* of the *7th Sasebo Special Naval Landing Force* (1500 men), *3rd Special Base Force* (300 men, including some personnel from *6th Yokasuka Special Naval Landing Force*), *111th Construction Unit* (800–900 men), and the *Suga Unit*, a construction force with about 750 conscripted Korean laborers overseen by 120 armed Japanese civilians. One prisoner stated that about 280 of the Korean laborers were armed with rifles, but received no training with the weapons. (This was unusual, since the Japanese ruled Korea as a colony with ruthless brutality, and Japanese often feared the less than docile Koreans).[62]

The exact types and numbers of weapons in the hands of the defenders are very difficult to assess. Many smaller weapons—machine guns and the like—were undoubtedly entombed with their users in buried or collapsed positions, and no real count was kept when the victors policed the battlefield. Even seventy years later, old weapons and human remains are still being recovered.

A document captured on Makin gives some indication of the Betio defenders' strength and weaponry, but should be viewed very skeptically. There are probable errors in translation, and this was an administrative document that appears to duplicate some entries, allocating weapons to two formations. For example, there are a total of 14 Type 95 *Ha-Go* tanks listed in the document: nine allocated to the *Headquarters Company, Special Base Force 3*; two to *Headquarters Company, 7th SNLF*; and three to *Company 2, 7th SNLF*. Subsequent analysis indicated that "It appears now that the documents apparently were proposed strength rather than actual strength."[63]

The Marines listed only seven tanks actually found on Betio. However, careful examination of photographs, comparing specific features such as distinctive types of damage, indicates there may have been as many as nine.

Most sources have attributed the tanks to the *3rd Base Force,* based on the memoirs of Petty Officer Tadao Oonuki, a Japanese tank driver captured after the battle. One was apparently fitted with a crude jib to serve as a tank recovery vehicle and repair vehicle. The Japanese did not have a dedicated tank recovery vehicle, as in most armies. The closest analog was three Type 95 *Ri-Ki* armored engineer cranes, but none were allocated to the Imperial Navy.[64]

The document is more useful for identifying the types—rather than numbers—of weapons. For example, Marine Corps survivors consistently mention Japanese mortar fire. No mention is made of mortars in the document, and none were captured. The document does list Type 89 Grenade Dischargers, or "knee mortars." This 50mm weapon fired timed-action

---

Opposite page: *A map of the facilities and defenses developed from air photos. The maps proved surprisingly accurate, and by knowing the number of bottoms per benjo (Japanese latrines), the T-shaped structures extending from the shoreline, the interpreters even developed an accurate assessment of the defender's manpower.*
—Archives and Special Collections, Library of the Marine Corps

OBJECTIVE: CODE NAME HELEN • 87

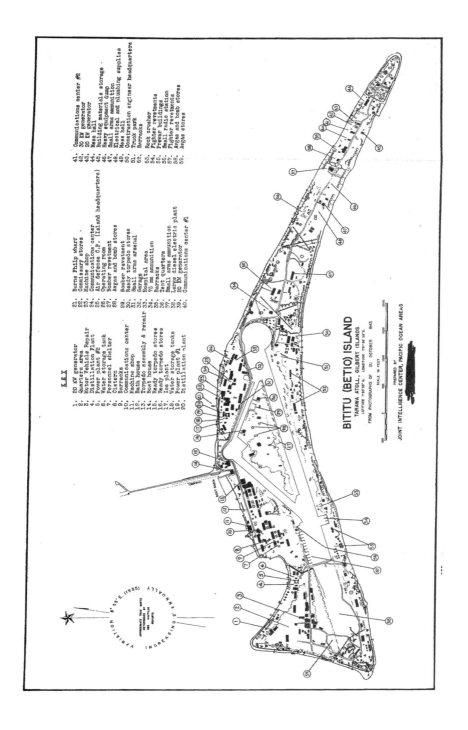

KEY

1. 20 kw generator
2. Quarters area
3. Motor Vehicle Repair
4. Distillation Plant
5. Power plant #2
6. Water storage tank
7. Personnel shelter
8. Cistern
9. Barracks
10. Communications center
11. Machine shop
12. Bath house
13. Torpedo assembly & repair
14. Boat house
15. Ready torpedo stores
16. Ready torpedo stores
17. Ice plant
18. Water storage tanks
19. Power plant #1
20. Distillation plant

21. Burns Philp wharf
22. Commissary stores
23. Machine shop
24. Communications center
25. Air defense C.P. (Island headquarters)
26. Operating room
27. Bomber revetment
28. Avgas and bomb stores
29. Bomber revetment
30. Ready torpedo stores
31. Small arms arsenal
32. Garage
33. Hospital area
34. 75 mm ammunition
35. Barracks
36. Tent quarters
37. Small arms ammunition
38. Large diesel electric plant
39. 20 KW generator
40. Communications center #1

41. Communications center #2
42. 30 KW generator
43. 20 KW generator
44. Mess hall
45. Building materials storage
46. Heavy equipment dump
47. Small arms ammunition
48. Mess hall
49. Electrical and plumbing supplies
50. Construction engineer headquarters
51. Truck park
52. Barracks
53. Rock crusher
54. Fighter revetments
55. Prewar buildings
56. Small radio station
57. Fighter revetments
58. Avgas and bomb stores
59. Avgas stores

BITITU (BETIO) ISLAND
TARAWA ATOLL, GILBERT ISLANDS
LATITUDE 1°21'30"N. LONGITUDE 172°56'30"E.
FROM PHOTOGRAPHS OF 20 OCTOBER 1943

SCALE IN FEET

PREPARED BY
JOINT INTELLIGENCE CENTER, PACIFIC OCEAN AREAS

The 75mm Type 88 anti-aircraft gun was the deadliest anti-tank gun in the Japanese arsenal. These guns were emplaced in pits around the periphery of the island, but their all-around traverse enabled them to fire inland. An aircraft sound detector, part of the battery equipment, is visible at upper right.—NARA

fragmentation, smoke, incendiary, and high-explosive rounds. The document lists 44 of these weapons.

This same document listed six 37mm Type 94 Rapid Fire Guns suitable for anti-tank defense; the 75mm Type 41 Mountain Guns (6) and 70mm Type 92 Infantry Guns (8) were obsolescent guns of limited tactical value. More questionable are eight "70mm anti-aircraft guns," a weapon that did not even exist in Japanese service. Contrary to some later writers, there were none of the latest-model 47mm Type 01 anti-tank guns on the island; these were all allocated to the Imperial Japanese Army.

To defend the airfield facilities the laborers and sailors set about building some of the most elaborate defenses in the Pacific to house a hodge-podge collection of guns. The centerpieces of the defense were the so-called Singapore guns, a pair of British-made eight-inch Vickers guns, popularly thought to have been captured at Singapore; in actuality they

The obsolescent 37mm Type 94 Rapid Fire Gun, like this one captured intact on New Georgia, was still an effective anti-tank gun at the near point-blank combat ranges on Tarawa. One or more guns like this one almost certainly destroyed COMMANDO.—NARA

had been purchased from the British. Open turrets taken from old ships, mounting single or twin 127mm dual-purpose guns, were sited to fire at ships or aircraft; there were twelve such guns in total.

Eight 80mm and ten 75mm Type 88 (1928) anti-aircraft guns were positioned to fire at either boats or aircraft. The 80mm guns were not the new Type 03 (1943) anti-aircraft guns, but obsolete guns removed from old warships. The Type 88 would prove to be the best anti-tank gun in the Japanese arsenal. In addition to their anti-aircraft role, they were positioned to lay down a deadly fire against landing boats. About thirty-one heavy 13mm machine guns in single and twin mounts were positioned to fire at boats or low-flying planes.

All these anti-aircraft weapons were of necessity positioned in open gun pits, protected only by coconut log and sand walls. In October, Marine planners requested a last-minute air strike by three Army Air Force heavy bombers dropping 2000-pound "daisy cutter" bombs. These bombs, fuzed to detonate in the air, would in theory have showered the open gun pits with deadly blast and shrapnel. Colonel David Shoup would later say that he had been told that the mission failed when one B-24 crashed on takeoff, a second crashed into the sea, and a third failed to reach the objective. No Air Force records indicate that the mission was ever flown.[65]

It is probable that such a raid would have had no significant effect anyway. The defenders had little regard for the heavy bombers, who on prior raids had most often missed the island entirely, dropping their bombs harmlessly into the sea.

Air photo analysis and examination of captured weapons indicated there were actually a dozen 70mm Type 92 Battalion Guns and nine "37mm Mobile Guns" emplaced to fire at landing sites and to protect the heavier guns. It is not clear whether these "mobile guns" were older Type 94 (1936) 37mm Rapid Fire Guns (an obsolete anti-tank gun reclassified as an infantry support gun) or Type 1 (1941) Anti-tank Guns, an improved version of the same gun with a longer tube and slightly higher muzzle velocity. The two guns were difficult to distinguish from each other, but it is likely that the SNLF formations were equipped with the older Type 94 as noted in the captured document,.[66]

Some of these guns had at least partial overhead protection, but could be quickly removed from their positions, as indicated by the "mobile guns" annotation in the intelligence reports.

The best-protected were the myriad of light machine guns and riflemen in sturdy bunkers constructed of two coconut log walls with up to 30 inches (76cm) of sand between, all heaped over with more sand and plant debris. These positions were difficult to detect and impervious to the American 37mm anti-tank and light tank guns, and usually defied even the M4's heavier 75mm cannon unless fired directly into an opening at point-blank range. American naval planners might have learned a lesson from America's own history. In 1776, a similar construction at Fort Sullivan, South Carolina defied prolonged British naval bombardment. Shell hits were absorbed by the soft sand, and the spongy coconut logs simply "healed" any shell penetrations. Only chance direct hits by heavy shells destroyed a few of these positions at Tarawa.

The Japanese anticipated landings on the seaward (southern) beaches. Most defenses faced in that direction, but the lagoon side defenses were strong enough.

Though many of the construction troops had already departed, the remainder worked tirelessly to further strengthen the defenses, leading the island's commandant to boast that "A million men cannot take Tarawa in a hundred years."

At the time, the reasons for throwing Marines against such defenses were both simple and complex. War Plan ORANGE had always assumed that seizure of the Marshall Islands—halfway between American bases on Samoa and the larger land masses of the Marianas—was essential. The Marshalls assumed even greater strategic significance after the unexpected loss of the American bases on Wake Island and Guam.

It was a given that both air and naval gunfire bombardment would be needed to help subdue the powerful defenses that the Americans expected to encounter in the Marshall Islands. The Marshalls had been held as a protectorate by the Japanese since they acquired them in the aftermath of World War I. The Japanese had essentially closed off any foreign access to the region, and no one knew what defenses the Japanese had constructed.

American naval leaders had correctly gauged that naval aviation would eventually be capable of subduing even land-based Japanese air forces, but that day had not yet arrived. In 1943, the US Navy still had relatively few carriers to risk lingering in support of landing operations. Aircraft carrier strike forces were also logistically weak, and unsuited to prolonged bombardment of Japanese bases. They had to refuel often, and onboard stocks of thin-cased high explosive bombs and ammunition were limited by magazine storage space. The need to stock torpedoes and armor-piercing bombs to respond to a potential Japanese naval counterattack further constrained munitions storage. As a result, aircraft carrier strikes at Japanese land bases were hit-and-run affairs of at most two days duration. Hardly the preparation the Marines thought necessary for an attack on islands that the enemy had spent a quarter of a century in fortifying. Prolonged attack by land-based aircraft would be necessary to grind down Japanese defenses.

Another, less obvious, reason was in many ways just as important—photography. The Navy and Marine Corps had suffered needlessly in the Solomons from a lack of useable maps. Maps had been notoriously unreliable, often based upon century-old naval charts, maps from National Geographic Magazine, photos of the coasts taken through the periscopes of submarines, and even hand-drawn sketches by former British and Australian traders and missionaries. (Most notably, the first Battle of the Tenaru

River was actually fought on the Ilu River, 3600 meters away along the coastline). This lesson had only been reinforced by Allied experiences in the Mediterranean Theater.[67]

Even less was known about the possessions long-ruled by the Japanese. The Marshalls were ruled in absolute secrecy by the Japanese and virtually nothing was known about them. Only land-based planes could provide the detailed and scaled vertical air photos necessary to make useful maps of the surrounding waters and reefs, islands and terrain, and Japanese defenses. With limited operational altitude and endurance, carrier reconnaissance aircraft were in large part limited to aerial oblique photography, photos taken over the side of the cockpit and of limited utility for mapping and intelligence analysis.

Raids by long-range American bombers commenced in mid-September 1943. In mid-October, carrier-based aircraft briefly raided Betio, damaging two ships caught in the lagoon. One was the supply ship *Saidu Maru*, damaged so badly that she was run aground to keep from sinking.

A tragic side-effect of the raids was that the Japanese used them as a pretext for murdering the prisoners held on Betio. One native watched as several were beheaded before he fainted. Another reported seeing the headless bodies, badly burned, in a pit. Despite searches, the bodies have never been located.[68]

Japanese occupied islands in the southern Gilberts were the objects of the usual photographic reconnaissance by submarines (a seemingly common mission for the old USS *Nautilus*, SS-168) and naval strike aircraft. Butaritari Island on Makin Atoll, and Betio Island on Tarawa Atoll, were some of the first objectives subjected to the scrutiny of the high-altitude camera's eye beginning with the B-24 bombing raids of mid-September.[69]

By late 1943, air photo analysis had already reached a high level of sophistication. Prior to the attack on Betio, photo analysts counted the number of privies (*benjo*) built on short piers extending into the water on both the southern and northern shores. Knowing the maximum number of bottoms per outhouse specified by Japanese naval regulations, they were able to make a surprisingly accurate estimate of the number of defenders. The highly-accurate maps of Betio's defenses were derived primarily from vertical air photos, and post-battle assessment indicated that ninety percent of defensive positions had been correctly identified and mapped. The detailed aerial mapping profoundly influenced the decision to land on the lagoon side of the island, less heavily fortified and with a narrower fringing reef.

In late 1943, detailed pre-invasion briefings using mosaics of high-altitude photos were already a part of most operations. What the photo interpreters could not determine was a critical factor for the tanks—water

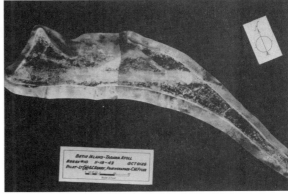

Tarawa was the first Pacific objective to be mapped in detail from aerial photos. Photo mosaics were used to create detailed maps of the defenses, and to brief the invasion troops.—NARA

depth. Various contingencies were developed, and it was accepted that the landing craft carrying tanks might have to divert to other beaches. Also unrecognized by the planners was that Betio has a dished reef. Because of wave action, the coral grows slightly higher at the seaward margin, with deeper water between the seaward edge of the reef and the beach. Like all such reefs, the reef margin is not a smooth line, but highly irregular. A landing craft may ground on an isolated coral head, while another boat a few yards away may find a reentrant and ground fifty yards or more closer to the beach. The constant action of waves stirs up fine coral dust and debris, limiting underwater visibility and concealing the bottom even in very shallow water. It was feared that debris stirred up by the pre-invasion bombardment might render the water even murkier. Submerged hazards such as craters caused by heavy shells would be invisible to men on foot, much less the tank crews.

After Holland Smith published *Coral and Brass*, Admiral Raymond Spruance commented that "I feel sure that he [Smith] would have been most unwilling to attempt the capture of any defended island without adequate aerial photographs...."[70]

Yet another critical problem was amphibious shipping capacity. One reason Allied naval planners had to be ever wary of a Japanese *yogaki* counterattack was the risk to the vulnerable transports, and the invasion of the Gilberts presented a prime example. Allied global shipping resources were stretched to the limit, and because of the "Germany first" policy, much of the available amphibious transport capability was committed to the Mediterranean, with more tied down in support of MacArthur's operations in the western Solomons and New Guinea.

Of the transports in the Tarawa invasion fleet, five were converted ocean liners (two launched in 1919), three were more recent conversions, and seven were civilian designs acquired under the Maritime Commission program.

Strategically the two most important amphibious transports for the Gilberts campaign were the USS *Ashland* (LSD-1) and the USS *Belle Grove* (LSD-2). The Navy had already deployed the British-designed Landing Ship Tank, or LST, the first seagoing landing ship capable of putting its cargo of vehicles directly onto the beach. But despite the name, the LSTs were considered too vulnerable to risk in the initial assault waves when tanks were most needed (the cynical crews swore that LST stood for Large Slow Target). For the duration of the Pacific war, the LSTs would be utilized primarily as mother-ships for the fleets of LVTs, or as transports for follow-on waves.

For the foreseeable future the limited number of LSDs, with their internal cargoes of LCMs (Landing Craft, Mechanized, up to 28 in the case of *Ashland*), would remain the only feasible way of putting medium tanks ashore with the early assault waves.

The shortage of LSDs might cause strategic planners the most sleepless nights, but each and every single transport—young or old—was critical, and they were not to be risked lightly. The loss of irreplaceable amphibious transport ships would have long-term strategic implications, forcing the delay of future operations and granting the Japanese even more time to construct defenses for their strategy of attrition.

Uncertainties as to how much transport would actually be available for the Gilberts frustrated planners until the very last minute. In the end

The USS Ashland, *shown here in July 1943, was the very first of many specialized amphibious assault ships. In late 1943 the US Navy could ill-afford to lose any of these strategically important vessels to a Japanese naval counterattack.*—NARA

there would be ships enough to lift only part of the Army's 27th Division to Makin. This forced Holland Smith to allocate the 6th Marines from the 2nd Marine Division as the Amphibious Corps operational reserve, to be committed at either Makin or Betio as the situation developed. This left only two rifle regiments to assault Betio.

The Betio landings would be carried out by the 2nd Marines, reinforced by the 2nd Battalion, 8th Marines (2/8). The assault troops would be augmented by contingents of artillery (10th Marines) with man-portable 75mm pack howitzers, the Pioneer (Shore Party) Battalion to handle logistics, and engineers from the 18th Marines. (At this time, combat demolitions and flamethrowers were still engineer responsibilities). The remaining two battalions of the 8th Marines, plus the regiment's headquarters personnel, would constitute a perilously small division reserve.[71]

A part of the initial plan was the preliminary seizure of an adjacent island to serve as an artillery base, since the Marines had less faith than the Navy in the ability of ship's guns to destroy shore defenses. Marine artillery could provide more precise fire to help neutralize beach defenses, and provide better support to operations once the troops were ashore. At an early October conference in Hawaii, the Division planning staff learned that the Navy feared that this would without doubt alert the Japanese and thereby increase the likelihood of a Japanese air or naval counterattack. There would be no preliminary land-based artillery bombardment.[72]

Apparently forgotten in the chaos of the planning was the link between tanks, artillery, and naval gunfire in the amphibious assault. The Marines had originally developed a tank force—and the means of landing it—because in numerous pre-war exercises naval gunfire had repeatedly proven incapable of the pinpoint accuracy required to reduce beach defenses. With artillery denied to them, and naval gunfire limited to 75 minutes duration of firing at general areas rather than at specific targets, tanks should have assumed even greater importance. But despite all prior experience, the battleship admirals were supremely confident their guns would obliterate even the strongest defenses.[73]

Despite the numerous pre-war exercises, the Marine Corps still had no formal tank doctrine. The tactical concept—such as it was—decreed that the division's own light tanks would land with the infantry assault waves. Individual light tank platoons would be assigned to support the infantry battalions; these platoons would land with their assigned battalions, distributed along the landing beaches. The light tank platoons were actually loaded aboard the same transport ships as the infantry battalions, and the tanks would have to be lifted out and into landing craft by ship's cranes.

Since powerful resistance was expected at Tarawa, the medium tanks would instead land with the initial assault waves, distributed along the landing beaches in support of individual infantry battalions.

The tidal cycle was the most contentious factor in planning, and as it turned out, the cause of near disaster. Shipping shortages and logistical problems precluded an attack before mid-November. The ideal time for landings would be on the spring tide (the time of highest monthly tidal fluctuation) but in November 1943, suitable high tides would occur in the pre-dawn darkness thereby limiting air and gunfire support, or twelve hours later in the afternoon, leaving too little time to secure a beachhead. The next suitable time in the tidal cycle, when the spring tides occurred in the early daylight hours, would be in late December. So the risks of landing on the neap tide, when tidal fluctuation would be at its lowest, were reluctantly accepted.

What few appreciated was that Tarawa is located on one of the very few positions on the earth's surface that, because of the configuration of the moon's cycle, are subject to unpredictable "dodging tides," periods when low tides are unusually low. Major Frank L. Holland, a New Zealander who had lived on the atoll, was adamant that at a dodging tide the water over the reef might be too shallow to allow landing boats to pass. Troops could be stranded at the reef's edge and left to wade hundreds of yards through machine gun fire. Holland Smith heeded Frank Holland's warnings, setting off a series of fiery arguments.

The eventual solution was to use amphibian tractors—LVTs—as assault vehicles. These tractors were designed as supply carriers, and their use as tactical vehicles met with considerable resistance. Eventually 125 tractors were made available, 75 older LVT-1s, and 50 newer LVT-2s. A major problem was that the division's older LVT-1s had been heavily used. The tractors had long since exceeded their expected service life, and despite heroic efforts by the maintenance personnel, most could not achieve anything approaching their theoretical top speed of 6mph/9.7kph in the water.[74]

The newer LVT-2s had more powerful engines, giving them a slightly higher speed in water (speed on land did not really matter), greater cargo capacity, and longer operating range. But there were as yet no LVT-2s west of California. The original contingent of LVT-2s was shipped directly from California to Samoa. Personnel from the 2nd Amphibian Tractor Battalion took over the tractors in Samoa, formed a new company, and conducted tests to verify that the amphibians could negotiate reefs similar to those at Tarawa. The frenzied schedule left no time for familiarization or infantry rehearsals with the new tractors. The new LVT-2 company would join the assault force on the morning of D-Day.[75]

A hundred amphibians would carry the first three assault waves, with 25 as a division reserve.

The role of the medium tanks was also hastily changed. Rather than landing later as reinforcements, the medium tanks would form part of the initial assault force, landing with the fifth wave. RED-1, where the troops would have to land in a small cove and therefore be potentially exposed to a cross fire, was thought likely to be the toughest objective. For that reason the First Platoon medium tanks, reinforced by the Charlie Company Headquarters Section, would support Major John Schoettel's 3/2.

Lieutenant Colonel Herbert Amey's 2/2 would land on the adjacent RED-2, which extended from a corner of land that formed the boundary with RED-1 to the base of the long pier, an easily recognizable landmark. This battalion would be supported by the Second Platoon medium tanks.

RED-3 was the widest landing beach, and closest to the center of the main Japanese building complexes. This beach would be attacked by Major Henry Crowe's 2/8, supported by the Third Platoon medium tanks.

The regimental reserve would be Major Wood B. Kyle's 1/2.

Subsequent waves would bring more troops ashore, and the assembled force would quickly push across the island to the south shore, turn left and right, and easily sweep toward the two ends of the island.

And so the plan was set into motion.

CHAPTER SIX

DAY ONE—THE REEF

Battle is an orgy of disorder.
—GENERAL GEORGE S. PATTON

As in most operations the Marines, too nervous to sleep on the night before a landing, spent their time doing anything to kill the time. Bale recalled that Lieutenant Sheedy "...won a lot of money playing poker the night before we landed."

The *Ashland* arrived off Betio and at 0345hours hove to several miles northwest of the island at the far northwestward corner of the transport area. Like all coral atolls, the water bottom dropped off very steeply on the oceanward side, so the ships could not anchor in place.[76]

Three troop transports began to swing the older LVT-1s outboard with cranes. Three brand-new LSTs, newly arrived with the fifty brand-new LVT-2s, began to launch their amtracs to take aboard troops from the troop transports.

Ed Bale recalled spending the final hours aboard ship checking and re-checking the condition of his tanks. Some like Harrell McNorton spent the final hours "Checking equipment, making sure that my tank COL-ORADO was ready for action." Corporal Olaf Johnson vividly recalled the traditional steak and eggs breakfast, and the detailed "Check of .30cal coaxial, seventy-five millimeter breech, radio settings." Joe Woolum also recalled the hearty breakfast, "... but wasn't very hungry."[77]

The infantry who would make up the assault waves were already clambering down into landing craft, and the boats circled in assembly areas near the ships. In the pre-dawn hours, the crew of the *Ashland* opened valves that flooded the well deck with seawater, floating the loaded LCM-3s and support boats off the steel deck. Other valves allowed seawater into tanks built into the sides of the ship and the ship ballasted down; the rear of the ship sank down into the sea. A huge ramp the full width of the ship's stern opened downward. Navy coxswains gunned their engines and attempted to back the boats backed out of the well deck and into the open sea.

The *Ashland* was anchored farthest out to sea, and the LCM coxswains quickly found that the rolling of the *Ashland* was making it hazardous to back their clumsy craft out of the crowded confines of the well deck. The only solution was to suspend unloading and stand farther inshore toward the reef where shallower water would lessen the wave action.[78]

Once free, the unwieldy LCMs formed up into an assembly circle to await their appointed time to move into the lagoon. The big landing craft were both faster and less maneuverable than the LVTs of the first waves. Finally, following behind the slow LVTs, the tank lighters had to wallow past the drifting transport ships and smaller landing craft milling about in the rough water. Bale was feeling miserable and worried by the confusion. Clifford Quine recalled being "Out in the water circling and waiting for the landing." Michael Shivetts thought "...loading went well. However, at the time, waiting your turn in choppy waters seemed to take forever."[79]

The careful plans for the invasion of Betio began to go awry almost immediately. In the pre-dawn darkness the battleship *Maryland* launched her gunfire observation floatplane. The island's defenders thought the bombardment had begun, and the eight-inch guns fired at the flashes of the powder charges from the *Maryland*'s aircraft catapult. American battleships and cruisers returned fire, and the battle was on, albeit prematurely.[80]

The cruisers and battleships of the bombardment group had opened fire prematurely, but continued to flail away at the shore batteries.

At 0550 hours the bombardment ships ceased fire. The strike from Admiral Frank Fletcher's three big aircraft carriers had been due at 0545 hours, but the aircraft were still nowhere to be seen, and some have erroneously attributed the Japanese shelling to this window of opportunity. The two officers in direct control—Major General Julian Smith and Admiral Harry Hill—were not able to contact the carrier group because the concussion from the *Maryland*'s big guns had temporarily knocked out her own radios. Worse, a stronger than expected current was carrying the unanchored

TABLE 2: DOCUMENTED TANK CREWS ON D-DAY AT TARAWA.

HQ SECTION

	CECILIA	COMMANDO
Tank Commander	1st Lt. Edward L. BALE Jr.	
Gunner	Pfc. Charles E. MARTIN	Cpl. Herman L. GRAVES?
Radio/loader	Sgt. Michael E. SHIVETTS	Pfc. Warren E. DUPLESSIS?
Driver	Cpl. Alfonso A. CHAVEZ	
Assistant driver	Sgt. Robert M. KELLER	Pvt. Paul F. BEABOUT?

1ST PLATOON

	CHICAGO	COUNT	CHINA GAL	CHERRY
Tank Commander	1st Lt. William I. SHEEDY	Pfc. Bruce J. SEWARD?	Pfc. Edward L. BAJUS	
Gunner		Pvt. John E. IRVINE	Pfc. Jack TANCIL Jr.	
Radio/loader		Cpl. Olaf G. JOHNSON		
Driver		Pfc. Donald J. McCONVILLE?	Pfc. Eugene M. JOSEFSON	
Assistant driver		Pvt. Earl J. ZBINDEN?	Cpl. William S. FORD?	

2ND PLATOON

	COBRA	CLIPPER	CUDDLES	CONGA
Tank Commander	1st Lt. Richard O. SLOAT	Sgt. Robert E. BAKER	PltSgt Hugh C. HAYCRAFT Jr.?	Sgt. Eugene H. ANDREWS?
Gunner	Pvt. Henry G. TRAUERNICHT	Pvt. Charles D. MASON		Cpl. Malcolm W. GARVOCK?
Radio/loader	Cpl. William H. EADS Jr.	Pfc. Donald W. PEARSON		
Driver	Cpl. Hester S. WEBB	Cpl. Antonio ALMARAZ		
Assistant driver	Pvt. Jack TRENT	Pvt. Clifford G. QUINE		

3RD PLATOON

	CANNONBALL	COLORADO	CONDOR	CHARLIE
Tank Commander	2nd Lt. Louis R. LARGEY	Sgt. John R. MARN	Sgt. Robert F. SHOOK	PltSgt. George TRINKA?
Gunner		Cpl. Edward M. PETERSON	Pvt. Joe D. WOOLUM	
Radio/loader		Pfc. William F. SCHWENN	Cpl. Herschel D. FULMER	
Driver		Cpl. Harrell O. McNORTON Jr.	Cpl. Raymond A. BARKER	
Assistant driver		Pvt. Robert L. FISHER	Pvt. Harry O. GREY	Cpl. William A. DUNKEL?

transports south, between the battleships and their targets. By 0550hours, Japanese shells were falling dangerously near some of the transports.

The ships at first maintained position, but eight-inch shells were falling too close for comfort. Hill signaled the transports to move north, and at 0616hours the ships steamed slowly north. Landing boats and LVTs struggled to keep up with their mother ships and reform their assembly circles in the open sea. Hill was now seriously concerned about the landing schedule.

Nevertheless, shortly after 0700hours two small Navy minesweepers began to scout a path along the unmarked channel that separated Betio from the submerged reef to the north. Close behind were two destroyers that would provide close gunfire support, USS *Ringgold* and *Dashiell*. The path of the ships through the channel brought them right under the noses of some of Betio's strongest defenses, and without doubt alerted the Japanese that the attack would come from the lagoon side. The respite from gunfire and air attacks provided Shibasaki with a priceless half-hour to shift some of his defensive arrangements to the lagoon side.

Finally, the carrier aircraft arrived at 0615 and began to pummel the island. Aboard the landing boats, those who had no immediate responsibilities observed that "They were bombing the hell out of the island" according to Ed Gazel. Others like nineteen-year-old Bill Dunkel spent the time "smoking my cigar and praying," and Mike Shivetts recalled that "After breakfast and a blessing and a bit of personal prayer there was cheerful talk of home and family." Shivetts also carried "A small GI prayer book."[81]

On shore, Japanese Navy Petty Officer Tadao Oonuki was helplessly enduring the final bombardment with others in a stifling hot air-raid shelter "like sheep in a sheep-fold." This was unlike the largely ineffective high-altitude bombing by American heavy bombers. Oonuki was a truck driver who had volunteered for service at a forward base, and ended up driving a Type 95 *Ha-Go* light tank of the *Third (Yokosuka) Special Base Force* assigned to Tarawa.[82]

One of the minesweepers, the *Pursuit*, had taken up position as a guide boat in the lagoon, and radioed the *Maryland* that the LVTs were hopelessly behind schedule. The first troop-carrying LVTs had been scheduled to cross the Line of Departure at 0750hours, with following waves at three minute intervals, but Admiral Hill decided to postpone H-Hour until 0845. He could not call off more scheduled air strikes because of the erratic radios.

Scheduled for the fifth assault wave, the LCM-3s carrying Bale's company waited as the slower amtracs carrying infantry of the first three assault waves churned along the cleared channel and into the lagoon. The amtracs advanced single file at low speed, guiding on buoys set by the minesweepers. Because of the configuration of the beach and channel, the lead tractors of each wave had to briefly drift off shore, under fire, until the rear tractors—with a final Line of Departure farther from the beach—reached their proper position. As each wave of tractors was properly formed up, at a signal from the wave guides the drivers gunned their engines and surged into the fire and toward the beach at top speed—a theoretical 7.5 miles per hour (12km/h).

The LVTs had started their runs ahead of the revised schedule, throwing the changed schedule further into disarray. The belated arrival of another air strike had to be aborted.[83] The LVT-2s had to slow to allow the desperately churning LVT-1s to catch up. The respite had allowed the Japanese to prepare, and shells began to burst over the amtracs. Most of the bigger shore batteries had been disabled by the American shelling, but those guns posed minimal threat to the LVTs anyway.

The first waves of infantry were being slaughtered, particularly on RED-1, where the LVTs were savaged by a deadly crossfire from three sides. As the LVTs crawled up onto the reef, machine gun fire began to rip through the thin aluminum sides, and through the steel plate welded on as supplementary armor.

Schoettel's battalion was the first to arrive at the beach at 0910hours. His King Company on the far left flank of RED-1 was supposed to link up with units on RED-2. Instead it was driven back to the right and never made contact with Amey's 2/2. The last to arrive at the seawall, at 0922 hours, Amey's battalion had been driven to the left by the same strong Japanese positions, some of its units landing on RED-3. Amey was killed on the reef, his battalion taken over by the senior officer present, observer Lieutenant Colonel Walter I. Jordan from the 4th Marine Division. On RED-3, Crowe's battalion had reached the seawall at 0917hours, aided by the fire of two destroyers that undoubtedly hindered the Japanese reaction. This battalion suffered by far the fewest casualties.

The LVTs had orders to carry the troops across the beach and inshore, but as many tried to mount the seawall at low spots, close-range fire ripped through the even thinner metal of their bellies. Some of the LVTs found breaches in the seawall and carried their troops as far as the edge of the air-field.[84]

Doctrine was for the light tanks of the Division's own tank battalion—presumably easier to land—to accompany the first assault waves, reinforced by the heavier M4A2s. That part of the plan also slipped into disarray. The light tanks were loaded aboard the ships carrying the infantry battalions they would support. Unfortunately the tanks were loaded deep in the cargo holds and had to be laboriously dug out and lifted over into bobbing LCMs by the cargo booms of the transports.

When the LCMs carrying the light tanks approached the landing beaches they were met by a hail of cannon fire. The light tank platoon, scheduled to land on RED-1, could not find a suitable landing site (their wading depth was less than that of the medium tanks), and moved east toward RED-3. The sight of large boats slowly moving broadside to the beach attracted the attention of Japanese gunners, and some of the LCMs carrying light tanks were sunk.[85]

The plan was for the LVTs to return to the edge of the reef, load up with more infantrymen from boats, and shuttle them across the shallow water. But too many had been destroyed or their crews killed. Many of the tractors that tried to return to the reef edge sank, or their engines failed from water pouring in through bullet holes, overwhelming their bilge pumps.

As the landings slipped further into confusion, the following boat waves, including the LCMs carrying the medium tanks—originally scheduled to land in the fifth wave at 0810hours—were held up at the Line of Departure. The file of LCMs had been led by those carrying the Third Platoon toward distant RED-3, with the boats carrying Headquarters Section and First Platoon bringing up the rear to land on RED-1. With Commanding Officer Lieutenant Bale on RED-1, the small company command group under Executive Officer Lieutenant Kent was assigned to land on RED-2. Their task was to find a centrally located position and handle logistics, communications, and coordination with the infantry. No one had foreseen that the battle would descend into such absolute chaos, throwing these well-laid plans out the window.

On RED-1, Major John Schoettel (3rd Battalion, 2nd Marines) hesitated to send his following waves into the carnage despite prodding from higher officers. Schoettel hovered offshore, with Bale's First Platoon Sergeant Charlie Sooter who was assigned as tank liaison instead of in his tank. Radioman Dodson Smith of Headquarters Company 3/2 was in the boat with Schoettel and Sooter: "We're on the Higgins boat. We didn't get in on the amtracs. They went on over the coral reef." One of Schoettel's company commanders, Major Michael P. Ryan of Love Company, took charge of the troops already ashore. Love Company was Dodson Smith's usual assignment, but that day Smith—who didn't even remember why he had joined the Marines at age seventeen—was assigned to the battalion headquarters group. The LCMs carrying the medium tanks still loitered at the Line of Departure under sporadic fire, further adding to the misery of the men in the boats.

Major Mike Ryan's informal command included not only the survivors from Schoettel's battalion, but many men who were supposed to have landed on RED-2. Extremely heavy fire from "The Pocket," a cluster of strong enemy positions near the boundary between the two beaches, had driven the LVTs far to the right and into the deadly cove. A single blessing in the confusion was that the 2/2 headquarters group, driven off RED-2, brought with them a single functioning radio, allowing Ryan to communicate with Shoup on RED-3.

The only battalion commander to get ashore in his planned position was Major Henry P. Crowe; his Second Battalion, Eighth Marines was attached to Colonel David Shoup's Second Marines. Crowe landed on RED-3 at the base of the "long pier." The first three assault waves, mounted in amtracs, got ashore in fairly good order, but as the boats of the fourth and fifth waves grounded on the reef, they came under heavy fire from every weapon the Japanese could bring to bear.

Bale recalled being held by the Navy control boat at the Line of Departure, and seeing the wreck of the *Saidu Maru,* but taking no fire from it. At last the medium tanks were given the order to land, but even before the LCMs approached the reef edge a murderous Japanese fire began to strike the boats. Colonel David Shoup later wrote that "It was intended that the tanks should hit the beach at about H plus 20. One tank was to precede the wave of tanks by at least 400 yards to test the reef condition, depth of water, etc. The amount, accuracy, and caliber of the enemy weapons brought to bear on the tank lighters rather disrupted the plan, and in general tanks landed when and where we could get them ashore."[86]

In an LCM off RED-3, Joe Woolum was sitting atop the tank turret: "We were all sitting up there watching the show. . . . First it was the ships shelling, then they shut down and then here comes the planes. As we got close to the shore, all of a sudden a big shell hit close to us. Water splashed up, and the concussion. So 'Psst!' We're like gophers" as they scrambled to get inside the tank.

"I turned on the electric traverse, and I'm trying to find me where I'm gonna start shooting. . . . I want to have me targets lined up. I'm turning like this and a big one hit. Either hit the aft of the landing craft, or it could have hit the tank. A big bang, and my electric traverse, I can't shut it off, and here we go, the turret's going round and around. So I have to turn it off and get the manual traverse." Woolum could not locate any targets amid the smoke and wreckage.

Some accounts have said that off RED-1, Schoettel intercepted the LCMs carrying Bale's tanks away from the beach. Bale disputes this: "At no time did Major Schoettel find any tanks headed back to the USS *Ashland.*" Bale was in an LCM that also included the *Ashland's* boat officer. Bale thought that Schoettel was interested in getting the tanks ashore as soon as possible because at one time he had been the executive officer of the tank battalion. Schoettel was laboring under the handicap of only having been in command of the battalion for a few weeks, with very little of that time spent in training or familiarization.

"I had a boat hook, marked in 4 inch increments up to forty inches. Had the depth of the water exceeded 40 inches we would not have landed. The USS *Ashland*'s boat officer, Noah Levine . . . and I measured a 36 inch depth and we disembarked."[87]

As Bale and the Navy crew were unloading the tanks, Schoettel appeared to tell Bale to get his tanks ashore as quickly as possible. "I responded we were doing just that." The boats could not have been headed back to the *Ashland*, because the LCMs carrying Bale's tanks had grounded on the reef only sixteen minutes after the first amtracs arrived on the beach.[88]

Casualties mounted quickly, and the worst carnage was on RED-1. Colonel David Shoup ordered Schoettel to land his reserve on RED-2 and attack westward. Just before 1000hours, Schoettel replied "We have nothing left to land."*

In an indication of how bad the situation was, Shoup ordered his only reserve, Wood B. Kyle's 1/2, to land on RED-2 and attack westward to assist Mike Ryan on RED-1. Instead, the fire from The Pocket split Kyle's battalion, with some landing on RED-2 but a substantial number driven to the right to land on RED-1.

As planned, the Recon Guides were among the first men from Charlie Company into the water. PFC Melvin Swango landed on RED-1 with twenty-one other Marines at H+14, a few minutes before the tanks. "Our mission was to guide the tanks around the bomb craters on the 800 yards of reef. They outfitted us with some floats about the size of a soccer ball. We each had three floats with about a six-foot cord and an anchor." Swango actually underestimated the difficulty of the assignment; the reef edge was about 1200 yards from the beach.

The original plan had been for the tanks to follow the walking men,

---

* Much has been inferred about Schoettel's supposed failings, but he deserves the benefit of the doubt. He was later transferred to the 22nd Marines, recommended for a Bronze Star on Eniwetok, wounded in action, and later killed in action on Guam. (See also Wright, *A Hell Of A Way To Die*, p. 30)

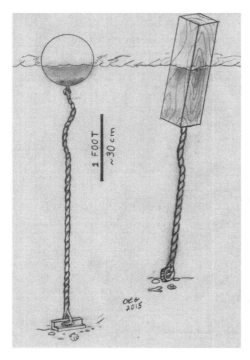

1 FOOT
~30 cm

oct
2015

Two reconstructions of the marker floats used by the Recon Guides, as described by Swango (left) and Bale (right). Weights were any sort of scrap metal—angle iron, broken gears, et cetera. Swango recalled the spherical float may have been painted orange, Bale recalls unpainted wood. The description by Bale is more probable for an item manufactured aboard ship.

but Ed Bale recalled the construction of the floats that, in theory, could be left to mark obstructions. "I also had fabricated some, I'd call floats, buoys, had pieces of scrap metal on the bottom and a 2 by 4 on the top connected by a piece of line or rope so that people could walk through the water and drop these things off so we could guide on them. Trouble is they dropped some of them off and they had to swim with the damn things and they floated away."[89]

The Recon Guides were supposed to mark a clear lane on RED-1, and then work their way east to mark paths for the tank platoons on RED-2 and RED-3. Clearly the difficulty of their assignment had been underestimated.

Swango: "There were about twenty of us, all in one Higgins boat. By the time we hit the edge of the reef the machine-gun fire was so intense it was tearing through the bulkheads of the Higgins boat. I would guess that maybe five or six of the men fell to the deck there, either killed or wounded. We just left them in the boat and they took them back to the ship.

"Sergeant [Kay A.] Zirker, who was in charge of our group, was hit by gunfire in the Higgins boat. He never left the boat. It didn't matter, because we knew what we had to do anyhow."[90]

Swango and the remaining guides took the floats belonging to the casualties. As quickly as possible the guides dove into the water where they would at least be smaller targets and avoid the fire directed at the boat. "We divided up those floats, but we soon found that they were all tangled in the salt water, and we couldn't do anything with them.

"They landed us right at the edge of the reef, and we started wading in." The plan to mark the craters with floats quickly deteriorated under the heavy machine gun fire, with the floats drifting away.

The concept was that "We spread out in a single line, spacing ourselves as far apart as possible while still being able to see any crater that might appear between us."[91]

Without marker floats, the guides became human markers. "Wherever we found a bomb crater, one man would stand there to wave the tanks around it, because if a tank got into that bomb crater the men couldn't get out. It would sink like a rock."

Swango continued: "Our tanks were watching for us as they ploughed through the water, exhausts roaring like some terrible denizens of the deep; occasionally one of the tank hatches would tilt slightly, and one of our buddies would wave a friendly salute from within the dark confines. Finally all the tanks had passed...."[92]

"Machine-gun fire was so intense it was like raindrops in the water all around us. Each time I looked around, there would be fewer of us. A man would simply sink beneath the water, and that would be the end of him. Most of the tanks got in.... Then it was up to us to follow the tanks in, if there were any of us left, and replace the tank crew casualties wherever necessary.

"I only know of three of us who survived. There was myself, [Corporal Charles T.] Charlie Kaiser, and another man.... Charlie Kaiser had his kidneys ruptured by underwater concussion while we were on the reef.

"I always thought of it as a suicide mission. I don't see how any of us could have survived."[93]

Another of the Recon Guides on RED-1 was Private Edwin H. Vancil, who had twice been reduced in rank while in training at Pendleton. Vancil was awarded the Silver Star: "Defying constant danger from enemy machine-gun and mortar fire while assisting his unit in laying a 1800-yard lane of channel markers over a shell and bomb-packed coral reef, Private Vancil valiantly made of himself a human marker in order to signal assault tanks to a successful landing on the beach-head when the floats were carried away by the heavy surf."[94]

If judged by the number of personnel, the Charlie Company Reconnaissance Guides were probably the most highly-decorated small unit on the bitterly-contested island. On RED-1, Private James W. Tobey, USMCR, "...unhesitatingly served as a human marker under intense, persistent enemy fire...." Tobey was awarded the Navy Cross for this and later actions.[95]

The company support personnel landed with the Recon Guides on RED-1, and Ed Gazel thought "The only ones that got ashore was the ones in our boat." Gazel recalled that they were loaded into an LCVP, the first boat to leave the *Ashland*. At the edge of the reef the support personnel were dumped out with the assault infantry. "There was myself, the two cooks, [company cook Staff Sergeant Carroll G.] Lusche, and [chief cook Staff Sergeant Ralph E.] 'Juice' Nelson, there was about eight or nine recon guys, and about fifteen mechanics, and I think the corpsmen [Pharmacist's Mate Second Class Johan Maewsky and Pharmacist's Mate First Class Lyle D. Sullivan] was with us too. One gunnery sergeant [Master Gunnery Sergeant Alphonse] Dumais...an old Frenchman and old China Marine. He was riding with us, but he got shot, too. There was about forty in the boat, but I think only about ten made the beach." Lusche was killed in the water, and Clifford Quine vividly remembered that one of the other men killed was Private Hubert C. Johnson Jr. "He was only seventeen years old. Had just turned seventeen."[96]

Gazel said, "We hit a reef about two hundred yards from the shore, maybe more. There was a lieutenant colonel riding with me. I don't know how he got on the boat. He came off another ship and rode in with us." Gazel did not recognize the officer. We have not been able to establish his identity, or how he came to be on the *Ashland*. "He (the colonel) said 'Let the ramp down.' Then he said 'Check the depth,' and the guy said 'Five feet.' He said 'Well, let the ramp down.' Five feet of water! We're two hundred yards away from the beach!

"He said 'Okay, let's go' so we jumped in. This guy got shot, too, this lieutenant colonel. We're walking in holding our ammunition and our weapons in the air. I looked down the line, and all these regular Marines, the infantry, was all lined up outside the reef. Walking in. We were the third wave, and we were getting picked off."

Private Scot Kinsman had been assigned to accompany and protect the Second Platoon tanks on RED-2. The landing craft grounded on the reef and the occupants spilled out into the neck-deep water:

We had to hold our rifles over our heads as we started in to that beach. This was the moment that we had trained for. The "Japs" had machine guns all along the beach pointing at us. There was a sunken ship to the right of us with "Jap" snipers shooting at us from it also. I heard the sound of a bullet, then another, and another. Then a Marine in front of me got it in the head and went under; then to my right, and then to my left. Marines were dropping like flies all around me. The water turned blood red. . . . Marines were floating back and forth like birch wood wrapped up in barbed wire, purple, bloated and unrecognizable. These were Marines from the first assault. I knew I was going to die.[97]

The landing boat Kinsman was in had stranded in the deadly space between the end of the long pier and the hulk of a grounded Japanese ship. The steel-hulled *Saidu Maru*, severely damaged by American air strikes in September and deliberately grounded on the reef, was still leaking bunker fuel into the water. Many accounts of the battle erroneously identify the ship as the *Nimanoa*, a wooden-hulled ketch used as a medical yacht by the pre-war colonial government. The *Nimanoa* had also been deliberately grounded to prevent its capture, but by D-Day the hulk had apparently been destroyed by the Japanese. The hulk of the *Saidu Maru* would be a constant threat, since Japanese snipers and machine guns occupied it until it was finally blown up by American aircraft.[98]

The planners had not anticipated the enemy's use of the wrecked ship, but could not ignore the threat posed by the long pier that separated RED-2 from RED-3. A scout-sniper section, followed by other Marines, had been tasked with clearing the pier, but it took time. Unlike Marines on the other side of the pier, those on the RED-2 side were blocked from seeking the shelter of the pier by a dredged channel parallel to the pier. The deeper water forced the men on RED-2 to the west, into more deadly fire from The Pocket. Like many, Kinsman was physically and emotionally spent by the trip across the reef. When he reached shallow water:

> I tried to crawl out of the water but I was so weak that I had to take my knife and cut my backpack off. It was full of water and heavy. I crawled on my elbows and knees on shore. You had to stay flat with the ground. If you as much as put up your arm, it would have been shot off. There were dead Marines everywhere on the beach. I dug a foxhole with my hands and feet to get below the ground level, as I lost my shovel. I used two dead Marines as protection from bullets in front of me. Then I heard my buddy, [PVT James W.] Red Mulligan, call out to me, "Scot, I'm hit!" I spotted him about five feet from shore with a fountain of blood coming out of the water from his body. I called to him and said, "Red, you can make it." "No, I can't" he replied. I reached in my back pocket and got my New Testament Gideon Bible. I said, "Red, you can make it. Grab this Bible," and I threw it to him. He crawled out of the water into my foxhole. I dug another one adjacent to it. There was blood on his buttocks. I cut his belt and pulled back his trousers. There was a clean bullet hole in the buttocks. I took his first aid kit and put sulfa on it with a large bandage. I then proceeded to clean my rifle as it was loaded with sand, to make it operable. There was so much sand in the barrel of the gun that it would have caused it to explode if I had tried to fire it.*

Amid the chaos and deafening noise, Kinsman saw one young Marine go berserk and jump to his feet, shouting. An NCO punched him in the face to quiet him. "... it was like a piece of hell and you were right in the

---

*Mulligan was officially listed as Killed In Action, with cause of death "gun shot wounds in abdomen." His grave site was lost and he is now listed as Missing. The New Testament that Kinsman refers to was the pocket-sized version provided free to servicemen.

middle of it. We were the living among the dead and I had a gut feeling we were about to join them."

The Second Tank Battalion commander, Lieutenant Colonel Alexander Swenceski, had asked for and received permission to land the battalion command group. The decision to land his command group and support personnel, as well as the Charlie Company support personnel, with the assault force was a grave error, since they had no clear role to play. Bale later told Swenceski "That was a damn fool request, and a damn fool decision. Two reasons. They didn't have any spare parts. All they had was a bunch of hand tools. There wasn't a thing in the world they could have done, and there wasn't a thing in the world his command group could have done."

In addition, Bale later wrote that "He had no means of communicating with me, the platoon leaders, or individual tanks. My maintenance people had only individual tool boxes, and no parts. Tank recovery vehicle left in New Caledonia due to shortage of shipping. Many died in the water attempting to wade ashore. Many wounded. Those that got ashore just cluttered up the Division CP until island secured." Years later Bale was given a tongue-lashing by Swenceski for his criticism of the decision.[99]

Swenceski tried to land by commandeering one of the LVTs that made it back to the reef edge. On the trip back across the shallow water the LVT was struck by a shell and blown onto its side, killing all but Swenceski. Gravely wounded, Swenceski dragged himself onto an island of dead bodies. Ashore, Shoup was told that Swenceski was dead, though he would be found barely alive 36 hours later. His executive officer, Worth McCoy, arrived at Shoup's command post along with three enlisted men from the battalion command group, but without the radios lost on the reef he could not play any role in the fighting.[100]

As Ed Gazel was wading in, "A guy on either side of me got shot. Either side of me! Blood in the water. We kept walking . . . When you see the guy next to you get shot—I was issued a forty-five, so the forty-five went back into my holster. The magazine was in my pocket and stayed in my pocket." Gazel was also burdened with a canteen and a machete. "Walking in I stepped into a hole, and I got rid of the nine-pound machete."

Most of the men hurried to whatever cover they could, but the Recon Guides did not have that option. Their suicidal duty was to wade slowly ashore searching the murky water for deep holes that might drown a tank,

Most of the island garrison's Ha-Go *light tanks were destroyed in the preliminary bombardment. One of these two tanks abandoned outside Admiral Shibasaki's command bunker likely belonged to Petty Officer Oonuki, one of the handful of Japanese survivors.*—NARA

There are no photos of the medium tanks in landing boats at Tarawa, but they were carried ashore in LCM-3s like this one. The markings indicate the USS William P. Biddle, *so the troops and radio car are from the HQ Company, 2nd Marines.*—NARA

The Recon Guides and support personnel were landed in wooden-hulled LCPRs and LCVPs; these LCVPs from the USS Doyen *are carrying men from the 8th Marines.*—NARA

Second Platoon tank CUDDLES partially submerged and abandoned off Red-3. Many men sheltered behind the sunken tanks on D-Day. Tanks sunk head-on to the beach were later towed out of shell holes using cables. Interestingly the headlights, normally kept stowed inside the tank, are still affixed.—NARA

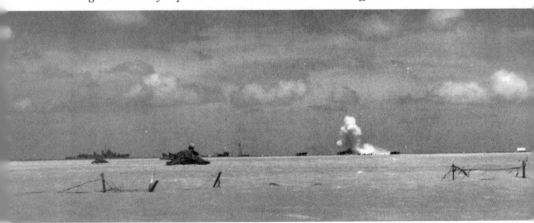

and wave the tanks around these traps. All this was to be accomplished under continuous machine gun and small arms fire.

PFC Joe Jordan, watching from the beach, later said that "Tanks which should have landed early were blown up during the time they were attempting to get in from the reef; their trip required men to guide the tanks around the craters caused by the naval bombardment—those guys should have gotten a Congressional [sic, Medal of Honor], the tanks and the guides were under constant fire from machine guns and anti-tank weapons."[101]

Implicit in Jordan's assessment was that the tanks probably began to save at least a few lives even before arriving at the beach or firing a shot. Throughout the war the Japanese would smother American tanks with intense fire, since part of their anti-tank doctrine was to blind tanks with smoke or intense fire. Marine infantry usually did not like to be in close proximity to the "bullet magnets," but in this case they were probably attracting at least some of the fire that would otherwise be concentrated on the infantrymen wading ashore.

But the carnage was still ghastly, and even from the land Japanese Petty Officer Oonuki could see the results: ". . . enemy landing craft began to run aground, and the US soldiers [sic] began to fall into the sea." Oonuki ". . . poured out shot until the barrel of my gun was red hot. . . ." but the Americans kept coming. Even the Japanese, indoctrinated with an irrational desire for self-sacrifice, were impressed with how ". . . they crossed the shallows to the shore, and then trod over the bodies of their fallen comrades, one after the other, until they managed to install themselves on one end of the island."

Gazel took shelter behind a disabled CHERRY about 100 yards offshore with the chief cook, Staff Sergeant Ralph E. Nelson, and one of the mechanics, Private Elmer J. Friedriechsen. "The three of us were behind this tank, with bullets coming at the other side of it. We had to make our way in, because we couldn't stay there all night long." Gazel estimated they were there about an hour or so.

Eventually Gazel thought he saw Mike Shivetts, whose tank had been disabled, waving his arms in a semaphore signal from the beach saying "Tank CP here!" Shivetts does not remember this at all. "He thanks me to this day for signaling him to 'Get over here, C Company's over here.' I don't recall doing that, but he swears I did it, so I guess maybe I did."

Friedriechsen went first. Gazel remembered that at first "All you have is your head above water. . . . You go in and the water gets shallower and shallower and finally it gets so shallow you got to stand up and run. [The last] thirty or forty yards the water is only two feet high so you stand up and start running toward the beach. You're trying to dive in. So I went next."

Gazel dove headlong into the cover behind the seawall, and "Those coconut logs made a hell of a fence. They were strung together with metal bars. . . . You could hear the bullets flying over the top."

The men in tanks were protected by the armor, but many feared drowning more than the enemy. Mike Shivetts had been in one of the tanks that practiced landing in New Zealand, so "Being under fire didn't mean as much as the coral breaking off and sinking into the water." Aboard ship "We had been told the island would be sunk by naval gunfire, so I wasn't worried about being killed or getting hit. Big mistake." Contrary to popular myth, no crewmen drowned in the tanks.

Some of the tanks did plunge into shell holes and were disabled when seawater flooded in, but it was not the reliable GM diesel engines that failed. As long as the air intake was not submerged they would continue to run for a short time even if the ignition system was damaged, firing by compression. The problem lay with the main electrical junction box low in the base of the turret basket. This simple piece of electro-mechanical equipment controlled the electrical systems of the tank, and allowed electrical connections between the fixed hull and the rotating turret. When it shorted out, everything electrical went dead. In the final analysis only two tanks, CUDDLES and CHERRY, were actually drowned out before reaching the beach, though several more would be lost moving parallel to the shore trying to locate a way off the beach.[102]

Off RED-1, loader Olaf Glenn Johnson in COUNT was hearing "Small arms and HE hitting the turret, with some sparks entering at the seventy-five millimeter pivot." Johnson's nervousness was indicated by "'Battle Hymn of the Republic' repeating in my mind."[103]

In CECILIA on RED-1, Shivetts remembered being "Hot, uncomfortable, sitting on a very small pullout pad [the loader's seat], but too busy to think about it."[104]

"We took a round through the left sponson, up fairly high in the sponson, nobody was hurt or anything," said Bale. "But the water got deeper. I was scared . . . I wasn't scared of the engine drowning out as I was of the electrical system going out because all the voltage regulators and everything were down here at the bottom of the hull."

The invasion plan suggested that the centrally-located and lengthy main pier, and a narrow dredged channel alongside would be the best route to bring supplies ashore. It quickly became obvious that the LCMs loaded with tank ammunition could not survive the approach, nor was there any way to move the heavy ammunition ashore. Several LCMs carrying light tanks and SPMs (halftracks mounting a 75mm cannon) had already been sunk off RED-2 and RED-3.[105]

On RED-3, the exposed beach between the water and the four-foot high coconut log seawall was about twenty yards wide, but the Japanese were dropping plunging fire onto Marines of the first waves who had taken shelter behind the wall. These were probably rounds from the ubiquitous Japanese Type 89 knee mortars. A few Marines braved the murderous machine gun fire, sweeping the top of the wall to gain the dubious shelter of an anti-tank ditch just beyond, establishing a precarious toehold on the island.[106]

Oonuki recalled that his tank penetrated into the shallow Marine beachhead, where the engine stalled, giving the three man crew a fright until Oonuki managed to restart it. Breaking free of the Marines who the crew thought had surrounded the tank, he drove back to the Japanese command bunker. No record from the American side documented such a deep penetration of the very shallow American position. Several accounts have stated that two Japanese tanks approached RED-3. Two 37mm anti-tank guns were hastily lifted over the seawall despite their 912 pound/414kg weight. The American account states that one tank was destroyed, the other "driven off."[107]

Some versions of Oonuki's memoir have him being recalled by a runner to cover the relocation of the garrison commander. Admiral Shibasaki had given up his command bunker to serve as a makeshift hospital. By this time Japanese communications were a complete shambles, and other prisoners reported that the landings came as a surprise because all communications had been knocked out by the preliminary air raids. All orders had to be sent by runners, many of whom were killed before delivering their messages.

At the main command bunker, two surviving Japanese tanks—now immobilized by lack of fuel—were supposed to provide covering fire for the evacuation. Soon after Admiral Keiji Shibasaki left, Oonuki climbed from the immobilized tank. A Marine naval gunfire observer had spotted all the movement in the open and called in shells from the two destroyers in the lagoon. Just as Oonuki reached the ground, a shell hit nearby with a "shattering roar" and his two companions, still atop the tank, were blown apart. Joe Alexander has speculated that the failure of the Japanese to launch a counterattack against the perilously thin Marine beachhead some hours later was the result of Shibasaki's death by a shell from the same bombardment.[108]

The intense fire drove the LCM-3s, carrying what was left of the Second Platoon tanks, from RED-2, and they landed a few yards east of the main pier. Lieutenant Colonel Evans Carlson, who had trained and led the 2nd Raider Battalion on the Makin Island raid and on Guadalcanal, was temporarily assigned as an observer with the 2nd Marine Division in the GALVANIC operation. In his report, he indicated that after committing his regimental reserve (1st Bn, 2nd Marines) to RED Beach-2, because of the intense fire coming off of this sector, Shoup ". . . directed the [Second Platoon] medium tanks to go in on RED 3 and work west."[109]

In CLIPPER ". . . we just hit the reef, gosh, it must have been three hundred yards from the beach," said Charlie Mason. "Of course that water kept coming up and bringing silt and stuff up." When the LCM grounded on the reef, a large-caliber round struck the boat and ". . . knocked the Navy crew right off in the water. The coxswain swam back, crawled aboard, and dropped the ramp for us. When we went out over that ramp, we dropped off in that hole on the other side of that reef—under water. That driver just gunned it, and came on up the other side. . . . We had the tank water-proofed, but that didn't mean much. It was coming in the top. We got wet. But we were alive."

In the same tank, Clifford Quine thought "We was lucky. We got dumped off the LCM about three hundred yards out on a reef. We didn't have the water or the shell holes to what the others up on the other end, so we made it in."

The extra men—replacement tank crews and support personnel—attached to the Second Platoon embarked aboard an LCVP landed on RED-2 as planned. The landing craft dropped their ramps about 1000 yards from the beach. As on RED-2, units immediately became intermingled in the immense confusion and carnage. Marines were shot down in the water by a deadly crossfire from the island and the *Saidu Maru*.

The Third Platoon arrived with the third landing wave, close to its designated landing site near the center of RED-3, and struck the reef about 500 yards from the beach. From his vantage point in COLORADO, Harrell McNorton could see "Gunfire hitting the boats. Men being killed and blown into the water." Like many, he found odors the most vivid memory: "Very disturbing. Gun powder smells."

Focused on their own approach, the Third Platoon tank crews apparently did not notice that the Second Platoon had landed at the same time, on the same beach. As on RED-1, tanks landing on RED-3 attracted heavy fire. A large-caliber round hit Largey's command tank, CANNONBALL, disabling her radio.[110]

Corporal Hubert D. "Doug" Crotts was one of the designated tank replacement personnel of the Recon Guide section attached to Third Platoon, and landed from an LCVP. Their primary assignment was to replace tank crew casualties, but they were also to act as supporting infantry and serve as foot guides as necessary. "The thing we were supposed to do there was go ahead of the tanks and look for any shell craters that would disable a tank. We got to that reef just about as the tanks did, and nothing went according to schedule for the next six to eight hours. Actually, the tanks, I saw some ahead of me, saw some completely dilapidated and rendered unusable.

"I took about three of my close friends, and we went over to the end of the pier. . . . We went down the pier, and we got in. I think it must have taken us four hours."

The long pier provided the only thing remotely resembling shelter, and it was a madhouse of troops trying to get ashore. "The water was just about up to our chins. I suppose we would have drowned, with the equipment we had if it had been even two or three inches deeper. . . . We were getting shot at almost constantly.

"I remember one of my buddies said 'Looky here,' and he had a spent shell in his hand he had caught kind of as it came into the water. It wasn't something we could do in a hurry." Crotts and the men nearby could see no functional tanks in the confusion.

"I know by the time I got in my rifle was rusty from the salt water and all. Wasn't really rusty, just brown. I remember throwing it away and picking up one from a dead Marine."

On RED-3 the water proved shallower than on RED-1, but there were no Recon Guides with their channel markers to guide the tanks. "No one was checking [the water depth]" recalled John Marn. Still, only one tank, Second Platoon's CUDDLES, fell into an unseen crater about 100 yards off RED-3.

It was about 1100hours before the medium tanks began to reach the various beaches, three hours behind schedule. The Headquarters Section of two tanks had started toward the right side of RED-1, with the 1st Platoon tanks to the left in the small cove.

Along all the beaches so many combat engineers had become casualties that the plans to breach the coconut log seawall had failed completely. In his account of the action on RED-1, Mike Ryan reported that the engineers had—as planned—blasted a gap through the seawall to allow the tanks to move inland. However, Bale and the other survivors recount having to search along the wall for a gap, and aerial photos show no such gaps blown in the seawall on RED-1.

When CECILIA got to the beach, "We got ashore, and I got out to try and find a way through that seawall," said Bale. "Hindsight's always best. The damn seawall was not a vertical seawall, [but] it was deep. Of course I never found the engineers.

"The [first] platoon leader, he landed west [sic, actually east] of me, to the left. Name was Sheedy. He landed up in the little cove. He came up and we talked, and he started back to his tank. . . ." Blocked by the intact seawall, under intense fire coming from Japanese positions at the junction of RED-1 and RED-2, and to avoid moving across the front of units landing on RED-2 (Bale had no way to know the landing force had been driven off the right flank of RED-2), there was no option but to shift to the right.

Unable to find a gap in the wall "I went back to the tank." Bale has been criticized for his decision to move parallel to the beach in shallow water, but ". . . the water was so high there was no place else to go, and you couldn't get through the seawall. There were almost no living Marines, except badly wounded, laying on that beach. So we went back in the water and ran parallel to the beach to try and find a place." Bale had instructed

Sheedy and the other tankers to follow his lead tank into the water.

At about 1130hours CECILIA and COMMANDO moved around the end of the small peninsula that formed the parrot's "beak" and located a narrow ramp through the seawall. Aerial photographs taken by a Navy observation plane clearly show that this gap is actually at the extreme end of GREEN Beach. The two tanks had moved beyond the area held by Marine infantry.

The reader should note that this is one of the mysteries of Tarawa—the identity of one of the tanks that moved inland is ambiguous. Ed Bale has recalled that the second tank was CHINA GAL rather than COMMANDO, and of course due credence should be given to first-person accounts. Our reasons for concluding the second tank might have been COMMANDO will be presented in the following chapter.

Bale: "About fifty yards from the intersection of RED Beach One and GREEN Beach we found a low spot on the seawall and were able to get through." This was apparently a spot used by the Japanese to move trucks and equipment out onto the reef at low tide. "We didn't see any Marines. . . . We saw a lot of Japanese running, and started shooting at them with the machine gun."

First Platoon was also shifting to the right to follow the Headquarters Section in search of a gap through the seawall. In the search for places where they could avoid braying their own dead and wounded, and find a gap through the seawall, several tanks were lost to shell craters. Unit cohesion was disrupted, and many of the tanks lost track of each other. COUNT made it ashore on RED-1, but Olaf Johnson wrote that "To rendezvous with Captain [sic] Bale, went back in water instead of along beach to avoid running over downed Marines. Hit a deep hole, had to bail out." [111]

In the confusion of abandoning the tank, one of the other crewmen inadvertently let go of a heavy hatch cover. It slammed shut on PVT John E. Irvine's hand, crushing bones. Like most of the injured and wounded, Irvine would have to endure a night on the beach before he was evacuated to the USS *Harry Lee* the next morning. [112] CHICAGO, maneuvering in the shallow water, was also disabled in a shell hole.

The LCMs carrying Second Platoon tanks had been driven to the left by the heavy fire from the right flank of RED-2. The LCMs veered left and put the tanks onto the reef east of the long pier, actually on the right side of RED-3. There the tanks also had to pick their way past dozens of dead and wounded below the seawall. Clifford Quine: "[Antonio] Almaraz was the driver, and I was the assistant driver and bow gunner. We went in and the first thing I remember . . . It was my introduction to combat, was two Marines face down in the sand. They got hit. They were gone."

The amtracs hung up on the seawall were a memorable sight for some of the men. "They had the amtracs," said Mason "and they were carrying troops in. They tried to get over, and when they'd come up on that seawall they showed the most vulnerable part—their belly. And those Japs would get 'em."

As on RED-1, the plan for the medium tanks to come ashore in a line-abreast formation had long since broken down because of the obstacle posed by the seawall. Tracks visible in aerial photos show that the Second Platoon shifted to the left, in single file, searching for a gap in the log wall. The three surviving tanks from the Second Platoon soon found a spot where the seawall was not continuous and the tanks could easily pass it. Charles Mason in CLIPPER recalled it as a spot where they could cross the seawall without unduly exposing the tanks belly. "It wasn't sticking up for very long. Up and over."

Bill Eads in COBRA recalled that "We were in a landing craft. The tank was in a landing craft and we were in the second or third wave to hit the beach. . . . We managed to get up over that wall that you see in so many pictures." Led by Lieutenant Sloat in COBRA, the Second Platoon tanks immediately proceeded toward an assembly area behind RED-2, located close to a big shell hole near the base of the main pier.

In the Third Platoon, John Marn in COLORADO thought that on the reef "We got lucky and didn't wash out." Once ashore, he quickly discovered "All we owned was twenty feet of beach and seawall."[113]

In this platoon, all four tanks safely arrived on dry sand in the area about 30 yards west of the Burns-Philp pier, and were also driven into a tight group while searching for an exit from the narrow beach. Quickly locating a gap, they easily crossed the coconut log wall. All four tanks made it ashore about thirty yards to the east of the Burns-Philp pier, and prepared to move inland.

Joe Woolum said that on RED-3 "...we were all in a line along here [pointing to a position on a map]...when we got ashore we got into more or less a line [parallel to the beach]."

Most accounts of the battle say that at this point, Major Henry P. "Jim" Crowe ill-advisedly "...ordered them to attack directly to the south and knock out all enemy positions encountered." [114]

However, the tanks already had clear instructions. Woolum recalled that "Our instructions were 'You drive across the island, don't even bother to shoot or nothing. Instructions were to push across the island as quickly as possible and return, firing only as necessary, turn around and come back. Then if you happened to see something, shoot it.'" This was the tank doctrine at the time, but in retrospect Woolum thought it was "asinine."

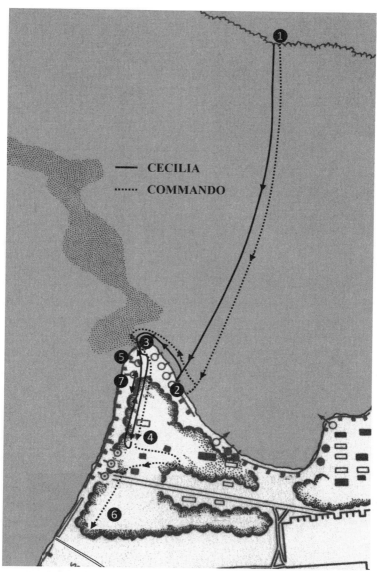

HEADQUARTERS SECTION, D-DAY AFTERNOON.

1: *CECILIA and COMMANDO disembark from LCMs.* **2:** *Both tanks arrive safely on the beach, but reenter the water and move westward to find an opening in the seawall.* **3:** *An opening allows the tanks to move inland.* **4:** *After shooting at the two big guns north of Green Beach, a Japanese Type 95 tank knocks out CECILIA's gun tube. COMMANDO returns fire, destroying the enemy tank.* **5:** *CECILIA returns to the beach to assess the damage.* **6:** *COMMANDO continues alone until knocked out by enemy fire.* **7:** *CECILIA is used to carry ammunition and water; she will spend the night near site 2 "for flank protection."*

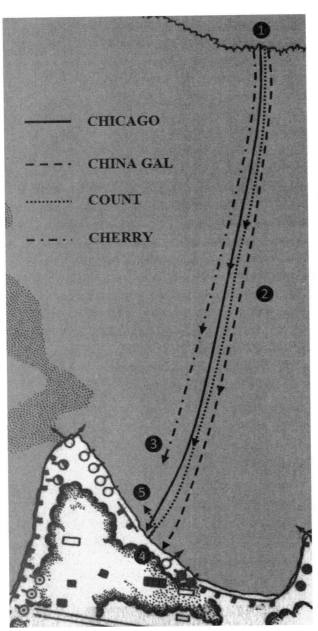

CHICAGO

CHINA GAL

COUNT

CHERRY

FIRST PLATOON, D-DAY AFTERNOON.
1: *LCMs unload tanks.* **2:** *Tanks are guided by reconnaissance personnel around submerged craters.* **3:** *About 150 yards from the beach CHERRY runs into a submerged crater.* **4:** *The other three tanks arrive at the beach east of Bale's position. The tanks return to the water and move west, parallel to the beach. CHICAGO quickly shorts out her electrical system in a submerged crater. CHINA GAL is disabled by a jammed breech block and sits immobile.* **5:** *COUNT tries to bypass disabled CHICAGO and runs into another crater. All tanks are now disabled.*

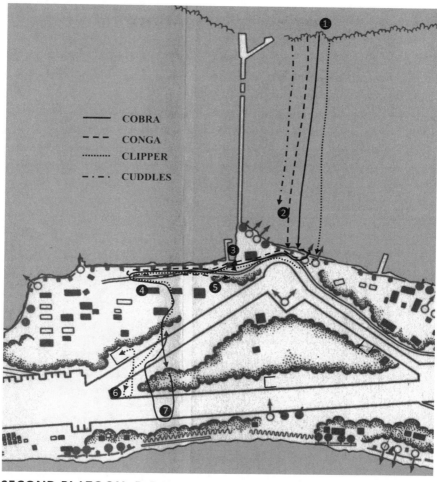

SECOND PLATOON, D-DAY AFTERNOON. 1: *All four tanks land east of the main pier.* **2:** *The four tanks cross the reef without guides. One, CUDDLES, falls into a shell hole; the others arrive on the beach and move inland.* **3:** *The surviving tanks gather at a previously designated assembly area near the base of the main pier.* **4:** *Tanks move west, but are waved back by infantry. Tanks are then attached to 1/2 and 2/2 to help them fight their way across the taxi strip.* **5:** *CONGA falls into a shell hole somewhere near the base of the main pier and is temporarily abandoned.* **6:** *CLIPPER loses one engine to a magnetic mine attack and finds cover in a revetment.* **7:** *COBRA crosses the main runway, and returns. She spends the night near the taxi strip, where the driver is killed.*

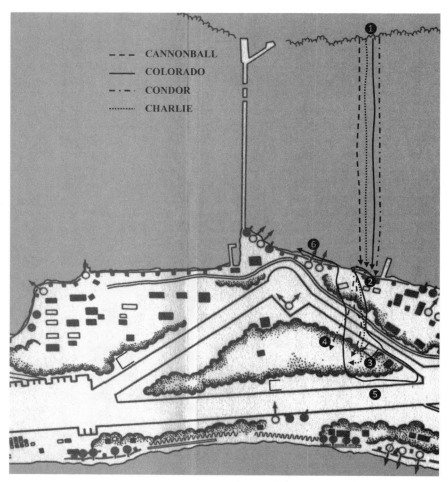

THIRD PLATOON, D-DAY AFTERNOON. 1: *Four tanks disembark.* **2:** *All four vehicles reach the beach, and about 30 yards west of the Burn's Philp pier find an opening in the seawall. The tanks form into a line abreast and cross the taxiway into the central triangle of the airfield.* **3:** *Soon after reaching the central triangle, CANNONBALL is hit by Japanese Type 88 guns firing across the runway. Maneuvering to avoid the fire, CANNONBALL falls into a fuel dump. CHARLIE positions herself between the disabled tank and the Japanese guns and is knocked out.* **4:** *CONDOR is hit by several rounds, and is abandoned.* **5:** *COLORADO makes her way east. Trying to cross the runway she is hammered by the Japanese guns and finally falls back, passing near the disabled vehicles.* **6:** *COLORADO returns in the water to prevent running over Marines below the seawall.*

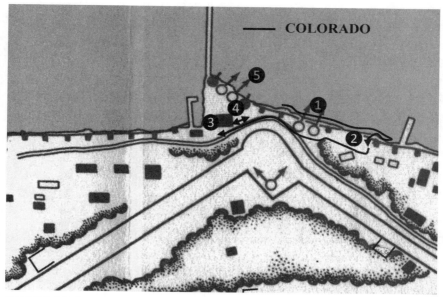

COLORADO, D-DAY LATE AFTERNOON. 1: *The tank remains in shallow water, moving parallel to the beach and firing inland.* **2:** *Tank commander John Marn is ordered inland to deal with Japanese positions.* **3:** *Moving west to defend the aid station near the main pier, COLORADO expends all her ammunition.* **4:** *On several occasions the tank falls back for ammunition, scavenged from disabled CONGA and CUDDLES. The tank commander and gunner are wounded near disabled CONGA.* **5:** *COLORADO spends the night in shallow water near the base of the main pier.*

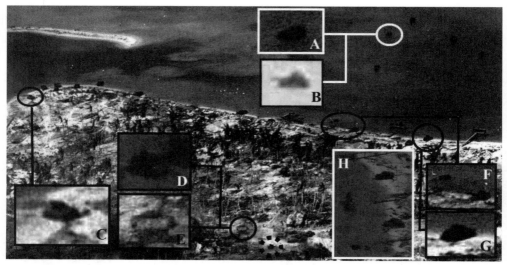

Photo taken by an aircraft from the USS ESSEX *on D-Day, early in the afternoon. It shows the western side of Red Beach One and the boundary with Green Beach, looking north.* **A:** *CHERRY drowned on the reef earlier that day.* **B:** *Photo showing the same vehicle, taken from the beach. The gun tube is lightly visible and is oriented westward.* **C:** *Located at the gap in the seawall used to penetrate inland earlier in the day, CECILIA fell back after having her main gun damaged.* **D** *and* **E:** *This medium tank located behind a small building could be COMMANDO. D was taken during the same sortie, from the north-west.* **F:** *At bottom right is CHICAGO, top left is COUNT's turret. Both were lost in the water during the morning.* **G:** *CHINA GAL on the beach, stopped with the main gun breech jammed.* **H:** *Photo taken during the same sortie, looking eastward. It shows from top to bottom: CHINA GAL, CHICAGO and COUNT. Other dark dots are disabled LVTs. Partial circle at bottom indicates a wrecked Japanese Type 95 tank.*—original photos from NARA and Marine Corps History Division

CHAPTER SEVEN

DAY ONE — INLAND

Cowards do not count in war; they are there but not in it.
—EURIPIDES

RED BEACH ONE

Before the two Headquarters Section tanks moved farther inland, Bale had ordered Vancil to ". . . work his way back . . . to locate the first platoon leader and have him bring tanks to my location."[115]

The radio net had already broken down. Bale had no way of knowing that the First Platoon tanks were all disabled, and he was wondering why they were not following.

Air photos indicate that for a time, CECILIA forged well ahead of COMMANDO, working its way through the rubble and fallen palms behind the intersection of RED-1 and GREEN Beaches. Eventually COMMANDO came on up and the two tanks moved inland to try and find friendly infantry. In fact, they had probably moved well ahead of the infantry.[116] From a post-battle interview, correspondent Technical Sergeant Samuel Schaffer wrote:

> 'There wasn't much we could see' said Bale. 'It was dark from the dust and smoke. Two of my men volunteered to get out and lead us on foot, spotting the targets for us. God, what guts they had to walk into that hell, in front of tanks and in front of infantry. And both were killed.'[117]

Shivetts, the loader in CECILIA, later said, in reference to moving without guides, "That was our downfall. Coconut logs. We got stuck on coconut logs. Chavez, our driver, he had that job because he was the best driver in the company—good enough that Ed Bale rode with him. We got hung up on coconut logs, and that's when we got knocked out of action."

Bale: "We started inland and suddenly a Japanese tank turret crops up over a revetment." The Japanese Type 95 light tank nosed up over the sand and log wall, its gun pointed straight at CECILIA. "They had a little 37mm gun that had a shoulder harness type thing that they elevated and depressed the gun with."[118]

What happened next was unique. "The CECILIA gunner [Charles 'Whitey' Martin] was excited and fired, missing the Japanese tank. Before the loader could reload, the Japanese tank fired."

Inside the turret, Shivetts had no clue what was happening. "The thirty-seven millimeter [round] entered the tube of the gun . . . and blew out the gun about six to eight inches down [the bore]. Unfortunately the breech was open, I'm sitting there with a seventy-five millimeter in my lap. There was a flash came through."

Bale: "His thirty-seven millimeter round hit the end of CECILIA's gun tube, broke into fragments, and came down the seventy-five millimeter gun tube. The breech was open, and the fragments bounced around the inside of the turret. The thing lit up like a Christmas tree, seven or eight different colors."

Shivetts: "I think it was Ed hollered something about flashback. Not being a tank man but a radio man, I hollered back 'Flashback my a-double-ess-ess, something hit me!' It was a piece of shrapnel, and hit me. Lucky as hell that there was no seventy-five millimeter in that breech of the gun. The breech was open."

Bale did not think that anyone was hit, ". . . but that driver [nearly] stomped me to death trying to get out of there. I had to put my foot in his chest."

COMMANDO fired back at the Japanese tank, ripping off the turret and ending the brief fight.[119]

Shivetts was not badly injured: "I knew something peppered me. That's all. Didn't even say anything to anybody." With the hull or tracks jammed on the log, "We were hung up and we were there for a while." Estimating time is difficult in combat. Shivetts thought they were stuck on the log for forty-five minutes or so, though Bale never even mentions being hung on the log.[120]

Bale: "A look down the gun tube by the loader revealed the inside of the tube was damaged. So then I said 'We're going back to the beach.' Leaving CHINA GAL [COMMANDO] to continue support of the badly-exposed troops, I returned to the beach with CECILIA to assess the damage."

Ed Bale has consistently refuted it, but some sources claim that the hit had also temporarily disabled the traversing mechanism. Shivetts said, "You couldn't traverse the turret. The gun was of no use for firing, so he [Bale] made the decision. Alfred [*sic*, Alfonso Chavez] got us off the coconut logs, and we got back to where we could bail out." According to one account written shortly afterward, presumably from an interview with the crew, the clutches were also damaged, taking CECILIA out of the fight for several hours.[121]

Recon Guide James Tobey apparently helped the tank to find its way back to the beach: "...after the tanks had safely reached the island, immediately made his way forward one hundred and fifty yards inside the hostile lines to a disabled tank [CECILIA?], guided it back through his own lines to the beach and was highly instrumental in restoring it to operating condition."[122]

At the beach, Bale dismounted and found that "A big hunk [had been] taken out of the muzzle. You looked down in there and the lands and grooves were gouged. I was afraid to try and fire something through there, afraid it would go off and wreck the turret."

Then "We went back in and worked with the infantry acting as a mobile machine gun. We worked until late afternoon of D-Day and ran into a young major by the name of Mike Ryan, who was the junior major of the 2nd Marine Division."[123]

This was another potentially disruptive aspect of the confused operational planning. "Mike Ryan, who had taken over that battalion, I had never seen before," said Bale. "I had never seen any of the company commanders, and this sort of thing."

Shivetts: "Then Ed [Bale] took off, and that was his own decision. We were left to do whatever needed to be done that we could do." Sergeant Robert M. Keller, the tank commander, had moved down to the assistant driver's seat while Bale was in the tank. Keller took over again, and Shivetts recalled that CECILIA would spend much of the remainder of the fight hauling water and ammunition to the infantry. We believe CECILIA eventually became stuck in a water-filled crater off RED-1, perhaps while maneuvering to attack enemy positions in The Pocket with its machine guns.[124]

COMMANDO forged ahead following the initial orders, and—with Ryan's infantry—pushed toward the southern, seaward beaches. In an account written just after the fighting, correspondent Samuel Shaffer credited COMMANDO with destroying "two five-inch anti-boat guns and five pillboxes" before it was put out of action.[125]

While we do not lightly contradict eyewitness accounts, our photo analysis suggests that the second tank that went on alone after CECILIA was disabled was indeed COMMANDO. Aerial photos taken after the fighting had moved on show a derelict medium tank sitting near the south end of GREEN Beach, with the turret slewed to the starboard side. Nearby are several distinctive very tall palm trees with preserved foliage (rare on Tarawa) and a tall pole with a tangle of wires and a possible power transformer atop the pole. This correlates with ground photos of the destroyed

COMMANDO landed on Red-1 Beach, destroyed a Japanese tank, several pillboxes and anti-boat guns, and penetrated far into Japanese held ground before being destroyed by fire from one or more 37mm guns.—NARA

tank identified as COMMANDO. The loss position of COMMANDO from air photos corresponds to that day's farthest advance of the infantry from sketch maps in after action reports.

Apparently unknown to the tank crew veterans, Major Mike Ryan, in a post battle report, stated that "We put three companies abreast, took two medium tanks, but the two tanks were knocked out. It was then about 1630." The loss of both tanks was likely the result of no formal training in tank-infantry cooperation.[126]

From COMMANDO's final position, it probably emerged from amid the wreckage and vegetation into a relatively open area, and took numerous shell hits on the starboard side, penetrating the sponson and perhaps the thicker turret armor. One contemporary account states that the tank was

COMMANDO came ashore near the Red-1/Green Beach boundary (top of photo) and was destroyed near the south end of GREEN Beach (left side of photo) on the afternoon of D-Day. Photo taken by an observation aircraft from USS Essex *after the battle.*—original photo from NARA

hit eighteen times. Despite the high number of rounds COMMANDO sustained, nobody was killed inside the vehicle.[127]

Measurement of the holes from photographs suggests rounds of approximately 37mm caliber. The position of COMMANDO further suggests that the strikes were likely from one or more of the four 37mm guns positioned to protect the bigger 200mm coastal guns on the south end of GREEN Beach (the crest of the bird's "head"). These 37mm guns—like most on Betio—had been emplaced in positions facing the sea, but after the battle analysts found that many had been hastily repositioned to fire toward American units advancing from the lagoon side.[128]

The loss of COMMANDO is another of the many conundrums of the battle. Intelligence reports did not accurately identify or break down smaller gun types, simply calling any smaller caliber weapon positioned to fire seaward an "anti-boat gun." As noted in an earlier chapter, the four "37mm mobile" guns identified in this position on one intelligence map probably refer to obsolete Type 94 (1934) Rapid Fire Infantry Guns. Originally designed as an anti-tank gun, the Type 94 had proven inadequate and been relegated to the general infantry support role.

The position of these guns was about 150 yards from the location of COMMANDO, and they were in theory marginally capable of penetrating the M4A2's sponson armor at this range, provided the gunner could achieve a perfect hit at ninety degrees to the armor. In other battles they usually failed to penetrate at even shorter ranges. Medium tank crews normally had little fear of this particular weapon unless a gun in a close-range ambush position could fire into the thinner armor behind the suspension units. Interestingly, in his post-battle analysis, the acting battalion commander of the Second Tank Battalion, Charles Worth McCoy, did not attribute any losses to the smaller guns: "Some mediums received numerous hits with about a 40mm which, although [they] did not knock any [out], penetrated the sides of the tanks.[129] Results of a post-battle examination of tanks damaged by similar projectiles is in the chapter entitled 'Aftermath.'"

RED BEACH TWO

By about 1130hours the Second Platoon tanks had worked their way back into their assigned sector behind RED-2, near the right-hand boundary of the shallow beachhead. The tanks drew so much enemy fire that the infantry in the area waved them back. The tanks were about to fall back when they were instead told to assist the infantry of First Battalion, Second Marine in their move toward the runway.

Once ashore, the tanks were still not out of danger from unseen craters. The three tanks from Second Platoon went on, accompanied by infantry, but without an integrated tank-infantry doctrine, both working as different entities. Tanks were sent in front of the American infantry lines and started to fire at enemy strong points. One Second Platoon tank, probably CONGA, tumbled into an unseen hole and was temporarily abandoned. Such losses were a recurring problem throughout the battle, attributed to the poor visibility from inside a tank.[130]

The crew escaped and fell back toward Marine lines. There they regrouped in a big shell hole where crewmen from other lost tanks were gathered with the supernumerary replacement personnel of the tank company. Because of heavy casualties among infantry ranks, they were helping them in holding the beachhead.

In CLIPPER, Charles Mason's first impression was "Old trucks knocked out, humps in the ground out there, and an airstrip across the way. You couldn't tell a heck of a lot...."

The lessons learned in the battles for the Solomon Islands had, to a limited degree, been carried back to the tank school. One weapon that particularly impressed the tank crews was the Type 99 *Hakobakurai* grenade-mine. A disc of explosive inside a canvas pouch fitted with four mag-

The Type 99 Hakobakurai *grenade mine, like this example captured on Betio, was a suicidal weapon with more psychological than physical effect. One of these weapons probably disabled one of CLIPPER's engines.*—NARA

nets and a time-delay fuze, it was supposed to be placed on the tank's armor and detonated. The magnets often failed to hold, and Japanese suicide attackers would hold it in place until it detonated. On New Georgia these devices had disabled several light tanks when placed against the thin rear engine hatches. It eventually proved far less effective against the thicker armor of the medium tanks, but it was still a very impressive psychological weapon.

Doug Crotts said that "We were supposed to get infantry working with us, especially if it looked like the tanks were in danger, to not let any enemy approach because one magnetic mine would have just devastated any tank.

"But it didn't work out that way. We didn't have any infantry working with us, because there wasn't any infantry that organized. We had to sort of protect the tanks ourselves."

CLIPPER and COBRA continued inland behind RED-2, with Lieutenant Sloat's COBRA in the lead. Mason: "These two Japs came out from I don't know where, a hole in the ground, and they was trying to get the grenades up into the radiator system of the tank that he [Sloat] was in. All at once it just snapped on me. They were just like shooting rabbits. I had no problem after that. It just boiled down to kill or be killed. And I didn't want to be killed."

Quine recalled that they went in "... probably wasn't over a hundred yards." Without infantry to protect them, "We shot some rounds off, some seventy-five.... and the next thing you know that magnetic mine, it was a suicide guy Jap, he put the magnetic mine on top of the engine [deck], and knocked out one engine."

In a separate interview Mason said he thought that several mortar shells struck the tank in quick succession. Mason recalled that the explosion "Knocked my loader colder than a cucumber."[131]

Quine: "There wasn't no communication. It was a SNAFU situation. As far as I know and I could tell we wasn't organized. We was all split up I think. Anyhow, that put CLIPPER out of commission." The explosion damaged the radios and knocked the loader-radio operator to the deck. Inside the tank, Quine clambered up to replace the loader. "I had to crawl up through the hole inside the turret. I loaded about three or four rounds ... in that seventy-five after we got hit."

Mason: "One engine was completely gone. The other was still running good. That driver [Almaraz] snapped the dead engine out and turned into one engine that was good. So fast that the tank didn't even quiver, keep it under rolling... That's why I say, an excellent tank driver.

"... it showed on the dash one engine was gone.... We pulled back and went into a revetment. It was kind of a fort.... We stayed right in the tank. The commander, which was [SGT Robert E.] Baker, we couldn't get nothing out of anybody. It was all screwed up.

"Pearson, who was my loader, he come up off the deck shaking his head. He says 'Them sons-of-bitches. My mother wouldn't like them for that!' It broke the tension in the crew, and we all started laughing." No one else was injured; Mason had "... a couple of burned spots on my arm. Nothing to even consider a wound. It was sometimes very comical. Sometimes shook you up." Baker apparently decided to sit out the rest of the day in the partially protected position.

The M4A2 was capable of operating on one engine if the driver used the transfer case to disengage the disabled engine. The loss of an engine made the tank underpowered and very hard to drive, and particularly hard to steer on rough ground or in close spaces. Many crews opted to declare the tank inoperable if an engine was disabled.[132]

Quine agreed that "With one engine, we made it to a revetment and stayed there all night."[133]

COBRA went on alone across the airfield, then turned to spend the rest of the afternoon shelling enemy positions.

RED BEACH THREE: THE MASSACRE OF THE THIRD PLATOON
All four tanks of the Third Platoon landed without mishap, and by noon the platoon was functioning as one of the few intact units on the island. John Marn said that once over the seawall "There were no Japanese movements in that area at the time, weren't any of them standing around there when we came in. A lot of gunfire."

In common with the infantry, the company's original orders were to rapidly push across and sever the island into two parts. After moving through the densely built-up but wrecked area north of the northwest-southeast taxi-way, the tanks spread out into a rough line-abreast formation.

Largey's CANNONBALL ran down the south side of the taxiway, turned right and overran a line of foxholes along the edge of the taxi-way, and moved into the triangle formed by the runway and the two taxi-ways. According to Woolum, CONDOR was on the extreme right of the line,

Lieutenant Largey's CANNONBALL tumbled sideways into a Japanese fuel dump and was destroyed by fire and internal explosion. The paint has burned away to expose an Army star and serial number, indicating it was originally issued from Army depot stores.—NARA

with CHARLIE to its left. This formation was ragged; there were fewer obstacles but the tanks still had to dodge raised sand berms and other obstacles, and CHARLIE eventually followed behind CANNONBALL.

The ensuing brief fight has been retold numerous times, and hopelessly garbled in the retelling. However, this is one of the few short and violent actions that can be traced out using the accounts of survivors, and aerial photographs taken during the battle (see Appendix E). In a few cases the paths of individual tanks can be followed in some detail.

"Okay, we're following orders, so the driver, here he goes," said Woolum. "I'm shooting. I don't know what I'm shooting at, if it's that hump over there or anything I'll blast it." Woolum estimated that "I fired maybe ten or fifteen rounds of seventy-five, and maybe one belt of thirty caliber. Never saw a Jap."

The tanks emerged into the more open area near the main runway, with few trees and structures, at the eastern end of the triangular central area. They were immediately hit by "enemy gun fire beleived [*sic*] to be of about 75mm caliber."[134]

CHARLIE moved into position to protect the crew exiting from stricken CANNONBALL, and was itself destroyed by several Type 88 guns. Several impact marks are visible. A penetration and hole from a fatal internal explosion are visible just above the pinch bar leaning against the tank.—NARA

The fire was undeniably effective, and it is likely that the tanks were taken under fire by four, and possibly as many as six, 75mm Type 88 anti-aircraft guns positioned about 360 yards/330 meters away on the other side of the open runway. This was point-blank range for such a weapon.

The Type 88 was the best anti-armor gun the Japanese possessed, capable of destroying American medium tanks at considerable ranges. It would continue to be one of the most feared anti-tank weapons up through the final battle on Okinawa, and tank crews habitually referred to it as "the Japanese eighty-eight." Like the German 88mm Flak guns, it was mounted on removable wheels. In action it sat on a tall pedestal with four cruciform legs that allowed 360 degree traverse. Unlike many guns on Tarawa, the Type 88s and the similar 80mm anti-aircraft guns were not dug in with overhead cover. Intended as both anti-aircraft and ant-boat guns, they were positioned in open pits overlooking the beach, and unlike the covered guns, could readily traverse to fire inland.

"They hit these first tanks over on the left of us" continued Woolum. After they hit some, here comes these guys trying to get out of the tank.

Some of them getting out, some of them getting hit. They keep banging, and they started hitting us."

According to most accounts, the first tank to be stricken was Largey's CANNONBALL. Hit several times, the driver maneuvered to avoid the incoming fire and veered to the right to take shelter behind a sand berm. The berm turned out to be a protective wall around a Japanese fuel dump—a pit filled with barrels of aviation fuel. As the driver pulled the tank behind the berm, the sandy ground collapsed and the tank tipped over on its right side and slid into the pit, rupturing the drums. Probably smelling the fuel, the crew began to bail out.

CHARLIE was following in CANONBALL's tracks. The driver, seeing CANNONBALL tip sideways, bypassed the disabled tank on the left. CHARLIE turned in front of CANNONBALL, and the driver positioned CHARLIE perpendicular to CANNONBALL, between the Japanese guns and the exiting crew. The Japanese guns started to hammer CHARLIE until hits quickly put the tank out of action. More strikes penetrated the hull side just below the turret, causing an internal fire and explosion that wrecked the tank.

In CONDOR, Woolum recalled that "When we'd get hit, you'd hear the horrible explosion, felt the [tank] shake. It would addle you for a while, and sparks would shoot off inside."[135]

Most accounts of the battle say that CONDOR was disabled by a bomb dropped from a Navy aircraft, but for decades Ed Bale has pointed out that there was no damage to the tank or surrounding objects consistent with that theory. Joe Woolum stated bluntly that they were hit by the enemy guns.[136]

Many of these misconceptions are probably due to Lieutenant Largey "...who was a talker, and Lou exaggerated" according to Bale. The civilian war correspondents and photographers were on RED-3, and "Lou could smell off a war correspondent a half-mile away" explained Bale, laughing. Between the inherent confusion of battle, Largey's flair for publicity, the understandably slightly garbled stories of on-scene reporters, but mostly because of the numerous retellings and embellishments by writers over the decades, considerable confusion has arisen.

CONDOR took several hits, and "That's when the driver [Corporal Raymond A. Barker] said 'we're on fire.'" The crews were trained to evacuate the tank if it caught fire; combat experience later proved that the diesel fuel was very difficult to ignite, but ammunition propellant fires were catastrophic. The concussion had apparently shorted out the engine fire warning system since photos of CONDOR from several angles show no penetrations of the armor.

Following the standard procedure would prove fatal for some. The tank commander, [SGT Robert F.] Shook, "...says 'Let's go!' and he bails out. I bail out right behind him. That's the last I saw of the other three guys."

Behind him Corporal Herschel B. Fulmer, the radio operator, was shot. "He was kind of a big guy, slower. He was slower. As he was trying to get out of the hatch a piece of shrapnel knocked him back down in the tank." Fulmer survived, but Woolum never knew how. The driver, Corporal Raymond A. Barker, was killed but is listed as Missing In Action since his body was never found. Woolum thought Private Harry O. Grey was also killed exiting the tank.[137]

CANNONBALL's crew quickly fled the tank after it tumbled into the

Numerous accounts say CONDOR was destroyed by a US Navy dive bomber, but veterans (including crewmen) say it was abandoned when a malfunctioning warning light indicated the engine was afire. The new cleated tracks and solid wheels are clearly visible. The tank commander oriented the hatch to protect the crew while escaping the tank. The gun tube was oriented in such a way that the driver (CPL Raymond Barker, KIA) could not open his hatch.—NARA

pit, but at some point the aviation fuel caught fire, and in the intense heat CANNONBALL's own ammunition detonated. The violence of the explosion ripped the starboard sponson plate loose from the front of the hull and twisted it out like soft metal. The tank burned, rendering it completely unsalvageable.

From their position on the ground about 100 feet away, Woolum and Shook saw ". . . a big hole where they had aviation barrels of gas around, and it was on fire, over there on the side. It got hotter and hotter . . . So Shook jumps up and says 'We gotta get outa here!' So he jumps up and takes off, and I'm right behind him." Shook was shot through the shoulder, and Woolum lost track of him in the mayhem.

Woolum spotted a long, shallow trench that he later thought might have been gouged out by a low-angle hit from a large naval shell. "I get in there. I holler 'Shook! Shook!' and I don't get no answer. I think he's dead too. I'm thinking about ending it [holding finger to right temple], and [I thought] 'No. When I see them coming after me I'll shoot seven times, and then I'll do it, you know, 'cause I wasn't gonna let them get me." Woolum was pondering suicide because the Japanese had a reputation for torturing prisoners in sadistic and grotesque ways.

COLORADO, on the far left of the line of Third Platoon tanks, had luckily escaped with little damage. Marn reported that "All on our own we caroused around knocking out several enemy artillery [pieces] still in action." In the process, "We were also hit several times the first day by the same Jap artillery, taking big gouges in our turret."[138]

Like most Marines, Marn only rarely saw the Japanese. "I didn't see them close up. Saw them far away when we fired into them [bunkers]." Struck by several rounds, Marn turned COLORADO back toward the beach.

Woolum: "About this time I hear this tank motor rev up. I look up and there's the COLORADO headed back for the beach." Woolum leapt up and raced to intercept the speeding tank, jumped and grabbed one of the lifting rings on the slope plate of the tank.

"I grabbed that and threw myself up on the front of the tank. Later Mac [McNorton, the driver] tells me . . . he just got a glimpse of me running up there, and he thought it was a Jap. So he tries to run me over . . . I looked in the periscope, I'm a-hollering 'Let me in! Let me in!' Things

Only COLORADO survived the massacre of Third Platoon, and retreated to the beach where it moved to and fro along the shore providing fire support. Contrary to myth, it drove into the water to avoid running over dead and wounded Marines, not to extinguish a non-existent fire.—NARA

were wild. About that time another shell hit probably the back of the tank or the side of the tank, and the concussion knocks me off. I hit on my feet. On my feet, and I was a going! I would bet I set records with them boon-docker shoes on, running in that sand. If they'd had a timer on me I'd have broke all damn records that seventy-five or a hundred yards to get back. You do things you would never do again."

Below the seawall was a line of nervous infantry, their rifles trained on Woolum. "I'm a hollering and waving. This is a matter of seconds, but over that wall I go." On the narrow strip of beach "It's just solid Marines—wounded and alive, and whatever. The corpsman, he doctored up my finger." Woolum had never noticed the end of his right forefinger was shot off. With other Marines, Woolum lay immobile in the shelter of the wall. Occasionally men would dare a look over the wall to be sure no counter-attack was forming.

Largey and eleven other men had made it back from behind Japanese lines on foot; three were missing. "It took us the rest of the afternoon, but at 6 p.m. eight of us broke through. Three boys pinned in a foxhole showed up two days later, unhurt," Largey later reported.[139]

The official report states that COLORADO was set afire by the enemy guns. Another of the persistent myths of the battle is that a Japanese attacker threw an improvised gasoline bomb against the side of COLORADO, setting it ablaze. No one knows the original source of the latter tale, but all of the men who were actually involved deny both versions. Marn: "Hell, no! They didn't have any gasoline to throw. They were just dug in like ticks. Sandpits and logs." Woolum (who leapt onto the supposedly flaming tank) went on to explain that "They say in that book that they drove out in the water to put the fire out. Untrue. He drove into the water because here [pointing to a photo] you can see the Marines, this is solid Marines, from the seawall to the water. So when he drove down getting away from the artillery, he couldn't park on the beach. He had to go out into the water a little."

Woolum said that shortly afterward, "[Major Henry P.] Crowe sent him [COLORADO] right back. . . . 'Get that goddamn tank back over that wall!' They went back over the wall, and they disappeared."

At some point Marn and COLORADO returned to help rescue another trapped tank crew. "Just one crew that was close. They were dug in after their tank got knocked out. We rescued them, and they were the only ones. Just crawled up to the tank, to the sides, off the ground. They weren't dug in." The men clambered up onto the tank to be carried to relative safety.

The number of Third Platoon tanks had dwindled to one, and out of touch with anyone else, for a time Marn thought that COLORADO was the only tank left in operation on the island. With darkness approaching, they again retreated back to the area of the beachhead.

Norman Hatch had enlisted out of high school and after a series of adventures was trained as a combat cameraman. He came ashore on RED-3 and recalled that the crew finally parked COLORADO for at least a large part of the late afternoon. "He fiddled around with it all day, about half of the tank in the water, the other half out. . . . "

Marn knew that Japanese were still holding out around the aid station, just east of the base of the main pier, and in his "fiddling around," "That's where I lost [used] most of my ammunition, shooting the hell out of things around them."

The senior officer ashore gave orders that the surviving tanks were not to be risked advancing without infantry support. COLORADO moved along the beach firing inland. A Recon Guide can be seen banging his rifle butt on the side of the turret to attract the attention of the crew.—NARA

Schoettel's landing boat, with Charlie Sooter and Dodson Smith aboard, had eventually arrived off RED-3. The boat grounded near the long pier at about 1400hours.[140]

Smith: "They were hitting our boat with machine gun fire, and mortar and those seventy-five [millimeter] mountain guns were firing shells all around us." Machine gun fire was striking the metal ramp—the only protection in the wooden boat. "Of course we didn't let any of them down, just went over the sides, because they were firing right on that ramp. A couple of the guys drowned."

Once in the water "We had to wade in from about six, eight hundred yards out. We had to leave one of the radios in the boat there, because the water was so deep that if we went over the side with the radio we would have drowned. We did get one ashore, a TBX, the bigger radio that had three parts to it, it had a transmitter, a receiver, and a generator—a hand-cranked generator. To send a message one guy had to crank the generator while the other guy either talked or used Morse code."

Carrying the heavy TBX—packed in two large, heavy waterproof chests—across the reef must have been a heroic struggle in itself.

"The little TBYs that were for each company, they wouldn't work. They were not waterproof, and you move three feet down on the land and you'd be out of communication. You had no communications by radio with the individual companies. The only communications we had was between the commanding officer and the ship." Once the radio was set up "We were sending some messages for Colonel Shoup. Of course he had another radio they got ashore but that was about it."

The carefully rehearsed logistics plan was a complete disaster. The Shore Party's demolition teams and the few small bulldozers ashore were supposed to breach the seawall, clear paths, and keep supplies flowing. Instead they were pressed into duty as assault engineers attacking enemy bunkers. The limited supplies coming ashore via the congested long pier were inadequate, and all efforts to sort out the confusion were stymied.

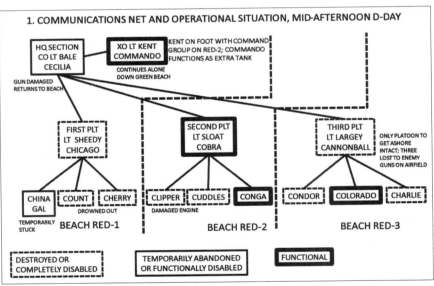

Although it is impossible to determine precise timing, by mid-afternoon of D-Day only four of fourteen Charlie Company tanks were fully functional. The rest were lost to deep water or enemy action.

The medium tanks, with their ammunition loaded onto LCMs that could not get close to the beach, were logistical orphans.

In the brutal heat, even drinking water was in short supply. Mike Shivetts recalled that for the tanks, without external water can racks, some water was carried inside the tank "But it was not much. A canteen apiece, I would guess." Marn added that in the brutal heat "We had no water in the tank at all. The infantry that happened to be dug in out there at the seashore [supplied some water]." Inside the tank it was "very warm" recalled Shivetts. "You could burn yourself on the metal of the turret."

Wounded, Woolum spent the remainder of the day lying below the seawall. "All day I'd see these boatloads coming in," said Woolum. "There'd be twenty or thirty men get out of a landing craft, way out there, this [chest] deep water, and you could see these bullets hitting in the water—psht—psht—psht—machine guns, rifles, whatever. These guys would start falling. And they kept on.

"As it got shallower, they fell worse. Maybe there would be two or three,

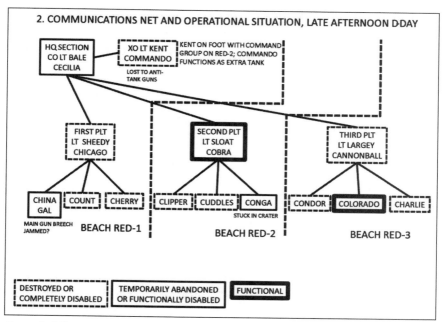

By nightfall on D-Day only two tanks remained fully functional, both isolated by the limitations of the company radio net.

or none maybe, out of a boat would get in. I'd watch it, and I wouldn't want to watch it."

CLOSE OF DAY—SITUATION IN DOUBT

By late afternoon the main beachhead along RED-2 and RED-3 was still only about one hundred yards deep. A basic part of the battle plan was to push across the island to the southern beaches as quickly as possible. In the massive confusion, some units—somehow meeting less resistance—forged far ahead of others. One group of about seventy men had pushed into the central triangle of the airfield. Even more exposed was a group of fifteen men from the Weapons Company of 2/2 stranded in a series of trenches on the far side of the main runway, near the south shore.[141]

The Japanese struggled to mount the *yogaki* fundamental to their strategy, but the counterstroke was fizzling out. At about 1800hours, American radar spotted a formation of fifteen Mitsubishi G4M "Betty" long-range twin-engine bombers approaching from the west, headed for the aircraft carriers—the *Independence, Essex*, and *Bunker Hill*—supporting the forces ashore. The planes that survived the hail of anti-aircraft fire concentrated on the light carrier *Independence,* CVL-22. The ship dodged four torpedoes but one ripped into the stern, blowing a forty-foot long hole in the ship's side and narrowly missing a torpedo magazine. With most of her propulsion damaged and listing heavily, the *Independence* was able to limp to Funafuti for temporary fixes by the repair ship USS *Vestal* (AR-4). The damaged *Independence* eventually made it away for more temporary repairs at Pearl Harbor, and permanent repairs in California.[142]

The Marines had to give up some of their hard-won gains in anticipation of a nocturnal counterattack. In addition, the Japanese kept filtering back to reoccupy positions, so that the withdrawing Marines had to fight their way back to the beach.[143]

Division commander MGen Julian Smith had asked for and received the corps reserve, the 6th Marines. They were not immediately available, but this did leave him free to immediately commit his last division reserve battalion, 1/8. The battalion was instructed to land to the east of RED-3 and attack west to relieve the pressure on RED-3, and the battalion was moved to the Line of Departure. But through yet another communications snafu attributable to the radios, the battalion never received the order to land. Consternation erupted at Smith's command center when an observation plane mistook artillerymen landing on RED-2 for the reserve landing on the wrong beach. Instead, the division's last precious infantry battalion would spend the night in the bobbing landing boats, wet, seasick, and miserable.

By the end of the day COMMANDO was destroyed, CECILIA's main gun permanently disabled, one tank (CUDDLES) stuck in a shell hole on the reef, two tanks (CHICAGO and COUNT) immobilized near the beach, and CHINA GAL temporarily out of action with a jammed breech block on its main gun. (The travails of CECILIA and CHINA GAL led some authors to conflate the two tanks, and write that CHINA GAL was damaged by the Japanese tank.) There were no fully functional tanks on RED-1.[144]

Bale: "Late afternoon, Mike [Ryan] cornered me and said, 'I'm going to try to pull all these bits and pieces of troops we had together and pull them back for the night.' So I took the two tanks [CECILIA and CHINA GAL] and went back almost to the beach where we checked status of ammunition and we moved 75 ammunition out of the one with the bad tube over into the other one [CHINA GAL]. Then I went on back to the beach, which wasn't more than 20 yards, and Mike came back and we rounded up every individual that could conceivably carry a rifle. We sent them over the seawall to get ready for the night. I stayed on the beach to catch anybody and anything that might be able to land before dark."[145]

Charlie Company—like every other unit on the island—was a complete shambles. On RED-2 Lieutenant Sloat's COBRA was still functioning, but there was no platoon to lead. On RED-3 only COLORADO survived. All three were isolated one from another by the breakdown of the communications system.

Efforts to land any more heavy equipment had been suspended. In a bobbing LCM offshore, SGT Peter Zurlinden, a combat correspondent attached to a platoon of Self Propelled Mount halftracks with their desperately needed 75mm cannons, was told that "With four tanks already gone, Lieutenant Robinson said we couldn't afford to lose any more equipment."[146]

In the late afternoon the tide began to rise. The bodies of dead Marines were floating about, and water was lapping against the wounded below the seawall. In the gathering darkness officers and NCOs were scooping up men and putting them to work at whatever task needed to be done, regardless of rank or normal assignment. On RED-2, Scot Kinsman was put to work gathering the wounded and moving them to the long pier where they could be put into rafts and floated to deeper water to be picked up by landing boats.

> When I came to Red Mulligan he had bled to death. When we got to the pier there were corpsmen loading the wounded on small craft to take them out to the hospital ship. I remember a Marine sitting on a 16-inch armor piercing unexploded shell as if nothing had happened, smoking a cigarette, with his eye hanging six inches down on his cheek. I had blood all over my arms and knees from crawling on the wet sand. I was told to go with them to help them unload. I talked to a corpsman later on about Red's wound. He said there was nothing I could have done because that fountain of blood that I saw coming out of his body into the water was because it had hit the main artery so he bled to death.
>
> When we got to the hospital ship it was quite an ordeal to get them aboard. I ended up in the room where they operate. It was unbelievable. A large area was filled with tables. The doctors were all covered with blood and they were going from table to table hoping to save the life of some young man. They were carrying them out as fast as they were carrying them in, some to be cared for by nurses, while some had died. I will never forget that sight. What happened after that or how I got back to my unit is a blank in my memory. Tarawa was a taste of hell! Many died and there were many missing in action. Those that went down in the ocean were most likely eaten by sharks for we saw many sharks around the islands. I can truthfully say this Island was no picnic.[147]

At about 1800hours Ryan on RED-1 decided to pull back even further to a defensible area along the seawall. Bale recalled that "The Japanese were as badly disorganized as we were, because if they could have formed a counterattack and came over that seawall, they could have wiped us out that night." Field sketch maps and the official history placed the farthest limit of the Marine advance about two-thirds of the way down GREEN Beach, to the area where COMMANDO was destroyed. In any case the Marines pulled back to a position around the bird's "beak" for the night.[148]

Fortunately there was no coordinated attack against the desperately shallow beachheads, but all night the Japanese dropped grenade launcher rounds into the Marines and a few foolhardy infiltrators probed the lines.

On RED-1, according to Bale, "It was a scary night because they kept throwing mortars. Mike Ryan and I got down for a while alongside an amtrac that had six or eight dead Marines in it. The Japanese kept throwing mortar shells at it, and we finally got up and moved."

Then Bale went down toward GREEN Beach, where he ". . . found an empty hole, went down in it, lay there and shook like a leaf. Some of the Marines had taken some machine guns out of the disabled tanks and amtracs and put them on ground mounts. We put them down on the left flank in case we got attacked from there."[149]

Bill Dunkel spent the night among strangers behind the low seawall on RED-3. In the darkness Dunkel dozed off, but ". . . heard a bang by my ear. Guy by me said 'Why the hell did you shoot him? I done had him with my knife!'"[150]

Bill Eads in the Second Platoon command tank, COBRA, was inland from RED-2. "We spent the first night in that tank on some kind of an airfield. I didn't get to see much of it. That's where [Corporal Hester S.] Buck Webb was killed. He got out of the tank for some reason. . . . I was still in the tank. He apparently went out through the bottom of the tank." Webb was shot through the neck. "I know Lieutenant Sloat was giving him morphine shots and stuff, because he was pretty bad hit." Webb died of his wound at some time during the night. COBRA was probably somewhere on the short taxi strip behind RED-2, but Eads never knew precisely where they were. "It was night-time, and there wasn't much to see from my point of [view]."

Also inland from RED-2, the crew of damaged CLIPPER sat out the night in a revetment. Quine "Just sat in the tank. We didn't get out. For air we kind of broke the lid, the hatch."

The crew and any available men worked frantically in the darkness to extricate CONGA from the shell crater. Whether or not they were assisted by towing the massive chunk of steel free with another tank is not recorded, but the next morning it was back in action.

Marines were not supposed to move about at night, but the situation on the tiny beachhead was desperate. The effort to salvage and resupply tanks on the first day also led to several awards for gallantry. His Silver Star citation stated that Largey ". . . fought his tanks well within enemy lines until three were destroyed and the fourth caught fire [*sic*]. He organized the crews of his destroyed tanks and led them back to his unit through enemy lines, exhibiting outstanding leadership and courage. While under heavy fire he salvaged ammunition from a disabled tank on the reef, giving small arms ammunition to an infantry unit and rearming his one remaining tank with heavy shells."[151]

On their own initiative, Doug Crotts and his small band of followers began to scavenge from the disabled tanks. His Navy Cross citation reads "During the first night, he salvaged urgently needed ammunition and fuel from wrecked tanks and, consistently exercising splendid initiative and expert technical skill throughout this vital period, was largely responsible for keeping the one remaining tank in the area in operation."[152]

Crotts just said, "We went in and got some ammunition two or three times in some rather precarious situations. We went from one tank to another in the late evening and got some, and also we got some fifty-caliber ammunition.

"I don't even know that I deserve it, and I'm a little bit uncomfortable even talking about it. The only thing I'll tell you, I just did what I had to do. I would have done it again. Some of the things anybody would have done—and did do."

Communications had broken down completely, and Lou Largey on RED-3 was unaware of what was going on even within his own platoon. Marn thought that "The radios were working, but we didn't use it to talk. Didn't have any idea to use it, even." Upon reflection about the radios, he added, "Hell, never used it so far as I know."

Unknown to Marn, "He [Largey] was hunkered down behind the seawall. . . ." In the darkness "There was no communications at all."

Being afoot on Betio held many hazards. Hatch remembered that "When we went to sleep that night we were given an order not to shoot our weapons because the Japanese were great on crawling in on things and we wouldn't know who was in there and we were likely to be shooting each other. The skipper said the only thing we were supposed to do was take our knives out, and if there was anybody like the Japs crawling around we should knife 'em. Not shoot 'em, but knife 'em. We slept with our knife in our hands. Sure enough, five of our men were killed that were wounded. Laying on the beach, because the Japs had gotten in."

On RED-1 the oldest man in Charlie Company, CPL Herman L. Graves (he was an elderly thirty-six and nicknamed "Pappy") had abandoned his tank and was lying below the seawall. He was mistaken for a Japanese infiltrator and nearly killed by the nervous infantry. The enemy made only sporadic individual forays against the men below the seawall, but Woolum said that "Graves was lying right there next to the seawall, and it was real moonlight." At some point "He hears something—he had his pistol—opens his eyes, and here's this Jap up on top [of the seawall].

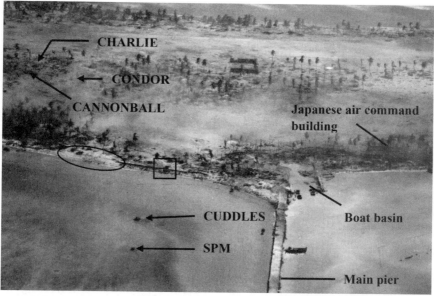

Aerial photo taken on D-DAY by a plane from the USS ESSEX. Vehicle tracks are visible on the reef off Red-3 Beach. An SPM is stalled a few yards behind CUDDLES. The oval indicates an opening in the seawall where 2nd Platoon tanks moved inland. The square shows Crowe's CP. Obscured by smoke, 2nd Platoon tanks are working inland behind Red-2. Three tanks from the 3rd Platoon are disabled on the central triangle and COLORADO is working with the infantry on the eastern side of Red-3, near Burn's Philp wharf.
—Original photo from NARA

Herman just shoots him. The Jap lunged over, fell right on top of Herman.

"These guys wake up all hollering at the shooting 'Who's that?' They think that Herman is the Jap, because he's old, and he's wrinkled, and his tanned face, at night they think he's the Jap. Some of the others are saying 'Shoot him! Shoot him!'" Finally "They told him take his jacket off. He took his dungaree jacket off and he was white as snow. He never got in the sun."

At some time during the night, Marn left COLORADO and was shot through the shoulder. "We were parked alongside a disabled tank, and I jumped out of the tank and a sniper got me right through the shoulder. It was a rifle shot. My gunner came out and he got wounded with a hand grenade." With no medical corpsmen available "People from the disabled tank bandaged me up for that night.... It was [men from] Largey's tank, actually." The men were undoubtedly sheltered near some Second Platoon tank, perhaps CONGA, since CANNONBALL, CHARLIE, and CONDOR were disabled farther inland.

Even in the close-in fighting "I had a Thompson submachine gun, but I never had to use it. I wasn't firing at anything outside the tank."

Theories as to why the Japanese never launched one of their preferred nocturnal counterattacks include the breakdown of their communications, or the death of Admiral Shibasaki already mentioned. On RED-3, infantryman PFC Joe Jordan thought it was naval gunfire from the USS *Ringgold*. "Several times we could hear the Jap troops beginning their *banzai* chant, and would call for fire towards that location. To this day I believe we would have been overrun that night if not for that naval gunfire."[153]

A nocturnal raid by a formation of Japanese aircraft approached the shipping area to the west of the island, but the bombers were forced to jettison their bombs harmlessly into the sea.

The Japanese failure to mount a land counterattack against the shallow and isolated beachheads remains one of the great mysteries of the battle—but it did cost the Japanese the battle.

CHAPTER EIGHT
DAY TWO—SECURING THE BEACHHEAD

Casualties many; Percentage of dead not known;
Combat efficiency; we are winning.
—COLONEL DAVID M. SHOUP,
21 NOVEMBER 1943

During the night, positions on RED-1 and RED-2 were vastly improved: five 75-millimeter pack howitzers were brought into action, and communications had improved. Communications with 1/8 offshore were restored, and the battalion was diverted to RED-2 at Shoup's request.

On the morning of the second day, The Pocket, the cluster of strong enemy positions at the junction of RED-1 and RED-2, was still a threat to the Marines ashore. Worse, machine guns in The Pocket relentlessly raked men wading ashore from landing boats at the edge of the reef. This fire took a particularly heavy toll on reserves wading ashore on RED-2. Major Lawrence C. Hays Jr.'s battalion lost almost all of its demolitions and flamethrowers. Hays was ordered to attack The Pocket in an effort to relieve Ryan and unite RED-1 and RED-2.

RED BEACH ONE

CECILIA's main gun was crippled, but there is some disagreement between Shivetts and Bale over whether the turret traverse was temporarily jammed. At any rate the traverse was restored by morning and Bale said that "... they used that one tank with a bad gun tube, moving up and down the beach and in the water firing at the Japanese positions [in the cove and

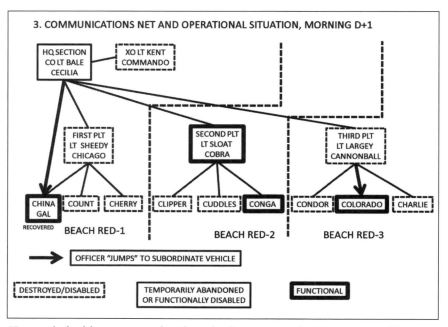

Two tanks had been recovered and put back into action by the morning of D+1. Lieutenants Bale and Largey both shifted to functional tanks, but communications were fatally disrupted.

The Pocket] with machine guns until it ran into a hole."[154] The unlucky tank tumbled sideways into an underwater shell hole only a few yards from the beach.

In the early morning hours Ed Bale took command of CHINA GAL, back in action and now the only fully functional tank on RED-1.[155]

"... the next morning I went back, started to pick up the other tank [CHINA GAL], and Mike said to me, 'The left flank is taking a lot of fire from the Japanese emplacements in that cove.' So I put people on top of the tanks that were in the water firing 50 caliber machine guns into these Japanese automatic weapons emplacements...."[156]

One of the men atop the tanks was company bugler PFC Jimmie Williams. "We needed a Field Music like a hole in the head ... but I put him in a tank crew," said Bale. Organizationally, as the company Field Music, he was in the Headquarters Section, but was a tank crewman in First Platoon. After his tank (possibly CHICAGO) was drowned out on

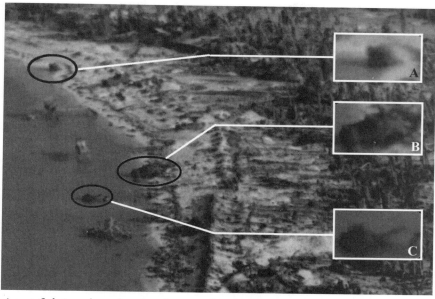

A post-fighting photo showing the cove of Red-1 Beach, looking eastward. A: CECILIA disabled in a shell hole on the morning of D+1. B: CHICAGO is stalled in a shell hole since D-Day. C: COUNT's turret is barely visible above the water line; it was immobilized in a shell hole on D-Day.—original photo from NARA

RED-1, "He was up on top of the turret manning the 50 caliber machine gun and firing it," said Bale. "He did some other things. He got a Navy Cross." The cove on RED-1 was swept by some of the most hellish cross-fire, so Williams' survival was little short of miraculous.

Five-inch naval gunfire from two destroyers pummeled the area behind GREEN Beach until Ryan decided that the Japanese had been subdued enough to begin his attack. Still hunkered behind the seawall, Gazel could sense "The Navy cruisers laying down shells about a thousand yards away from us." The crewmen of an abandoned tank were with him, but there were no duties for them to perform. "We sat there. We didn't have any food, but who cared? We were still alive."

"Along about daylight I took CHINA GAL and we started across parallel to GREEN Beach," said Ed Bale. "We operated with six people in there... There were some readjustments on the tank crew because the tank commander whose name was Bajus ... he took over as a gunner and the gunner moved over to help . . . with the communication [the radio operator/loader] . . . We had four people in that turret."[157]

Official reports state that at about 1120hours Mike Ryan's infantry and Bale's lone tank attacked south on a 100-yard front behind GREEN Beach.[158] Bale ". . . ran into an infantry company commander [Ryan] and we designed, in about sixty seconds, the tank-infantry tactics the Marine Corps would use the rest of World War II."

The Japanese positions faced the water, so "[We] fired the tank gun into whatever entrance, or opening there was," recalled Bale. "The infantry would get as close to that enemy position as they could, so as soon as we fired they could throw in there whatever they had. Since so much had been lost in landing in the way of demolitions, satchel charges, and flamethrowers, it depended on what they had. . . . They were taking things off the dead back on the beach, and this sort of thing."

The tanks were also short of 75mm cannon ammunition since the LCMs could not land on D-Day. Marn said, "Hell no! There was nobody around to supply [us]. They were all dug in, trying to protect themselves. They couldn't stand up on the beach. . . . That's why I stopped at the beach down there and caught Largey."

On RED-3, Largey and men like Crotts could scavenge from drowned or wrecked tanks, but on RED-1 Bale was in dire straits. "Some of the ammunition we got was seventy-five millimeter pack howitzer. Which would work. It didn't seat the same way, it didn't fire the same way, but it worked."

With no rhyme or reason as to what was coming ashore, "We used whatever the stuff was fuzed with. . . . It didn't matter because the object was to shoot as much as you could."

The ammunition consumption was so high in part because of the construction of many Japanese positions. The soft sand and coconut logs effectively absorbed the blows of the cannon shells.

It was a slow process because ". . . everybody checked every hole, every emplacement. We fired a lot of ammunition. The big bunkers were not only concrete, but they were covered with deep sand."

By 1235hours, Ryan's battalion had seized enough of a beachhead that Ryan sent a runner back to have his single operational radio report the news to the division commander. Ryan, and Bale in his lone tank, had achieved a major coup. Despite the discovery of large horned anti-boat mines that littered the reef off GREEN Beach, troops could land there unopposed. Smith now felt confident enough to order a battalion of the 6th Marines to land across GREEN Beach, with light tanks in support. The importance of GREEN Beach being opened cannot be overestimated, since it allowed fresh troops to come ashore as organized units. Division commander Julian Smith called it "the most cheering news of D plus 1."[159]

Bale commented that "... nobody including Mike Ryan was conscious of clearing GREEN Beach. That wasn't the issue. The issue was killing the Japanese to survive yourself. That was the issue."

During the process of clearing GREEN Beach, Bale was frustrated by the lack of communications with the infantry. "On that beach . . . it was either some infantryman crawling up on the back of that tank and talking to me, or me getting out on the ground and taking to the infantry. It was about half and half."

With no usual duties he could perform, Ed Gazel—like many men—was scooped up for burial detail as bodies were gathered up and brought in on stretchers. "I spent the second day burying the dead. . . . I was standing on the beach with the chaplain. The guys were bringing the dead in. They would bring 'em up, over to me, and I would pick 'em up by their belt, and I would lower 'em down into the sand. The chaplain was right there, cutting their dog tags off and recording. Then we'd move to the next guy."

The chaplain's duty was to keep one of the dead man's identity tags. The second identity tag was interred with the body. The chaplain also had to record the nature of the dead man's mortal wound as best he could, and make a map of his hasty gravesite. Unfortunately many of these hasty gravesites were lost, so that many men known to be dead are officially listed as Missing In Action.

In the stifling heat bodies decomposed rapidly. "That smell of death, you don't forget it." Gazel recalls burying about twenty-five bodies and that many still were wearing their packs, complete with shovels.

RED BEACH TWO

Two companies from 1/2 somehow held their positions in the central triangle of the airfield through the night. Their mission now was to extend their position to the south shore, a task they would have to complete despite machine gun fire across the open airfield, and with salvaged CONGA in support. The need for tanks to attempt to break through The Pocket to reach RED-1, and to help break out of the precarious position around RED-3, was too pressing.

About dawn, the crew of incapacitated CLIPPER on RED-2 was broken up.

Charlie Mason: "Another tank crew [from CONGA] come over. Some way a round had got under the gun shield and exploded inside and hurt the gunner and the tank commander. They needed a replacement while they got patched up. So I and my assistant, the loader [Pearson], he took over as tank commander.... He says 'The tank commander's just a figurehead anyway. Let me take it.' So he did."

Quine and the rest of the crew of CLIPPER "... got out of the tank and went over and joined with some of our tankers was in a big shell hole. ..." Over the course of the battle most of these crewmen stayed together.

In COBRA, Dick Sloat had PVT Jack Trent take over for the dead Webb. Bill Eads: "The next morning we got that tank back to a point close to the beach, and some officer—I'm not sure who he was—instructed us, told us to go around a point to fire at some kind of a blockhouse or something up there. We did, and our tank at the time was being driven by Jack Trent who was the assistant driver." Eads was replaced in his own position by another crewman, but he does not recall the name of the replacement. At about 1500hours, "We went into a shell hole in the water and we had no choice but to leave the tank. Water was coming in pretty heavy....

"I got out through the top of the tank, and I was [already] wet. I swam towards a place away from the beach a little bit. Apparently Jack Trent came out the same way. Him and I ended up at the same place..." The two men decided to head back in, and "While I was heading for the beach I got shot."

The shallow water was still swept by machine gun fire. "I was swimming toward the beach, and I got hit in the back. When I came up out of the water to get some air, it must have been something like a fifty caliber that hit me, it was a pretty big slit in my back. That's about all they could see when I got to the beach." Trent and Eads made it to the seawall together. "When we crawled up on the beach they put Jack and I both in a landing craft and took us both out to a hospital ship of some kind, I forget the name of it."

Crewmen were finally gathered up and assigned to get another tank back into in action, probably salvaged CONGA. Mason and the cobbled-together crew were attached to the combined 2nd Battalion 2nd Marines, and the 1st Battalion 2nd Marines were to help them cross the airfield toward the southern beaches:

> ... then we had to go across the airstrip and help old Major Crowe and his group. Up along the airstrip they were trying to clear 'em all out, so they could move on up. Crowe wanted to talk to the tank commander. Well, Don was not really a tank commander but he was acting so, he went out to talk to Major Crowe. Crowe wanted him to go on up and they'd come up later. Don says "Hell no!" he says "Suicide. We go up with and keep 'em pinned down, you come up. You keep 'em pinned down and we go again." And Crowe threatened to have him shot for disobeying orders. He said "Shoot and be damned! I'm not gonna kill my crew!" And Crowe went with his idea.*

CONGA's new crew found that "The Japs had a whole bunch of guys pinned down in a shell hole out there. They wanted a tank so they could protect them while they got out of there. Every time they stuck their head up they got it shot off. He stuck a stick up, [and] that gunner in that pillbox out there just cut the stick off. He was good.

"We pulled up there between the shell hole and the pillbox, and boy it sounded like hail on a tin roof. . . . So I turned over to see where it was coming from. And that was when that little [power traverse] handle came in handy." At first Mason had trouble locating the enemy gunner, who would cease firing when the tank gun was pointed in his general direction. "So I said 'I'll fix him.' So I started to turn back it over and whipped it back right quick. I was just guessing at the time when he'd start firing. I guessed right.

"He was firing out of a little hole in that pillbox; it was about six inches

---

* Crowe was still on Red-3 Beach, busy reducing strong points at the base of Burns-Philp pier. This was more probably Major Kyle or possibly Lieutenant Colonel Jordan, commanding the remnants of 1/2 and 2/2 respectively.

wide and four inches high. And it was so close, not over twenty-five yards."
At such close range Mason could only guess at the correction for the par-
allax, the misalignment between the line of sight and the actual shell tra-
jectory. "I fired one high explosive round. It went right through that hole
just as perfect—you couldn't have made it any better. Of course it exploded
inside. We had no more trouble with that pillbox."

Like the other gunners, Mason quickly discovered that "They were
buried in so good. They had a lot of time to do it. All their emplacements
were built with coconut logs and sand. You shoot a hole through those coconut logs they'd just open up and close right back up and fill up with
sand. They were good. Good for them. Not good for us."

At some point, CONGA was hit by several rounds coming from surviving Japanese heavy guns positioned along the Black Beaches.

". . . Just a little while later that tank r[e]ared back; we got hit right
squared in the front. We found out later the seventy-five millimeter, approximately a seventy-five, I think they had them numbered a little different, hit us right square in the front. Where'd it come from? We had no
idea. Well, I was looking through the periscope. And 'bang' again. Hit us
again. And that time, the only thing I could see was a little puff of dust, or
maybe smoke. I didn't know. Up quite little ways. So I fired at it. His third
shot, my first one ran off right together. It just happened to pick that doggone seventy-five millimeter mountain gun up, flipped it up in the air and
set down right on the crew upside down. Killed every one of 'em." The
"mountain gun" was probably a Type 41 (1908) field gun with its distinctive spoked wheels, peculiar box trail made of tubular steel, and single
spade. At least one was captured intact. Not really an anti-tank gun, it was
provided with a shaped-charge anti-tank round, but was probably firing
high-explosive.

At about 1430hours, CONGA was finally knocked out of action
again—this time for good—by "what is believed to be our own mortar
fire/round" that fell onto the engine deck. The weak armor of the ventilation grill was penetrated by a round that disabled one or possibly both of
the engines, rendering the tank inoperable.

CONGA is the only tank whose final loss site cannot be identified
from photographs. It is possible that Pearson recalled the location of the
revetment where CLIPPER had sheltered temporarily the night before,

and made for the relative safety of that position. Despite the loss of the supporting tank, infantry from 1/2 and 2/2 made it to the southern shore.

RED BEACH THREE

To the east, Woolum and many of his comrades were still huddled under the dubious shelter of the seawall. Woolum, the shattered bone sticking out of his finger, was finally evacuated to a ship.

In the dim pre-dawn light Largey found the wounded Marn. "I was getting some new ammunition for my tank, and that's when Largey found me and took my tank." Relieved of duty, "I took one of my injured crew out to the end of the dock to a small rescue boat, and went to a hospital ship out in the bay." Carrying his wounded gunner [Corporal Edward M. Peterson] over his unwounded shoulder, Marn later recalled walking on the bodies of dead Marines and thought, "I'd do the same for them [act as a stepping stone], if I had to." Marn walked through what seemed like "…miles of neck-deep water." At the end of the pier "I got him on the rescue boat. Boat turns around and comes back and picks me up, and took us both to the hospital ship."

Scavenging along the seawall for crewmen, Largey found Bill Dunkel and others to fill out a crew. "Lt. Redy [sic, Largey?] came down beach and recognizing me as a loader for a tank he put me in the tank COLORADO to replace their loader."

Norman Hatch: "When we woke up we saw that there was something going on in the tank [COLORADO]. We didn't pay too much attention to it.... We looked at it, and all of a sudden the big gun began to revolve, he was moving it, turning it around." Everyone in the shallow beachhead was still on edge. "We didn't know who was in the tank. We immediately suspected that a Jap had gotten in there and was going to fire down the beach with this tank.*

"We all dove for cover one way or another. All of a sudden this First Lieutenant [sic, Largey was a Second Lieutenant] pokes his head out of the

---

* In later battles the Japanese did occupy and use the weapons on some abandoned tanks. The crews had instructions to, if feasible, disable all weapons and secure the hatches with heavy padlocks before abandoning a tank.

tank, and says 'Hey! I'm not gonna shoot ya.' For a while the beachhead there at number three was really upset."

COLORADO was soon back in action. Dunkel: "We went to this giant pillbox, fired [a] half-dozen rounds. All they did was fall off."[160]

Despite the scavenging from disabled tanks, ammunition for the tank cannons soon ran out on RED-3. Bale said Charlie Sooter, the First Platoon sergeant who had been with Major Schoettel as tank liaison and landed on RED-3 "On his own initiative started trying to find ammunition. Weren't concerned about fuel because we weren't going anywhere. In fact we never refueled throughout this thing. On D Plus One he got hold of a jeep and a jeep trailer, and brought us ammunition." Dodging through enemy held ground to resupply the tanks, "He was quite a guy. I got him made a second lieutenant before the war was over." Eventually, "When they began to get some supplies in, directly into RED Beach One, he got word out to the LSD, and they sent some more in."

Like most Marines ashore, Charlie Sooter was just doing whatever was necessary to survive and prevail. William Sooter was an engineer corporal in Able Company, 18th Marines. On the second day ashore, [Will] Sooter was carrying a box of ammunition on the beach when he heard someone call his name. He turned to see his younger brother, Charlie. Sooter had no idea his brother was among the men in a tank outfit his ship had picked up en route to Tarawa.

"I had a good cry," he said about the reunion. "I hadn't seen him in a year." The brothers spent that night together in a foxhole, getting little rest because of nearby machine-gun fire. In the morning, they discovered their foxhole was next to a Japanese pillbox. Charlie approached the pillbox and dropped in a grenade. The Japanese kept firing. He got some dynamite from his brother and again sneaked up on the pillbox to drop the sticks in. This time the firing stopped. Charlie later would be given a Silver Star for heroism.[161]

With few radios in action, Sooter's boat mate radioman Dodson Smith was also pressed into duty supporting the tanks. "I had to go back and carry ammunition to them. We got behind them going down the beach. We had to go down and pick up cloverleafs." The ammunition for the tank cannon came in wooden crates, but pack howitzer ammunition was handled in bundles of three rounds called cloverleafs because the end of the bundle looked like a shamrock. "Each shell weighed twenty-five pounds, so that was seventy-five pounds. You couldn't crouch. You just had to stand straight up, and it's a wonder we didn't get shot going back and forth. But those tanks would knock out the pillboxes. . . . "

PFC Howard 'Tex' Rudloff, a replacement crewman who had reached the shore, was one of the men Largey had found on the beach; he was now the driver for COLORADO. Like the gunners, drivers like Rudloff had a role to play in the tank's offensive capabilities. Before the war, a much-publicized tactic—but one unproven in actual combat—was to crush enemy positions under the weight of the tank; to bray them by spinning the steel tracks and ripping small bunkers and other positions apart. But the official battalion report from Betio concluded:

b. Medium tanks were incapable of crushing the pillboxes, and the only effective method they could use was their own tank fire. This

Their onboard ammunition quickly exhausted, the medium tanks were forced to fire 75mm pack howitzer ammunition like this being brought ashore in three-round "shamrocks" from an LCVP. The working party includes sailors (white markings on helmets), Shore Party (camouflage helmet covers and stripes on trouser legs), and other Marines pressed into duty.—NARA

Cannon ammunition fired by medium tanks on Tarawa, from left to right: High-Explosive; Armor-Piercing, Tracer; and Canister. On firing, the thin metal shell of the Canister broke apart to release hundreds of steel balls like a huge shotgun shell. At far right is a 75mm Pack Howitzer round. The shorter casing and misalignment of the rotating bands (indicated by dashed line) meant the round would not seat properly in the tank cannon's chamber. The tool at upper right is a fuze wrench used with High-Explosive shells.

was done by sending tanks to a definitely located enemy emplacement with orders to destroy it. In some cases, as much as forty (40) rounds of various types of 75mm ammunition would be required to thoroughly clean out such positions, for instance the numerous times one (1) tank was sent to the Burns-Philp pier to clean out a well constructed position in this area. Finally the entire pier had to be shelled by a medium tank.

c. It was definitely determined that the 37mm gun on the light tank was ineffective insofar as permanently knocking out pill boxes and various Jap emplacements. . . .[162]

David Shoup was pessimistic about even the capabilities of the 75mm cannon:

> . . . 37mm AP bounced off; also 75mm AP did the same thing. However, if continuous fire from the 75s was directed at the same spot eventually you could blow away the sand and concrete and penetrate the steel. The ammunition expenditure for this kind of pillbox treatment is prohibitive. In one case it was reported to me that they had used 112 rounds of 75s to do this kind of job.[163]

Later a deadly standoff quickly developed around the huge sand-covered Japanese command bunker that the Marines eventually called "Bonnyman's Hill." COLORADO would fire several rounds and the infantry would rush the positions, only to be immediately driven back by fire from surrounding positions. Crowe had learned a lesson from the loss of so many tanks on the first day, and forbade the tank to operate forward of the infantry.[164]

Largey also found Doug Crotts, one of the much-needed Recon Guides accustomed to working with tanks. Largey was such an overpowering personality that Crotts did not remember any of the other tank crew members in COLORADO:

> At one stage he said, "Doug, you've got to get in the tank and go with me. I've got to show you what we're looking at here, so when you give me signals you'll know what I can see, what I can't see, and what happenstance will enable me to see."
>
> I got in . . . I said "Lou"—I was turned around, not being familiar with the inside of a tank—"is this our lines straight ahead?"
>
> He said "Oh, no. Japanese."
>
> I said "Well, there's Japanese soldiers going over a little mound, one after another."
>
> He threw the turret over in that direction. The Japanese were just like marching, only on their stomachs. Lou just took a machine gun, and he could almost just close his eyes after the timing started. It was almost like a dance. As they would climb over he'd just roll them over. After they quit coming he just threw a seventy-five into the group.
>
> He said "I just want you to see." I thought boy, I'd rather be outside than in this thing. . . . I think I had claustrophobia, to tell you the truth. I never did relax inside. I felt better outside.

Crotts's claustrophobia must have been really severe, as one of the guides' tasks was to go ahead of the tank and move dead or wounded Marines out of its path, a near-suicidal endeavor. "My job, once we got started, was first of all be sure the tank didn't run over any Marines, wounded or even dead. We'd move them, and they would protect me while I was out there with my other two friends, cleaning the way for them."

Following a rather naïve drill worked out in training, Crotts would stand in front of the tank. "When we could spot anything we thought they ought to see, I would lay my rifle down as if I was sighting. . . . He could look at my rifle, and I would hold up fingers for how many yards out there it was."[165]

A safer way to communicate was by shouting through the pistol port, a small hatch on the left rear side of the turret that the loader used to discard spent shell cases. Crotts quickly found a new way to communicate. "I took a seventy-five millimeter shell and beat on that tank until they acknowledged that they saw us. That was very risky. Those Japs saw you out there and they knew damn well what you were telling them."

A major problem was that the Japanese continued to filter in and re-occupy the positions cleared at such great sacrifice. Finally the Marines resorted to using the light bulldozers of the Shore Party to heap sand over the "destroyed" positions near the base of the Burns-Philp pier.

THE CLOSE OF DAY TWO

At about 1500hours, civilian correspondent Robert Sherrod unexpectedly encountered two other civilians—a correspondent and a photographer—near Colonel Crowe's command post in the shallow RED-3 beachhead. Given the two days of carnage, each thought the others were surely dead. As they compared impressions, Largey sauntered up:

> Lt. Largey sits down beside us. "Were you ever inside a tank when it gets hit?" he asks. "The spot inside the tank where the shell hits turns a bright yellow, like a sunrise. My tank got two hits a while ago." Largey walks back to his iron horse. Says Johnson, "That guy is a genius at keeping his tanks running. He repairs the guns, refuels them somehow, and reloads them with ammunition."[166]

By 1800hours, the American toehold on RED-2 and RED-3 was barely expanded from the first day. Near the base of the Burns-Philp pier the Marines still faced numerous intact and mutually-supporting pillboxes and bunkers. The most formidable was Bonnyman's Hill, the huge concrete structure heaped over with sand to form an artificial hill, the highest point on the island. Unknown to the Marines, Admiral Shibasaki had moved his command center to this structure.*

---

*This was actually a power plant housing three generators.

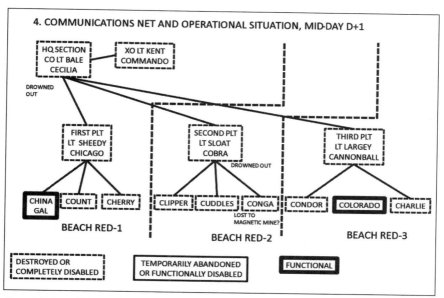

*By mid-day of D+1, CONGA had been disabled by enemy
action, and COBRA tumbled into a water-filled crater
while trying to reduce Japanese positions in The Pocket.*

Thanks to the efforts of Ryan and Bale's single supporting tank, the
Marines now had control of GREEN Beach, as yet unrecognized as a turning point in the battle. Control of the beach allowed the First Battalion,
Sixth Marines to come ashore as an intact, fully-functional formation. This
unit was known to its detractors as the "condom Navy" because it was
trained to use rubber rafts in the assault. Fortunately the scorned rafts were
ideal for landing through the highly-variable water depths over the
GREEN Beach reef. The M3 light tanks of B Company, 2nd Tank Battalion were not so fortunate.

The tanks had been loaded at the bottom of the cargo holds, and it
took hours to dig them out. Strong currents parallel to the shore made it
almost impossible to hold the LCMs in position long enough to unload,
the water over the dished reef was too deep, and there were numerous deep
potholes. Only two light tanks made it ashore, several were lost on the reef,
and the remainder diverted to RED-2. At 1815hours, the troops landing
over GREEN Beach reported that the light tanks had not been able to ne-

gotiate the reef. A handful of light tanks of C Company landed on RED-2 at about 1700hours and dug in, probably somewhere near the base of the long pier. The B Company light tanks continued to dribble in throughout the night; many were lost on the reef during the darkness, and some finally landed as late as 0730 the next morning.[167]

On RED-1, Bale again pulled his remaining tank back for the night. "When it got dark, or before dark that night, we pulled back almost all the way to RED Beach [One, near the bird's "beak"], and holed up for the night. We had a few infantrymen nearby, and we slept under that tank."

The situation had definitely turned in favor of the Americans. At 2030hours, Colonel Merritt A. "Ed Mike" Edson arrived to take over from Shoup, who had not slept—or even been off his feet—since the landings. Communications, though still clumsy, were improving, though Edson had to contact some battalion commanders, particularly battalions of the 6th Marines, by officers assigned as messengers. More reinforcements would come ashore over GREEN Beach.

Plans were drawn up for air and naval gunfire bombardments the next day. Artillery was at last emplaced on a nearby island.

The feared *yogaki* had fizzled, at least at Betio. Bale: "That was the night the Japanese airplane flew over dropping flares and some kind of light bombs."[168]

The nuisance air raid caused a brief interruption in landing artillery on nearby Bairiki, but little else.

To add insult to injury, the bombs fell into ground still under Japanese control.

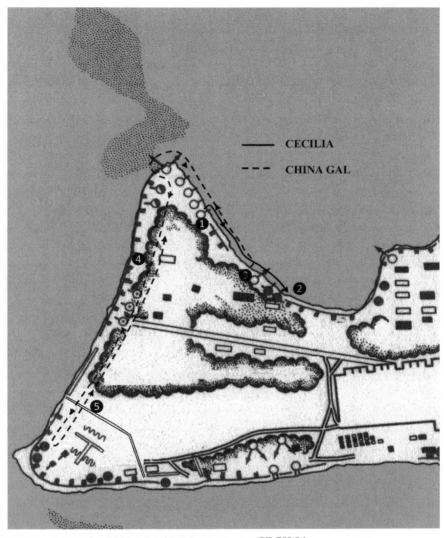

RED-1 AND GREEN BEACHES, D+1. 1: *CECILIA moves east to attack The Pocket from the water* **2:** *While firing with her machine guns, CECILIA falls into a submerged shell hole and is abandoned.* **3:** *Bale takes over repaired CHINA GAL and moves west to find the infantry and push south along Green Beach.* **4:** *With Mike Ryan's infantry, CHINA GAL clears Green Beach, attacking enemy positions from behind.* **5:** *At nightfall CHINA GAL falls back to spend the night in a safer area.*

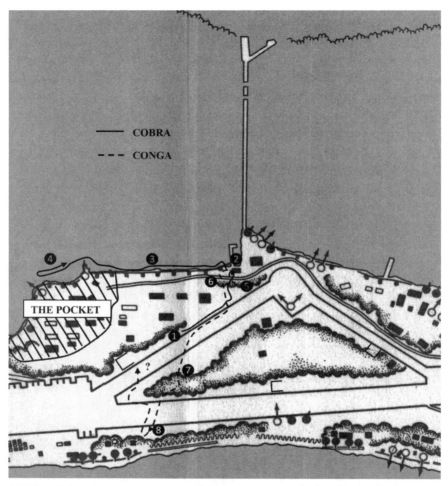

SECOND PLATOON, D+1. 1: *COBRA returns to the beach to unload the body of Cpl. Webb.* **2:** *A new assistant driver is added to the crew, and COBRA is ordered to attack The Pocket from the water.* **3:** *The tank runs parallel to the beach in shallow water, to prevent running over dead and wounded.* **4:** *On her way back from shelling The Pocket, COBRA falls into a submerged shell hole and is abandoned.* **5:** *CONGA is returned to action, out of the shellhole.* **6:** *CONGA's wounded gunner and tank commander are replaced by two of CLIPPER's crewmen.* **7:** *CONGA is attached to 1/2 and 2/2 to assist them in crossing the airfield.* **8:** *CONGA is hit by a US mortar round in one engine, and falls back to a revetment, possibly the same one where CLIPPER sheltered.*

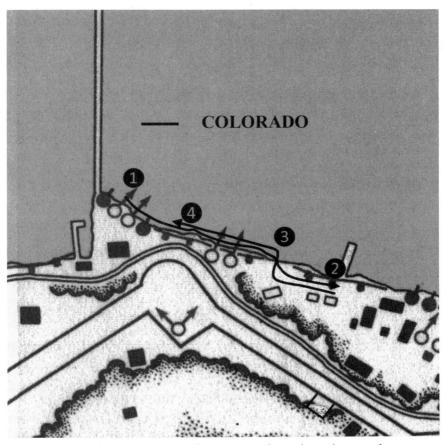

COLORADO, D+1. 1: *Early in the morning, the tank is taken over by Lieutenant Largey, who creates a new crew.* **2:** *The tank assists the infantry near the base of Burn's Philp pier.* **3:** *On several occasions, the tank falls back to scavenge for ammunition. COLORADO shells enemy along the long pier.* **4:** *The tank eventually returns in the water to spend the night.*

CHAPTER NINE
DAY THREE—SWEEPING THE ISLAND

In every battle there comes a time when both sides consider
themselves beaten, then he who continues the attack wins.
—GENERAL ULYSSES S. GRANT

RED BEACH ONE

B
ale: "During the night the First Battalion, Sixth Marines had come
ashore. I met Mike Ryan and Bill Jones. Jones was under orders to
relieve Ryan and push down between the airstrip and the beach.
They got into an argument over who got the one tank. Ryan wanted to
keep it.

"Jones had a radio and contacted Shoup." Colonel David M. Shoup
of the Second Marines was still exercising tactical control ashore. "Shoup
issued the order that Jones got the tank. It took them a couple of hours
to get organized, because in coming ashore in those rubber boats, units
got mixed up."

There was still fighting around The Pocket, but most of the scattered
Marine units were now at least in communication with each other. The
main thrust would be by Jones's fresh troops, moving along the strip between the southern beaches and the main runway. This narrow front—
about one hundred yards—meant that the front would be covered by a
single company. The main issue was ammunition for the 75mm guns of
the medium tanks, the only weapons capable of dealing with the hardened
positions.

CHINA GAL moved primarily along the margin of the runway so that
suicidal enemy attackers would have a more difficult time rushing the tank.
"We ran a lot on the airstrip, firing off the airstrip." This placed the Marines

176

On D+2 chaos still reigned supreme at the Long Pier as sailors (dark belts and white markings on helmets) worked with Marines of the Shore Party to sort the mass of supplies coming ashore. Note the boxes floating in the water and the group of Korean prisoners under guard.—NARA

As the fighting moved farther inland, beaches like Red-1 were left littered with debris, bodies, and abandoned vehicles like CECILIA.—NARA

in an unusual tactical situation. On the north shore, infantry supported by a few light tanks were attacking west, trying to eliminate The Pocket. Scarcely two hundred yards away other infantry—supported by CHINA GAL—was attacking toward the west. "It could have gotten real hairy," said Bale. "It was hairy, but it could have gotten worse."

Once the attack got rolling, "We pushed relatively fast, because all these things you see here (pointing to map) above ground had all been destroyed. What you were contending with were fortified positions, dug in, with about this much of them (a few inches) sticking up above ground, and they had these firing ports. They were oriented toward the sea. . . .

"You went after the back of them where the entrance was; those that had the side firing ports, you went after those."

Bale had several good friends in Jones' battalion. "One of them was following that tank closely. . . ." when a Japanese machine gun opened fire at close range. "His pack got almost shredded. He hit the deck."

By 1100, Jones's infantry and the tanks reached the trapped pocket of the 1/2 and 2/2 Marines in the central triangle of the airfield. This allowed Kyle's tired Marines to have ammo, water and other kinds of resupply, and to evacuate their wounded. By now the tanks and infantry were working smoothly together. Infantry was definitely needed for tanks, which ". . . do not discover and destroy more than seventy-five percent of the emplacements" without them, according to William Jones.[169]

On this day the light tanks had finally made it into action. "On D+2, we were the only tank operating in that area with 1/6 until early afternoon, when we were joined by one light tank that landed on GREEN Beach. When the light tank showed up, I talked with the tank commander kneeling behind CHINA GAL and instructed him to stay behind CHINA GAL, using his 37mm gun and his machine guns as he saw fit, while being prepared to fire on CHINA GAL if the Japanese attempted to swarm her or place magnetic mines on her."[170]

PFC Arnold Gladson of Weapons Company 2/2 recalled one incident that conveys the dark and fatalistic brand of humor that so often characterizes Marines: "There was the Oklahoma sergeant who volunteered to walk between tanks, guiding them from one pillbox to another, 'They asked for an intelligent Marine,' he said. 'I ain't very smart but I went.'"[171]

Some of the infantry, like Ralph Browner of Able Company 1/2, had more vivid memories:

> Then the CHINA GAL pulled up along side me and asked where the Japs were. After telling them, they pulled forward about 20 yards and fired their cannon down the opening into the bunker. Immediately after they fired, the Japs came boiling out, about fifteen of them and started hacking at the tank with bayonets, rifles, and sabers. The tank started going around in circles and running over the Japs. Between the tank and the Marines that could fire, we soon wiped out the Japs. I remember one Jap threw a land mine up on the back of the tank but it rolled back off, hit him in the chest, and blew him apart. I was firing at the Japs all the time and believe that I got some.[172]

Clifford Quine had been reclaimed by Bale and added to CHINA GAL's crew as a replacement assistant driver, and recalled that the new tank suffered the same kind of suicidal attack that had disabled CLIPPER:

> Darn if the same thing didn't happen to that tank. We made it to the airfield on the third day and were starting to go right down the runway. I can still see this swarm of Jap soldiers running at us through my sights. One of the Japs put a magnetic mine on the slanted part of the tank above the hull. When it went off, we had nuts and bolts flying all over the inside of the tank. None of us were hurt too badly and we made it to safety.[173]

Bale had no memory of either incident, but "The one thing I do clearly remember is that there was no running in circles. Not enough room due to trees, bunkers, etc."[174]

RED BEACH TWO

At 0700hours, 1/8 attacked to the west, into the teeth of The Pocket, in yet another attempt to eliminate that hellhole. They were supported by five light tanks from C Company, 2nd Tank Battalion. (The official Marine Corps history says three light tanks, but the platoon leader, Warrant Officer

LVTs were used for the first time as assault vehicles on Tarawa. This photo was taken at the boundary between Red 2 and 1, looking west. In the background, the turret of COBRA appears above the water.—NARA

William "Mac" McMillian, stated that five tanks participated.)[175]

The light tanks proved incapable of destroying the stubborn enemy positions, even by firing multiple rounds into a pillbox's firing ports at point blank range. In one case McMillian fired ten or more rounds directly into a pillbox only to have the defenders emerge—quite unscathed—and try to swarm onto his tank. McMillian thought the 37mm cannon did little except to suppress Japanese defensive fire long enough to allow demolition and flamethrower teams to close with and destroy the positions.[176]

At 1130hours, the light tanks were withdrawn and replaced by two Self Propelled Mounts. The thin armor of the SPMs proved unable to withstand the intense, close-range fire. One had its radiator holed by heavy machine gun fire, and the guns were withdrawn.[177]

At nightfall The Pocket had still defied all attempts to subdue it.

RED BEACH THREE

At the position where they had destroyed the artillery piece the previous day, Mason and others "...went over and looked around. One of those Jap officers had a medal. It looked odd. I just took a liking to it, and I picked it up. Stuck it in my pocket."

Near the base of the Burns-Philp pier, COLORADO and the tired infantry from 2/8 and 3/8 were still trying to reduce the complex of mutually-supporting fortifications. Among all these fortifications, three were particularly lethal for the Marines: a steel pillbox, a bunker constructed of coconut logs and sand containing several machine guns, and Bonnyman's Hill, the large bombproof monstrosity covered with a deep layer of sand that effectively absorbed cannon fire. Mutually supporting, all three would have to be attacked simultaneously.

At about 0930hours the attack commenced. Protected by infantry and led by Doug Crotts, COLORADO approached the steel pillbox, firing point blank into the opening. The coconut log bunker was luckily destroyed when a mortar round penetrated it, detonating ammunition stored inside.

The last of the three emplacements—Bonnyman's Hill—dominated the local terrain and was the most important. Largey's tank was sent to destroy it, but the soft sand absorbed the rounds fired by the 75mm gun without effect. Finally, the tank used machine guns and 75mm gun to cover the infantry rushing up and onto the top of the "hill."[178]

An observer attached to the assault battalion stated that "75mm fire from medium tanks failed to penetrate the walls and it was only by the use of TNT and flame throwers through the ventilators that troops housed there were finally subdued."[179]

Once these emplacements were reduced, COLORADO worked during the remainder of the day alongside Crowe's infantry, making their way slowly eastward. By the end of the day, 2/8 and 3/8 reached the turning circle of the airfield. The whole central triangle was now under American control, but Japanese holdouts still made the areas secured by the Marines quite deadly.

One reporter wrote that:

Late in the afternoon, he [Largey] got an urgent call from across the island to knock out a "steel turret." He raced "Colorado" across and let fly. His target turned out to be a Japanese tank.[180]

This entrenched Type 95 may have been either on the eastern corner of the central triangle or on the opposite side of the main runway. The two medium tanks had assigned operating areas on either side of the runway.

SWEEPING THE ISLAND

By 1300hours there was a flock of seven light tanks, plus one used as a communication base according to Jones's report, but "We didn't know what to do with them," said Bale. The 37mm gun was just too puny to deal with hardened positions. Finally "What we did was we teamed up like a mother hen with two or three chicks. We would go places and they would protect us with their machine gun fire. The Japanese really didn't have anything by then that could have harmed any tanks. You could have gone in there with armored cars—thin metal."[181]

The paths and actions of the very busy medium tanks were certainly not as simple as might be envisioned from Bale's description. Nor were their advances in a simple straight line as the tanks maneuvered as needed to support the infantry. In general, Bale in CHINA GAL was operating with Jones's infantry south of the main runway, with Largey in COLORADO to the north of the runway. Photos taken by an observation aircraft captured one tank—probably CHINA GAL—maneuvering on the main runway twice, while the other—probably COLORADO—replenished ammunition from an amtrac parked under trees near the RED beaches on the north side of the runway. The same set of images show the light tanks in an impromptu assembly area on the north side, probably before joining up with the medium tanks.*

The covey of light tanks suffered damage from enemy fire and the usual mechanical failures. Perhaps the most unique loss was due to a collision with a medium tank sometime before noon. The incident was so minor that none of the medium tank crews ever remarked on it. The bomb and shell craters continued to pose a hazard; Bale recalled the unmerciful ribbing suffered by a light tank commander, George Watson, whose tank was immobilized after driving into a deep crater on the wide, open main runway.[182]

Bale recalled that in the afternoon, "Bill Jones, the battalion commander, he came over to my tank, and said he had gotten the message to report to Shoup at the command post over here on RED Two. Could I get him there, because they were still taking fire across that airstrip? So I put him in a light tank and sent him over there. He was probably gone about an hour, hour-and-a-half and came back. He had his orders about not advancing much further, holding up for the night."

Jones was also told he would be relieved in the morning, but that night

* The identifying markings are of course not visible, so the two tanks may be reversed, but this would be inconsistent with Bale's account.

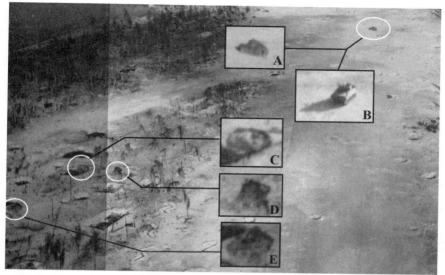

Photos taken by an observation aircraft from the USS CHENANGO *on D+2 late in the afternoon showing the main runway and the central triangle. A:* CHINA GAL *on the airstrip en route to support LT 1/6 after having reloaded with ammunition. B:* CHINA GAL *(from another photo), taken by the same plane but above the northern shore.* CANNONBALL *(C),* CHARLIE *(D), and* CONDOR *(E) were all wrecked on D-Day.*—original photos from NARA

COLORADO *parked near the Japanese air operations building, reloading ammunition from LVTs that carried supplies ashore on Red-2 Beach, in the background. USS* CHENANGO *photo sortie, late afternoon, D+2.* —original photo from NARA

"I had that one medium and two light tanks so we stayed out on the airstrip. . . . because there was so much garbage and junk and deep sand in here." At about 1830hours the Marines stopped for the night near the east turning circle of the airstrip. "I got thirty or forty yards behind the main line the infantry had. . . . We figured there would be a counterattack, because anything that was left was down in that end of the island. The Japanese had a history of these things. . . ."[183]

THE JAPANESE NAVAL COUNTERATTACK

Badly battered in the Solomon Islands and at Rabaul, the Imperial Navy was slow to react to the Gilberts invasions. Nervous gunners on the American ships fired on US Navy aircraft, but no daylight air raids materialized. At noon Navy destroyers reported sound contacts near the transport area, and for four hours the destroyers stalked the intruder.

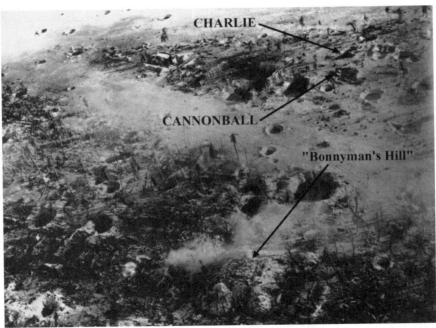

Air photo taken by a plane from the USS CHENANGO *on D+2 shows the eastern side of the central triangle (top) and Bonnyman's Hill. Note the tracks that trace the paths of CANNONBALL and CHARLIE. Most of the other tracks were left by COLORADO during later fighting.*—Original photo from NARA

At 1627hours two destroyers depth charged the contact, forcing the *I-35* to the surface. The destroyers, the USS *Meade* and the USS *Frazier*, smothered the submarine with a hail of five-inch shells, but still it refused to die. Finally the *Frazier* rammed the submarine, which immediately sank leaving a handful of survivors to be captured. It was the only naval counterattack launched at the Tarawa shipping.

THE END OF DAY THREE

At the close of day the division was confident that Betio could be secured. A battalion of artillery had been emplaced on a nearby island to provide more accurate fire support, but the division staff estimated that five more days might be required to eliminate the smaller but still deadly enemy enclaves. The largest was still The Pocket, followed by the eastern end of the island, as well as isolated pillboxes and bunkers.[184]

The gruesome job of burying the dead continued relentlessly, and Olaf Johnson was also drafted for burial detail. "The bad smell of decomposing bodies began the second day and never let up." One of the dead he buried was Lieutenant Sheedy, shot through the abdomen. Private Vancil, who had been sent to find Sheedy, was also found dead lying side by side in front of a machine gun emplacement. Bale recalled: "This kid [Vancil] had his arm like this [gesturing] on Sheedy's back and they were shot from a machine gun position across the cove. . . . And we buried them on the beach." Listed as killed by "gunshot wound in the abdomen," Private Vancil, former disciplinary problem, was posthumously awarded the Silver Star.[185]

The Marines had now pushed the remnants of the Japanese garrison onto the low-lying "tail" of the bird-shaped island. Little more than a sandbar, the tail was separated from the rest of the island by a deep anti-tank ditch and a wire barrier. Several other anti-tank ditches formed trenches for the defenders driven from the rest of the island, and more wire barriers further compartmented the long, low lying area. There were other powerful positions including big guns and ten heavy machine gun positions.

Anticipating the usual apocalyptic *banzai* counterattack, the Navy and Marines relentlessly plastered the "tail" of the bird with air attacks, artillery, and naval gunfire. Petty Officer Oonuki, who had joined the infantry, was caught in an open trench and knocked unconscious.

Bale: "That counterattack came at night. It was a hell of a fight. Pretty hot." At about 1930hours a small force of Japanese probed the lines of 1/6, penetrating the position before a scratch force from the Headquarters and Weapons Companies—the small battalion reserve—wiped them out and restored the line.

The Japanese main attack opened with a hail of machine gun fire at about 0300, and at 0400 some three hundred Japanese rushed the lines of Able and Baker Company, 1/6. Artillery and naval gunfire thinned the Japanese ranks. The Marines countered with small arms and mortars, and knives and bayonets when the enemy penetrated their lines. By 0500hours the attack had been broken, and Red Mike Edson commented that the Japanese "...gave us very able assistance by trying to counterattack."[186]

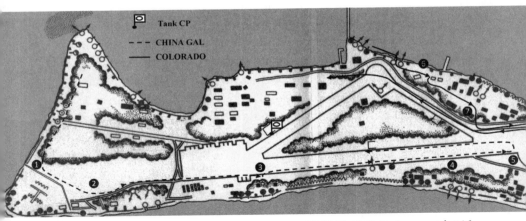

CHINA GAL AND COLORADO, D+2. 1: *CHINA GAL links up with 1/6, landed in the night.* **2:** *The attack to the east starts late in the morning.* **3:** *CHINA GAL, assisted by light tanks, maneuvers on the south side of the main runway to avoid soft sand and suicidal attackers.* **4:** *On several occasions, CHINA GAL falls back to pick up ammunition. The tank CP is established near the large revetments south of The Pocket.* **5:** *At about 1800hours the attack halts and the tank falls back to a position behind the front line.* **6:** *In the morning COLORADO attacks a large bunker. Ammunition expenditure is extremely heavy. The tank picks up ammunition from the disabled tanks, and uses pack howitzer ammunition brought ashore near the Japanese air operations building.* **7:** *COLORADO assists the infantry in their attack eastward throughout the day.* **8:** *At about 1800hours the attack stops and the tank falls back to the base of the main pier.*

CHAPTER TEN
DAY FOUR—THE FINAL CARNAGE

The victory of endurance born.
—WILLIAM CULLEN BRYANT

The slaughter of the Japanese in the climactic *banzai* had, as usual, broken the back of significant resistance. The diehards in The Pocket had to be eliminated by Hays's 1/8, Schoettel's battered 3/2, and skilled demolitions experts from the 18th Marines. By 1000hours the two battalions had closed the noose, and at 1305hours the western end of the island was declared secured.

The low-lying sand spit at the eastern end of the island was so narrow that only limited forces could be brought to bear, so McLeod's relatively fresh 3/6 was selected for the final push to eliminate the estimated 400 to 500 Japanese trapped there. They would have the support of all the light tanks and both medium tanks, all the flamethrowers from Jones's spent battalion, and all the air, artillery, and naval gunfire support they could wish for.

The narrow eastern end of the island had remained Japanese-held ground through three days of constant shelling and aerial bombing. The intensity of that bombardment is obvious in aerial photos. The advancing tanks could negotiate the Japanese anti-tank ditch, but afterward they would have to work their way through a moonscape of craters.

"I don't know why they call it an attack," said Bale. After the brutal fighting of the previous three days, "It was like a walk in the park. I moved over to that other battalion that Lou Largey in COLORADO was with. I moved over there because they pinched out the First Battalion, Sixth

Marines. . . . They call it an attack. There wasn't a damn thing there."

The final effort began at 0800hours. Before the attack started, COL-ORADO was parked, waiting in the turning circle. Then, Bale in CHINA GAL ". . . went on down and we joined up with the one remaining [medium] tank out of that tank company."[187] Light tanks quickly joined and "We went in a formation of iron. They [the medium tanks] were not out front or behind us, they were about on the same line with us," explained McMillian.[188]

Just past the ditch the Marines were temporarily halted by a cluster of mutually-supporting defensive positions. McLeod decided to leave his Item Company and the tanks to isolate this hornet's nest, and push on with the rest of his force.

The Japanese unexpectedly played into the Marines' hands. The occupants of the largest position came boiling out to attack the Americans. COLORADO fired a high-explosive round into the midst of the frenzied crowd. Largey estimated that the shot killed from fifty to seventy-five of the enemy. His estimate was probably wildly inflated, but at any rate the counterattack marked the end of any significant resistance.[189]

At 1310hours, the first Marines waded into the shallow water at the eastern tip and the island was declared secured. True to their corrupted modern version of the ancient *Bushido* warrior code, the Japanese had fought virtually to the last man. The Marines found that many had committed suicide, shooting themselves under the chin or clutching an exploding grenade to their bodies. Only seventeen Japanese and 139 Korean laborers had been taken alive, including survivors who were captured or surrendered days later.

The Marines now owned a charnel house, reeking of decomposing bodies and human excrement. Men assigned to burial details scavenged for gas masks, wore rags with a few drops of gasoline over their face, or stuck broken cigarettes up their noses in attempts to allay the stench. The sense of smell is hard-wired into the limbic brain, the most primitive part of the human nervous system, and odors can trigger powerful memories. Fifty years later Jim Carter, a light tank crewman, commented on the war film *Saving Private Ryan.* "They had the noise . . . but they couldn't duplicate the smell. That was something else you had to get used to. It was the dead bodies, dead seaweed, and diesel fuel."[190]

Private Howard E. "Tex" Rudloff in battered COLORADO. After landing from an LCVP, Rudloff took over as driver on D+1. Note Rudloff's P1942 utilities, the impact marks on the driver's hood, and the padlock used to secure the tank when the crew was absent.—NARA

The Marines had won the airfield site thought essential for the invasion of the more strategically valuable Marshall Islands group, but at a terrible cost. Some 1,696 Marines and supporting Navy personnel had been killed (after a thorough search of the island, the missing were declared presumed dead), and 2,101 were wounded. This latter number did not include those with injuries too minor to receive a corpsman's attention.

The Navy was sufficiently anxious to move aircraft onto the newly-captured facility and to use it as an emergency landing site, so the first plane was assigned to land before the fighting had entirely ended. At about noon, an F6F Hellcat single-engine fighter piloted by Ensign William W. Kelly (VF-18, flying off the fleet carrier USS *Bunker Hill*, CV-17) touched down and dodged around the craters and the bulldozers already working to repair the landing strip.[191]

Over the next hours and days a steadily increasing stream of aircraft arrived.

As bad as it was, the toll for the capture of Betio could have been far worse. The expected large *yogaki* never materialized, only sporadic Japanese attacks. Holland Smith had fumed at what he saw as excessive Army caution in the attack on far more lightly defended Butaritari Island on Makin Atoll. The large island had also been secured on 23 November at the cost of 66 killed or died of wounds, and 152 wounded. But the worst of the carnage at Makin was not on the island.

Three escort carriers and their protective destroyers lingered twenty

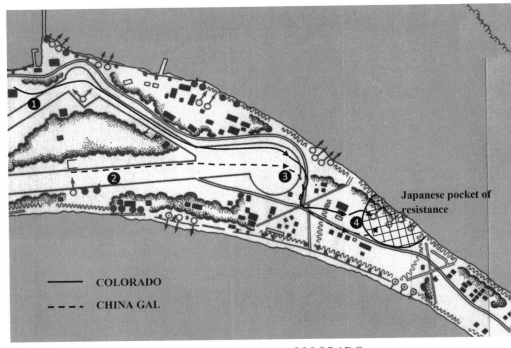

COLORADO

- - - - CHINA GAL

CHINA GAL AND COLORADO, D+3. 1: *COLORADO moves toward the front line and waits for orders at the edge of the airstrip.* **2:** *CHINA GAL moves toward the frontline.* **3:** *Both tanks form up with infantry on the turning circle and cross the large anti-tank ditch on a path used by Japanese for their own vehicles* **4:** *Both medium tanks work with infantry to reduce a final enemy pocket of resistance. By the time the pocket is eliminated infantry have already reached the eastern end of the island.*

miles off Butaritari to provide continued air support as Army troops cleared nearby islands. On the morning of 24 November, the crews went to work early as the carriers prepared to launch the routine dawn air patrol. A lookout on the USS *Liscome Bay* spotted the track of a torpedo fired by the Japanese submarine *I-175* at 0510hours only seconds before it exploded near the aft engine room.

As men rushed topside the stricken ship's main aircraft bomb magazine exploded, possibly the result of a second torpedo strike. The titanic explosion engulfed the entire ship, showering nearby ships with debris and pieces of bodies. Twenty-three minutes after the first torpedo impact the ship sank, taking down its 28 aircraft and 644 officers and men. Among the dead were the ship's captain, Captain Irving D. Wiltsie, Rear Admiral Henry M. Mullinnix (commander of Carrier Division 24), and Ship's Cook Doris Miller, who had won the Navy Cross at Pearl Harbor.[192]

What the Marines did not win was intelligence information. The carnage was so complete that unlike on nearby Makin, few documents were captured.

CHAPTER ELEVEN
AFTERMATH

There are only two kinds of people that understand
Marines: Marines and those who have met them in battle.
Everyone else has a second-hand opinion.
—UNKNOWN

The tank battalion had set up an assembly area behind the large aircraft revetments just south of the bird's "neck," and as many tanks as could be driven or dragged were brought there. On the fourth day, said Bale, "I was told where my people were, that they had been put in an aircraft revetment. We holed up in there until we were loaded out. Worked out of there salvaging tanks."

The ravaged island might have been declared secure, but the Navy and Marines were still wary of a possible Japanese counter-landing. In prior operations the always aggressive Japanese had been quick to counterattack. The weary Marines were organized to repel such an attack as indicated by a hand-written note from the acting CO of the 2nd Tank Battalion:

> Unit report covering period from 0500 Nov. 25 to 0500 Nov. 26.
> (Yoke) Bn reorganized into 4 platoons of light tanks, reinforced with 3 medium tanks. Two platoons of 5 light tanks each and 2 medium tanks are dispersed in southeast end of island with 1/6 for defense of area. Two remaining platoons plus 1 med. tank dispersed in Bn. area. All other vehicles being maintained. Bn. strength: 13 Off., 3 Warrant., Navy 5, Enl. 261, Aggregate 282. Tanks ready for combat: 20 light tanks M3 (illegible) 3 medium tanks. McCoy"[193]

Sailors from the USS Sheridan *work to recover bodies floating in the lagoon. Some were so badly decomposed they disintegrated when touched; they were weighted and sunk in place.*—NARA

At the end of the battle Charlie Company established an assembly area near Red-2. Three medium tanks were reported operational— COLORADO (front), CHICAGO, and CHINA GAL (rear). Note the elephant symbol and the calligraphy used for the tank names.—NARA

Almost every structure on the island had been destroyed in the fighting, or was filled with enemy bodies rapidly decaying in the brutal heat. The few remaining trees had mostly been stripped of their foliage, so there was no shade from the relentless sun. Most men were assigned to some sort of labor duty in policing up the battlefield.

"We went back to try and find as many bodies of our people as we could," said Ed Bale. "Every outfit was doing that. And the object was to get the people under ground. Buried."

Decades later Bale still recalled that although Master Gunny Alfonse Dumais is still officially listed as Missing In Action, he was confident that Dumais's partial remains were located. But since only the body from the waist down was located, the remains could not be conclusively identified.[194]

Charlie Company had suffered about one-third of its strength in casualties, greater than some infantry units. The recovered dead were hastily interred, the precise cause of their death recorded. But many had been killed while in the water, their bodies often unrecoverable. Despite their efforts, "We were too far from the shore to recover the bodies" recalled Ed Gazel. Aerial observers reported "Japanese bodies" drifting out to sea—but there were no Japanese in the water. Other accounts recorded that bodies in the water too badly decomposed to recover without disintegrating were simply weighted down and sunk into the sea.[195]

Officially, eight Charlie Company men were listed as Killed In Action. Five more were known to have been killed and interred, but their gravesites were later lost and they are now officially listed as Missing In Action. Probably as a result of the hasty burials, subsequent construction on the island, and confusion in post-war removal and reburial, remains were lost. Lieutenant Sheedy's original burial site was known and his remains recovered, but Vancil, who died with him and was originally buried alongside him, is now listed among the missing. The bodies of six more men, some likely lost in the water and others known to have been killed ashore, were never recovered or identified. They were and still are listed as Missing In Action. When the unit left the island, the missing were listed as presumed dead, their status later changed to presumed Killed In Action.

The wounded are a special case. The thirty men listed as Wounded In Action represent only those men wounded badly enough to be treated, have their wounds recorded by a corpsman, and evacuated for further treatment. The official list of wounded does not include those men who never sought treatment for minor wounds. For this reason the list of casualties in Appendix D can never represent a complete list of the wounded. One additional man was evacuated for severe heat exhaustion.

Enemy dead were buried in mass graves, often dumped into bomb craters and sand bulldozed over the corpses. Others were loaded onto boats and dumped at sea.

The more fortunate Marines were set to work salvaging useful equipment from rifles to tanks. Engineers and Navy Seabees accelerated the construction work they began even before the fighting ended. The hulks of the M4A2s were difficult to deal with in the absence of the retriever. The Japanese had apparently jury-rigged one of their light tanks with a recovery boom, but it had no chance of budging the big mediums.[196]

The crews were trained to recover stuck tanks with cables and chains. Once recovered the diesel engines could be jump-started by towing the vehicle up to speed, and thereafter it would continue to run, firing on compression.

Ed Bale: "I can say that my maintenance people had the majority running. There were a few that were pushed into the LCMs using CB [Navy Construction Battalion] dozers." Bale credited much of this to his maintenance chief, Warrant Officer Roger A. Massey, who he had promoted from staff sergeant at Pendleton. Massey was a fellow Texan who had dropped out of high school to enlist during the Great Depression. ". . . Massey was an old Marine who had been a motor transport sergeant. He was a genius at keeping things running. He figured out a way to take all the towing cables off the tanks and rig two or three tanks on the shore and pull these things out." Massey performed prodigious feats of repair. "If it could be fixed/repaired, he could do it. Took voltage regulators that had been wet, dried them out and rebuilt them. I was extremely fortunate to have him all the way through Okinawa."[197]

CHICAGO was probably one of the first tanks recovered on the afternoon of D+3. This tank was lost on RED-1, in a shell hole close to the beach. The tank was canted in such a way that the rear was sunk into the hole but the raised front, facing the beach, was easily accessible, and could be towed forward by cables hooked to functional tanks. According to Bale,

Massey and his crews eventually managed to salvage all but two tanks and prepare them for transport off the island.

Canted sideways and broadside to the beach in a crater, there was nothing on the island capable of budging COBRA's mass. It sits off RED-1 today, firmly embedded in the coral. Bale recalls that "After the fight was over I went back to it because when I left it [CECILIA], I left a pint of Scotch in my dispatch case. And I went back to get that pint of Scotch." CANNONBALL was destroyed by fire and an internal explosion; the right side sponson armor was ripped open and peeled back like rubber. Its armor compromised by the flames, it was abandoned as a total loss.

To minimize sunburn most men wore their utilities—by now encrusted and stiff as leather with dirt, dried sweat, blood, and often with urine or diarrhea caused by the flies that feasted on the dead—with the jacket sleeves rolled down despite the heat. Most men had left their cloth caps aboard ship, or lost them in the landing. Photos show men who (probably despite orders) had discarded the heavy steel helmet, wearing only the fiber liner and the cloth cover with the cloth flaps, normally tucked between the helmet and liner, hanging down to shade the neck.

The *Ashland's* boats returned to pick up the medium tank company, and Gazel recalled that four or five men were sitting around waiting. "They brought a number ten can [three quarts/2.8 liters] of pears, and it was like manna from heaven."

FINAL OPERATIONS AND EVACUATION

Throughout the fierce battle, MGen Holland Smith had been cooped up and fuming aboard Admiral Richmond Turner's command ship standing off Makin Atoll. Early in the day on 24 November he flew in from Makin, and with 2nd Division commander MGen Julian Smith toured the island and inspected Japanese defenses. The tour was to climax with a flag raising ceremony, so the Marines scoured the island for the items necessary for the formal event.

Bale recalled something far more welcome to the Marines: "I had left 2 clean sets of dungarees aboard the *Ashland*. The morning of D+4, the boat officer, Noah Levine . . . brought cases of cold pineapple juice for the company and a clean uniform for me."[198]

An American flag for the planned ceremony was no problem, and New

Zealander Major Frank Holland contributed a small British Union Jack. The only field music the Marines could locate was Jimmie Williams, with the battered bugle he had rescued from a sinking aircraft carrier. But like many Marines, Williams had rummaged through the Japanese storehouses and replaced his grimy utilities with a brand new white Japanese sailor's uniform. There was probably considerable shouting and scurrying, and Williams changed back into proper uniform. From somewhere a Marine dress uniform barracks cap appeared, perhaps brought ashore by Levine.

Two tall palm trees, stripped of their branches and foliage but still standing, were rigged as crude flagpoles. While Williams played "To the Colors," the American and then the British flags were raised over the island, formally signifying the change of ownership.[199]

Field Music PFC Jimmie Williams played To the Colors *for the flag raising ceremony, wearing clean dungarees and a salvaged barracks cap. Williams caused a furor when he first appeared wearing a Japanese sailors dress uniform, the only clean clothing he could find. Image from a 16mm movie film.*—NARA

The capture of smaller outlying islands and the total elimination of the smaller Japanese garrisons had begun on 21 November when Dog Company, 2nd Tank Battalion (Division Scouts) landed on Eita, east of Betio. This island was seized to provide an artillery base to support the Marines on Betio, but it triggered a pursuit of fleeing Japanese from island to island to island up the eastern side of the atoll. The lengthy chase ended only on 28 November when the last Japanese were trapped on Naa, the most northerly island of the atoll. More time would be spent checking smaller atolls of the Gilberts until the entire chain was declared secured on 1 December.

On the morning of 23 November following the failed *banzai*, Petty Officer Tadao Oonuki had dug himself out from under a pile of corpses in the trench. Burned on the face and head, and just ahead of the Marines'

CHINA GAL in the assembly area. The clean dungarees
suggest the man on the tank may be Ed Bale.—NARA

The smoke of battle was still rising when Navy Seabees set to
work improving the airfield. This bulldozer is passing salvaged
CHERRY, with another tank barely visible at left.—NARA

A photo taken from across the western taxi strip shows the tank CP in the large revetments after the battle. CHERRY and CONGA are parked in the front, CHARLIE is on the far right, and an unidentified M4A2 can be seen inside the revetment.—NARA

This tank is generally thought to be CECILIA because of the position and damage to the cannon muzzle. The man on the right wears a tanker's helmet, the man on the left has cut his trousers off leaving a ragged lower edge, and wears the helmet liner and cloth cover without the steel helmet as protection from the sun.—NARA

Salvaged CHICAGO traversing the reef to be loaded back aboard an LCM in foreground.—Official photo via Tarawa on the Web

When the survivors arrived at the new Camp Tarawa on Hawaii, the site was completely barren. A tent city was eventually built. Ed Gazel— shown here while still at Camp Pendleton—was made Company First Sergeant after his predecessor was killed at Tarawa.—Gazel

A medium tank, from the nature of the damage probably COMMANDO, sits stripped and abandoned long after the battle.—Kim Harrison

CONGA and three other medium tanks sit amid a row of light tanks awaiting transport off the island. The medium tanks will be refurbished and used in training, but the light tanks were already completely obsolete.—Kim Harrison

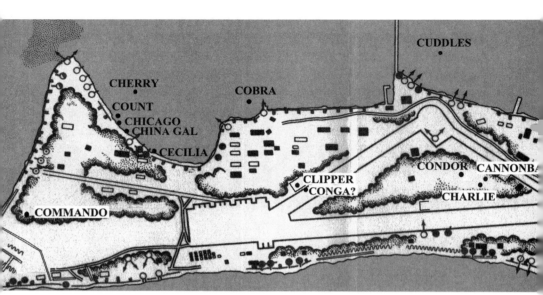

POSITIONS OF DESTROYED AND DISABLED MEDIUM TANKS ON THE ISLAND. *CHINA GAL was temporarily disabled on D-Day but put back into action early on D+1. The position where each individual tank was lost or abandoned was determined from aerial and ground photos, official reports, and interviews. Loss sites of all but one, CONGA, were identified with some certainty.*

final attack, he waded to the nearby island of Bairiki and spent nearly three weeks trying to evade capture by the Marines who were using the island as an artillery base. Desperate, unable to find food or even fresh water, he and his comrades decided to risk a return to Betio. While wading across the reef, Oonuki found some shellfish and ate them raw. Badly depleted by his ordeal and now suffering from food poisoning, once back on Betio he lapsed into unconsciousness. Not knowing how long he was unconscious, he awoke to find himself a prisoner. Treated with unexpected kindness by his captors, he spent the remainder of the war in several prison camps, eventually ending up in Texas.

On the morning of 27 November, the hand-written 2nd Tank Battalion Unit Report indicated that the light tanks had been reorganized again, and "Medium tanks attempting to re-embark aboard LSD#1." The next morning's report indicated "C Co. (medium) tanks embarked aboard the U.S.S. *Ashland* with 6 tanks and personnel, consisting of 4 officers, 1 Warrant, 68 enlisted and 1 Navy, aggregate 74. Eight (8) medium tanks left on island for salvage."[200]

There was still a considerable rush to move the vulnerable ships away from Tarawa, and this has led to another of the minor discrepancies in the records. On 27 and 28 November the *Ashland's* log records are somewhat ambiguous, but indicate loading six medium tanks and ten light tanks for immediate return to Hawaii.[201]

The Marine Corps is notoriously stingy with salvageable equipment. Bale—who although attached to 2nd Tank Battalion for the operation, bore final responsibility for disposition of the tanks—has consistently maintained that only two tanks were ultimately left on the island as unsalvageable. This is consistent with the single tank that today remains canted sideways in an old shell crater off RED-1.[202]

Although official documents indicate that only one tank was burned, photos clearly indicate that COMMANDO probably burned and CANNONBALL was destroyed beyond repair by fire and internal explosion. The second tank left behind, CANNONBALL, was rumored to have been used as fill by Navy construction troops during later extension of the long pier, but there is no traceable record to verify this. The remaining six must have been temporarily left to await return on another trip.

On the voyage to Hawaii, Shivetts thought "The trip was fine but somewhat somber. Had a lot to think about, especially what was coming on future invasions."[203]

Even as the Marines back-loaded onto the transports and set sail, the construction crews were already hard at work. The crude Japanese airstrip on Betio was hastily extended and paved. Two new airstrips were constructed on Buota. The soft soil of Butaritari could not support a runway capable of handling heavy bombers, but another bomber airstrip was built on Apamama. The first twin-engine bombers—B-25 Mitchells—arrived on 15 December and by early January big four-engine B-24 Liberators were operating from the Gilberts. Before year's end these long-range aircraft were systematically bombing and photographing the Marshall Islands.

HAWAII

On the afternoon of 9 December, the *Ashland* arrived at the port of Hilo on the big island of Hawaii and the company personnel were disembarked and loaded onto a long convoy of trucks. Just before midnight, the *Ashland* got underway for the short trip to the tiny port at Kahului on the north coast of Maui where the *Ashland* "Hoisted out six medium tanks." Less than an hour and a half later the ship was underway again, bound for Pearl Harbor. The *Ashland* was simply too valuable a ship to be left idle.[204]

A sixty-mile trip in the jouncing trucks led around the island and up the slopes of the Mauna Loa volcano to the Parker Ranch. The cattle ranch was situated in a topographic saddle between two dormant volcanoes on the "dry" side of Hawaii, where the terrain resembles Oklahoma more than a tropical paradise. Ed Gazel: "When the six-by-six trucks got up there, all you could see was rolling grass."

The next day the Marines set up their own tents, but "We had no water.... One guy went down the road [to where] there was a little Hawaiian grocery store. He came back with a case of pineapple juice. We were brushing our teeth with pineapple juice." But the next day "Two truckloads, six-by-sixes, came up loaded with beer. The third day the Seabees came up and started digging for water." Eventually the construction troops did erect some semi-permanent structures, but the troops continued to live in pyramidal squad tents at what became known as Camp Tarawa. "One day they did take us to the Parker Ranch for a barbecue. One day out of six months."

The wounded had begun their treatment and rehabilitation in makeshift hospitals aboard the transport ships. Bill Eads said, "There was a plastic surgeon, I guess he was from New York or someplace, that worked on me. I ended up going from there to Hawaii, to the Civilian Hospital 128." After a month or so of recuperation Eads was sent back to his unit, to Lieutenant Sloat's crew. Marine Corps policy was to send wounded men back to their original unit and friends for morale purposes.

In the naval hospital in Hawaii the surgeons wanted to remove the end of Woolum's finger up to the joint, but "I talked them out of it.... For a long time it was just the bone sticking out. You couldn't touch it." Woolum began to regret his decision, since the nerves were exposed. Unknown to him, "I had a little piece of shrapnel in my head but that was all. I was the least wounded of the crew." Eventually thin tissue grew back over the dead bone at the end of his finger, and Woolum was returned to the company.

There were also the countless administrative details to be attended to.

New uniforms and personal gear were issued to replace that lost in action. Men were transferred in and out of the unit. Veterans, green replacements from the tank school, and men reassigned from other units had to be integrated into the company.

The men were told to turn in any souvenirs to be examined for potential intelligence value, so Mason turned in his scavenged medal. "Wasn't a few days later a general called the company, and wanted to see me. I had no idea what it was about. General 'Howlin' Mad' Smith; he was a rough old son-of-a-gun. So I went over to see him, as appointed.... It was all because of that stinking doggone little medal. There was only five of them ever issued to the Japanese Army in history. And I had got one of them.

"He thought it would be wise to have that in the Marine Corps Museum in Quantico. Actually that was the best place for it, and I knew it, because I would probably have lost it before I got back. So I agreed to it. ..."

A whole new complement of tanks was issued to replace those expended on Tarawa. Countless parts had to be cleaned of preservatives and inventoried, lubricants and fluids drained and replaced, and every part inspected. Mason recalled that "Those [new tanks] had to be all fixed up, tuned up, 'cause they're sure not tuned at the factory. So that was a big job. And had to go out to the range and [bore] sight them all in. All kinds of maintenance. You checked everything right from the track all the way up."

For the officers there was a new invention. In the pre-war Corps there were so few officers they were known only by name. On Hawaii, officers learned that they would now be enumerated like all other military property, and assigned serial numbers. The new numbers were still not the impersonal sequential numbers of enlisted men, but instead was the number of their personnel file at Headquarters Marine Corps.[205]

For some there were promotions and advancements. Ed Gazel was made Company First Sergeant. (Unfortunately the new billet did not come with advancement in pay grade commensurate with his new duties). Bale was promoted to captain, the appropriate rank for the billet he had been filling as a lieutenant. The promotion list was dated 1 December, but "I learned about it on the seventh of December, but it must have been close to the fifteenth before it became effective because battalion headquarters was travelling."

INCORPORATING LESSONS LEARNED

The Marines had learned valuable lessons about what went right and what went wrong in their new doctrine of amphibious assault, albeit at a terrible price. Though fundamentally sound, there were major problems with ship-to-shore logistics. Logistical shortcomings had not mattered much at Guadalcanal where the defenders fled into the jungle, leaving huge heaps of supplies piling up on the beaches unmolested. At Tarawa they had nearly led to disaster when critical items like ammunition waited aboard ships while cargo like crates of toilet paper were ferried ashore in the rush to unload the transports.

Improved Army Signal Corps SCR-series radios were already in the procurement pipeline, though because of shortages, the old TBX and TBY radios would continue to serve until 1945. The radios were cited as a significant problem in all units. Some radios did survive the trip across the reef, but the radio net failed because of severed links; see the "Communications Net and Operational Situation" diagrams for Charlie Company. All units encountered similar situations ashore, from company to regiment level. Some units managed to get functional radios ashore, but after action reports indicate that communications were sporadic and ineffective. The radios were mentioned in virtually all after action assessments. For example, George Company 2/2 managed to get a functional TBY ashore, but their report suggested that they could receive communications from ships offshore but could not communicate effectively by radio with their own battalion and regiment.[206]

One major failure was that of the limited amount of intelligence information garnered. An exhaustive study was done of the defensive works and the weapons captured, but in truth, examples of most of these weapons had been captured elsewhere. Japanese language specialists scoured the island, but the extreme violence and near-total destruction of structures assured the loss of most documents of any importance. A thorough analysis of defensive structures led to the construction of duplicate defenses, and weapons and tactics would be tested against them in advance of future operations. Reports on the Tarawa defenses would provide the basis for intelligence reports and field manuals on Japanese defenses for the remainder of the war.

In retrospect, most analyses later concluded that the medium tanks, though few survived the first days, had played a crucial role. COLORADO had played a pivotal role in reducing Japanese positions behind RED-3. More important, but less heralded, on GREEN Beach CHINA GAL had provided the firepower to destroy the defenses from behind. It was across GREEN that fresh and critical replacements arrived as coherent fighting units.

Though it has been given little credit in the ensuing years, the exploits of CHINA GAL were dramatized in a CBS radio program that aired on 10 August 1944. Typical of wartime propaganda, it is both cheesy and revolting to the men who served on the island.

As the survivors struggled to assess all the things that had gone so disastrously wrong, there were clear indications that many still did not understand the flaws in tank doctrine. The Division's D-4 (logistics) officer, Lieutenant Colonel Jesse R. Cook Jr., was a former tanker trained at Fort Knox. Bale said he "…sat down with McCoy and the company commanders. One of the things he asked was 'Why didn't you cruise on the objective?' That was the term that was used for running around on the objective. That was a tactic that the Army taught. I don't know whether it came from the horse cavalry running over a hill and riding around on the hilltop, or what the hell it came from." Clearly many did not yet understand that sending tanks unaccompanied into Japanese-held ground was virtually suicidal.[207]

The M3s of the division's light tank battalion were clearly inadequate for the job. "They were good people, well-trained, but they had the wrong equipment" was Bale's assessment.

One of the major concerns was why medium tank losses were so disproportionately heavy, and what Japanese weapons had disabled the tanks. Inspectors examined the six tanks turned over to Tank Company, 22nd Marines for use in the upcoming invasion of the Marshall Islands. Four had already been refurbished, but examination of the other two indicated the following damage from rounds of "about 40mm caliber" to one tank:

(SPONSONS)—The 40mm hits (approximately 1-1/2 inch diameter)* penetrated the two inch armor, in that the inside of the armor was pierced and a small hole about 1/4 inch in diameter

---

* 40mm was a familiar U.S. caliber; "about 1.5 inches" equals 38mm.

was made. The projectile itself did not pass through. A very careful study of such hits was made and it is known that the inside of the armor plate did not chip or fragment from such hits.
(TURRET)—Holes caused from 40mm projectiles in the turret were observed. The projectile did not penetrate and only a small paint scorched spot showed on the inside. There was no bulge on the inside, visible to the naked eye, as a result of such hits. In some instances it appeared as though the hit was scored at an angle and the armor showed scars of glancing hits. In some cases these scars were about one inch deep and from two to three inches long.
(GUN SHIELD)—Two glancing strikes of 40mm shells were observed in the 75mm gun shield. It was apparent that the projectiles scored at an angle and scars as mentioned above were visible.

The report went on to describe the effects of small arms, high-explosives, and plunging fire on the tanks. The latter included one large caliber round that went through the rear hull deck, penetrated a fuel tank, severed fuel and ignition lines, and sent shrapnel into both engines, all without destroying the sturdy tank. The report concluded that the most effective Japanese anti-tank measure was the four-foot coconut log wall.[208]

The Marine Corps was quickly transitioning to medium tanks. With no future role, the I Corps Medium Tank Battalion was formally dissolved on 15 February 1944. Charlie Company was transferred to the Second Marine Division to become Able Company, 2nd Tank Battalion. Training began in earnest for the invasion of Saipan, in the Marianas. "But now we've got a little sense," thought Woolum. In retrospect, "I was glad that Tarawa was my first one, because there was nothing else ever like Tarawa to me."

In an interview by staff of the National Museum of the Pacific War that followed a symposium on the battle, Bale said:

Probably some of the best combined arms training I've ever been through took place up there in the Second Marine Division. I attributed it to several things. We had lost so many people and learned so many lessons following Tarawa, and we didn't know where we were going, but we wanted to apply all those things and did not want to make the mistakes, and did not want to lose the lives. Before the division embarked and left there, the division staff laid out on the ground, using a chalk line, and said "this is the beach, and over here is something else, and over here is a road" and this kind of thing. It duplicated where we were going to land. Then everybody walked through it. Didn't make any difference whether you were in tanks or the artillery or what, you walked through it. I've often said, I didn't say it today because I have friends out in that audience, and also panelists who would disagree violently with me, but I also think that, and I've served in four Marine Divisions at one time or another between World War II and Korea and Viet Nam. The 2nd Marine Division when it left Hawaii going to Saipan was probably the best trained Marine Division I've ever seen.[209]

The renewed and realistic training itself was dangerous, and men who survived Tarawa were killed and maimed elsewhere. Lou Largey was severely injured on Hawaii. Stories differ as to how he was injured—some say a machine gun round cooked off in a hot barrel wounded him. The more likely story is that he was struck by the cleaning rod and propelled from the barrel by the recoil spring, while the gun was being cleaned. At any rate, Largey was sent Stateside to help sell War Bonds.

Modifications to the tanks were the result of the hard-won lessons of Tarawa. Doug Crotts said that there were three recommendations. "One, put a bulldozer on the front of one tank out of each company so we could cover up [positions]. The Japanese would come out of foxholes. We'd thrown grenades in there and thought they were empty, and they had a bunch of tunnels and they'd come back and shoot us in the back." During the battle, engineers and Seabees had ridden atop unarmored bulldozers to bury troublesome positions. "Of course that was deadly for them."

Telephones for communicating with the infantry, an idea first tried on New Georgia in June–August 1943, were fitted to the back of the tanks and connected to the intercom. "A light would come on so they'd know we'd pulled the phone off the hook." Bale said that "The battalion communications officer and his people wired every one of those tanks with sound-powered telephones. We worked out a system for the infantry designating targets, which should have been done before...."

The third recommendation was to mount a flamethrower. This last change was only partially implemented. The light tanks would continue to serve as specialized Satan flame tanks (converted M3A1s with a Canadian-designed "Ronson" flame gun) and as escorts for the flame tanks (the new M5A1s) in a new D Company of the Second and Fourth Tank Battalions.

The official recommendations went much further: better ammunition supply, an improved intercom (when the GF-RU failed, the integral intercom went with it), and more integrated training with infantry.

The outmoded aircraft radios were singled out for special attention. Worth McCoy, who had assumed command of the 2nd Tank Battalion when Swenceski was missing and presumed killed, apparently saw no significant problems with the GF-RU, and concluded that "The RU/GF is a good radio but trouble was experienced with the dynamotor." But significantly, the Division report recommended a new radio "...compact, capable of easy change of frequency, and rugged enough to withstand the hardships encountered in an armored vehicle."[210]

A post battle interrogation of tankers on Tarawa (24 November 1943), conducted by a Major Woodrum (USMCR) stated that the number of spare periscopes should be increased in the tanks. Tank crews reported that "the Japanese snipers and automatic weapons concentrated their fire on the periscopes and that the tanks were able to continue operation only through removing extra periscopes from tanks previously disabled."[211]

Tank crews undertook their own unofficial modifications. Charlie Mason: "To start with they had racks for ninety-seven rounds of seventy-five millimeter. We modified those racks and put a hundred and twenty-five rounds in. It started out twenty-six belts of thirty caliber . . . We had fifty-two belts of thirty."

THE MARIANAS, OKINAWA, AND OCCUPATION DUTY

Most liberties were in the small town of Honokaa, but just before departing for the invasion of Saipan a lucky few went to Hilo on the other side of the island. Olaf Johnson ". . . 'had a few' and had words with and resisted Army MPs. I was locked in a brig all night. Our company was pulling out the next morning. They verified this, and drove me to camp and to Captain Bale just before muster. Instead of being angry (my greatest fear) he seemed to be amused. *No punishment.*"[212]

Others, like Jimmy Williams, went into the ship's brig on the way to Saipan because "...he was drunk, stole a Jeep and wrecked it."

The company fought again on Saipan, where Dick Sloat was killed in action. Among his other duties, Sloat was the company supply officer and worked with Ed Gazel, helping to shuttle supplies from the beach to the tanks aboard amtracs. "We're interested in getting the bullets and ammunition and water to the tanks."

One day Gazel went back to the beach for more cannon ammunition. A platoon from C Co. 4th Tank Battalion under Lieutenant Gearl M. "Max" English was waiting to cross an open area they thought was a mine field. Ed Bale remembered that some of his tanks had been in the area just hours earlier, and he knew that the road was free of mines.

Bale was about to relay the information to English. Instead, Sloat volunteered to go. Bale: "It was my job to go. I didn't go simply because he wanted to go so bad. And he was that kind of officer. I've had lieutenants that I've had to fire in combat. He was very different. He was very devoted to duty. You could rely on him. You didn't have to tell him but once. He was always pleasant and enthusiastic, even under the worst of circumstances."

Arriving in the area where several of English's tanks were waiting, Sloat moved carefully toward English's tank, easily distinguishable thanks to the light brown camouflage paint daubed onto the turret of English's tank, KING KONG. Sloat grabbed the rear telephone out of its box on the rear of the tank to communicate with the crew and tell them the path was safe. For whatever reason, the telephone was not functional so Sloat decided to crawl onto the tank to talk to English. A Japanese sniper spotted the young lieutenant and shot him through the head. The company had lost one of its best officers. "We lost a lot of good people there," recalled Bale.[213]

Doug Crotts's phenomenal luck also ran out on Saipan. Still a recon guide, he scouted paths for the tanks through the jagged terrain and directed fire onto targets. In the flatter terrain around Lake Susupe, seven tanks advanced through muddy ground, but the first was hit, blowing the track off.

Crotts moved in to help: "We were drawing fire from across a big open field. I had my rifle down showing them where the fire was coming from, and dadgum if I didn't forget the sonofagun could shoot. All of a sudden the guy just tore my legs up. Went through one leg and seared the other one."

Bale moved his own tank up to help Crotts and the crew of the disabled tank. "They moved the tank up right over me so I got some protection." Carried to safety in the tank, Crotts was put onto a bouncing jeep ambulance and carried to a succession of medical aid posts. Each post declared they could not help him, so the jeep moved on. "Finally I burst into tears. I said 'You sonofaB, don't you put me back on that jeep! I have had it with the on and off of jeeps!' I just couldn't stand that vibration anymore."

Crotts started through the long evacuation pipeline, ending up in the United States, his war over.[214]

Melvin Swango was put back into a tank crew, in Shook's AMAPOLA. On Saipan, the tank's suspension was blown off by a 250-pound bomb rigged as a mine. None of the crew was injured and they began to strip the disabled tank of guns and other equipment to make it useless to the enemy. While they worked several Marines arrived in a jeep. One walked over to a nearby shed, kicked the door open, and sprayed the interior with his BAR.

"He motioned for us to come over there. We went over and looked. Inside were five dead Japanese soldiers, all fully armed. Why they didn't come out and kill us, we don't know."[215]

The company went on to fight on Tinian, just across a narrow channel from Saipan, from 24 July until 1 August 1944.

The final fights were on the tiny island of Ie Shima near Okinawa, and in the last phase of the last battle of the war, on southernmost Okinawa. Elements of the 2nd Marine Division were the operational reserve for Operation ICEBERG, the capture of Okinawa and nearby islands. On Ie Shima the tanks supported Army troops in the brief struggle.

With Army and Marine Corps divisions bloodied in the protracted struggle for Okinawa, the 8th Marines, with Bale's tanks in support, were committed to the final stages of the campaign. The commander of the 8th Army, Lieutenant General Simon Bolivar Buckner Jr., was particularly impressed by the 8th Marines and asked specifically for them. Buckner would be the most senior American officer to die in action during World War II, killed while watching Bale's Able Company tanks in action.

"I sat up on a ridge line at the 8th Marines CP," said Bale, "and directed the tanks for a couple of days." The CP had a pair of large, tripod-mounted Japanese binoculars captured on Tinian, and Bale believed that the sun glinting off the brass binoculars attracted the attention of Japanese gunners.

"Right after General Buckner showed up, we got these three rounds of direct-fire artillery." The explosions, probably from a Japanese 47mm anti-tank gun, threw shards of sharp stone. Only Buckner was seriously hurt, but "You could have put a beer bottle through his chest," said Bale.[216]

By the time of Okinawa, the Japanese had fully recognized the dominance of the medium tanks and would go all out to develop ways to counter them—improved suicide weapons like the lunge mine, and huge mines made by burying aerial bomb or torpedo warheads with a regular anti-tank mine as a detonator. These early improvised explosive devices could lift the thirty-two ton M4 tanks high into the air, ripping off the turrets and tearing the hulls apart. The crews were rightfully cynical about their chances of survival. Charles Mason: "It was just normal. If one of those got hit and blown up, it's five dead men. That was just normal, and we expected it."

Despite the unrelenting savagery that was to come, many like Joe Woolum thought that none had the intensity of Tarawa. "Tarawa was just a mass of shooting and bombing and all, never a split *second* that there wasn't hundreds of explosions, shellfire, rifle fire." He thought Saipan was easier, Tinian easier still, and "By the time we went to Okinawa we was old hands, and it was just a day's work more or less."

The Marine Corps was converting to the long-awaited M4A3 medium tank. Some units continued to use the reliable old M4A2, but the production lines for that vehicle were shutting down and replacement parts would no longer be available. Able Company converted to the new tank in time for the Okinawa campaign.[217]

When Japan surrendered, the rumor immediately arose that they were going home immediately. But Gazel recalled that on the beach at Okinawa "There's an LST, with the ramp open": a vessel not designed for long voyages. "We're old salts. We know where we're going. We're not going home." They were headed for occupation duty in Nagasaki. The LSTs were manned by new sailors commanded by youthful NROTC officers, and "We had more time on the water than they did."

Woolum was eventually discharged at Camp Pendleton. Robert L. Bergeron's cousin had a car, so four of them drove across the country to Fort Worth, Texas. He was waiting to catch a bus to Oklahoma City when he gave his last change to a panhandler "...but now I'm broke." In Oklahoma City "I can't catch a cab. Hell, I can't even call anybody. I hitchhike out, get home, I'm hungry and Mom she feeds me." His father told him he didn't have to go to work, but after six weeks Woolum went back to work as a journeyman painter for the city. He moved to California where he stayed for sixteen years, then back to Oklahoma and eventually to Texas.

Looking back from the perspective of seventy years, Woolum could probably speak for many: "I should have died when I was nineteen years old. I should have never got off Tarawa.... It's been borrowed time since then."

EPILOGUE
THE LEGACY OF TARAWA

God grant me a good sword and no use for it.
—POLISH PROVERB

After Peleliu, Tarawa remains the most controversial Marine Corps campaign of the Pacific War. One part of that controversy can be traced to Holland Smith's postwar comments on whether the battle was necessary, and the confusion that was part of the first experiment in amphibious frontal assault. Another part of the controversy undoubtedly dates back to a single decision made in the immediate aftermath of the battle.

Tarawa was the first battle where gruesome photos of dead Americans were released to be shown to the public in theater newsreels and print publications. Marine Corps and civilian correspondents had documented the battle extensively, and Commandant Thomas Holcomb authorized the release of their images because he felt the public needed to know the price to be paid for defeating Japan. The images profoundly shocked civilians whose concepts of war were derived from Hollywood films, where men suffered curiously painless shoulder wounds, or gave a brief but noble speech, closed their eyes, and quietly died.

Another factor may have been simple timing. Tarawa was fought at a time in the war at which there were no distractions to the public's attention.

In truth the toll for two other Pacific battles fought for murky reason was significantly higher. The final toll at Tarawa was 1696 dead or presumed dead, 2101 wounded, and one escort carrier lost.

In late 1944, Peleliu, in the Palau Islands, was taken to secure the sea-

215

ward flank of Douglas MacArthur's return to the Philippines. But Bill Halsey's Navy carrier strike forces had discovered that the Palaus were an empty shell, and he urged that the operation be cancelled. The Peleliu operation went ahead anyway, at the cost of 1336 dead or presumed dead, and 5450 wounded. But the horrific battle was overshadowed by the triumphant return to the Philippines, and the victorious march of Allied armies across Western Europe.

Iwo Jima, the bloodiest battle in Marine Corps history, cost 6821 dead or presumed dead, 19,217 wounded, and an escort carrier lost. It was fought to secure an emergency landing strip for B-29 bombers, and as a base for fighter planes to escort the bombers over Japan. The cost of Iwo has often been justified by saying that the number of bomber crewmen's lives saved outnumbered the Marines killed, an assertion seldom questioned. In reality there were just not that many bomber crewmen, and most of the landings on the island were routine, not emergencies. The capture of that blood-soaked island did make the bombing campaign less costly and preserved aircraft. Iwo would have been an important forward base if the United States had been forced to subdue mainland Japan by blockade and invasion. But the assertion that the cost of Iwo Jima was justified by the saving of aircrew lives cannot be proven.[218]

In the final analysis, for the men who fought there, the cost of a battle like Tarawa can never be measured by any such simple cost versus benefit calculation. The physical and emotional investment is simply too great.

It is that emotional investment that draws so many back to the battlefields of their youth. There is truth in the adage "you can't go home again"; home has always changed, and usually not for the better. For the survivors of combat, old battlefields are even more depressing, given the price that was paid for them. Some battlefields are preserved as now-peaceful monuments, but veterans of the horrific battle on Bititu are invariably disgusted at the sordid mess it has become.

Much of the remaining debris of battle is long since gone. Some was hauled away and sold for scrap metal in the days when scrap still had a dollar value. More was used as fill in later construction, or simply dumped into the sea. Some of the larger emplacements, like Shibasaki's command bunker, now serve as trysting places, or as convenient impromptu toilets. Massive naval guns still sit rusting away in their emplacements simply because they are too big to make it worthwhile to remove them.

"There's an awful lot of junk still on that island," said Ed Bale, who returned for the fiftieth anniversary of the battle in 1993. "They just dragged LVTs out in the water, because the place is so crowded with people." The displaced local population was allowed to return after the war, and the ensuing population boom has made the tiny island one of the most densely-populated places on the planet.

"It's sad to go back there and look at the way they're living. Shacks. No toilets. They build a house that has no running water, a hydrant out in front of the house.

"There's a fish-packing plant and it's owned by some Australian company, and the unemployment is seventy-five, eighty per cent. Alcoholism is high. Outside the bars there's [piles of] beer cans as big as a house. Empty beer cans.

"The people are malnourished, because they eat mostly rice, coconut, breadfruit, fish. The lagoon is contaminated because that's everybody's bathroom. You lay in your hotel room, you look out and see them out doing their business in the lagoon. I've seen them reach down and grab a handful of sand and—that kind of thing.

"It's an interesting place to go back to, particularly if you always had the desire to go back. I wouldn't want to go back again."

Things have only gotten worse, with an ever-growing population and a worsening economy.

The United States military and private organizations still conduct efforts to locate the remains of those still missing from the long-ago battle, but the effort is itself a losing battle. Remains lie somewhere underneath the random jumble of bars, shacks, chicken coops, pigsties, and gardens that cover every square inch of land. Most remains located are those of the Japanese and Korean defenders, entombed in their positions or hastily dumped into mass graves. Those remains are repatriated to Japan.

Perhaps it is better to follow the course advocated by some: to let the dead rest in peace. The enduring monument to those who died there and those who survived is far greater than any physical edifice we might construct. It is a hallowed tradition of endurance and valor.

But whatever our puny efforts, in time Tarawa will experience the geological fate of all coral atolls. It will slowly sink beneath the waves to become one more silent seamount in the broad ocean that bears such a deceptive name: Pacific. Peaceful.

LATER LIFE

Ed Bale—photo courtesy of Ed Bale

ED BALE remained in the Marine Corps for "30 years 1 month and 16 days." He served as a battalion commander in Korea and as a division chief of staff in Vietnam. He then worked in the banking business for several years before his second retirement.

DOUG CROTTS was severely wounded on Saipan and spent the rest of the war recuperating. He later earned Bachelors and Masters degrees in English and History, and taught high school. He died in February 2011.

WILLIAM A. "BILL" DUNKEL started an electronics company and an alarm company, and after retirement realized his dream of cattle-farming. Bill died in April 2013.

BILL EADS became a prison guard at San Quentin, including a tour on death row, and helped open several new prisons.

ED GAZEL eventually became the company first sergeant. After the war he became quite successful in the grocery business.

NORMAN HATCH made warrant officer and transferred to the Reserves where he rose to the rank of major. He worked with the Department of Defense and was a consultant to the White House and Congress. The footage shot at Tarawa was the basis for the Oscar-winning documentary "With The Marines At Tarawa."

OLAF GLENN JOHNSON was reassigned to another company, and given a dozer tank (the company executive officer's tank). We have no further information on him.

ORELL F. KENT went on to win the Silver Star on Saipan. He returned to Mississippi where he died in 1988.

WILLIAM R. "SCOT" KINSMAN returned to Illinois and became a graphic artist, eventually starting his own art and print company. He died in June 2010.

John Marn—courtesy Barbara Nevala

JOHN MARN was returned to duty after his wounds healed. Returned to the company, he fought at Saipan and Tinian, but was assigned to duty at Pearl Harbor before the invasion of Okinawa. He was a ranch manager in Montana, and died in June 2013.

HARRELL MCNORTON had his most frightening moment on Tarawa when the Japanese rushed his tank. Reassigned as a tank crew instructor at Camp Pendleton after the battle for Saipan, he later became an optical technician. He passed away in 2012.

Harrel McNorton —courtesy Barbara Nevala

CHARLES D. MASON; we have no additional information on him.

CLIFFORD QUINE went back to the same factory, under a job-protection program for veterans.

MIKE SHIVETTS, at Bale's insistence, later became a tank commander. Like many, he ". . . chose to forget about it completely, as best possible, and that was the end of it." After a brief experience in college, he went back to the steel mill "Much to my Dad's chagrin."

WILLIAM DODSON SMITH was wounded by a grenade on Saipan but stayed in a forward position for a day and a half despite his wound. For this he received the Bronze Star which made him one of the lucky men with enough points to be immediately shipped Stateside at war's end. He retired from the office machine business at age seventy-five.

CHARLES A. SOOTER received a commission and was a captain in Korea. He was awarded the Silver Star and Bronze Star. He died in 2003.

MELVIN SWANGO entered the hotel business, his "lifelong love affair." He managed ten properties in a major market. Melvin died in 2003.

JOE WOOLUM acted as a gunner in the tank Amapola from Saipan to Okinawa. After being discharged, he stayed in Oklahoma and worked as a painter. Joe died in December 2014.

APPENDIX **A**
CHARLIE COMPANY CHRONOLOGY

---

18 JANUARY 1943: Lt. Col. Bennet G. Powers activates the 1st Corps Medium Tank Battalion composed of a Headquarters Company and four tank companies (A through D) at Camp Elliott California.[219]

FEBRUARY/MARCH 1943: The battalion receives its first diesel powered M4A2 tanks.

1 JUNE 1943: Charlie Company transferred to Jacques Farm (now part of the US Navy Recreation Center), San Diego, California.[220]

22 JUNE 1943: C Company receives a complement of new tanks for combat service.[221]

19 JULY 1943: Men and equipment of C Company ship out of San Diego aboard the SS *John McLean*.[222]

15 AUGUST 1943: C Company arrives at Noumea, New Caledonia. Men live and train in Camp Magenta, a temporary transit camp located north of Noumea. The tanks are parked a few miles away from the camp.

11 SEPTEMBER 1943: The battalion is reunited at Camp St. Louis, the old Marine 2nd Raider Battalion camp, northeast of Noumea.[223]

16 SEPTEMBER 1943: Company C, 1st Corps Medium Tank Battalion is attached to the 2nd Marine Division.[224]

27 SEPTEMBER 1943: Men and material from C Company leave New Caledonia for Wellington, New Zealand, on the SS *Mormacport*.

6 OCTOBER 1943: C Company arrives and disembarks in New Zealand. The same day, the company is attached to the 2nd Tank Battalion.[225]

9 OCTOBER 1943: 146 men from C Company leave New Zealand aboard the SS *Mormacport*. One officer, eleven men, and two tanks are left in New Zealand for fording tests with the M4A2s.[226]

14 OCTOBER 1943: The bulk of C Company arrives and disembarks from the SS *Mormacport* in New Caledonia.[227]

1 NOVEMBER 1943: Twelve personnel and two tanks left in New Zealand sail on USS *Doyen* and USS *Zeilin* for Efate, New Hebrides.[228]

3 NOVEMBER 1943: C Company consisting of five officers, 132 men, two Navy medical corpsmen and twelve tanks embark aboard USS *Ashland,* leaving on 4 November for Efate. Some personnel remain behind as a rear echelon and the VTR is left on the island for lack of space in the transport.

6 NOVEMBER 1943: USS *Ashland* arrives at Efate, New Hebrides; men and tanks remain aboard.

7 NOVEMBER 1943: Men and equipment aboard the USS *Ashland* disembark and take part in a practice landing at Mele Bay (Efate).[229] USS *Doyen* and USS *Zeilin* arrive at Efate.

8 NOVEMBER 1943: Twelve men and the two tanks from C Company disembark from USS *Zeilin* and USS *Doyen* to re-embark on USS *Ashland.*

9 NOVEMBER 1943: Tanks and men from C Company take part in a second landing exercise at Mele Bay. During both rehearsals, tanks remain on the beach and never move inland.

13 NOVEMBER 1943: USS *Ashland* leaves Efate, New Hebrides with 151 men and fourteen tanks of Charlie Company.

20 NOVEMBER 1943: USS *Ashland* arrives off Tarawa. Charlie Company's men and tanks take part in the battle of Betio (20–23 November 1943).

27–28 NOVEMBER 1943: USS *Ashland* moves into the lagoon and a hundred surviving Charlie Company personnel and six medium tanks re-embark. The USS *Ashland* departs Tarawa lagoon. The Division wounded will sail aboard ships to which they were taken for care. USS *Hayward,* USS *Sheridan,* USS *Zeilin,* USS *Middleton,* USS *Doyen* and USS *Harry Lee* transport wounded to Pearl Harbor and Hilo, Hawaii.[230]

7 DECEMBER 1943: USS *Ashland* arrives at Pearl Harbor (island of Oahu), Hawaii Territory. Troops remain aboard.[231]

9 DECEMBER 1943: USS *Ashland* arrives at port of Hilo (island of Hawaii), Hawaii Territory. The tanks remain aboard ship. Battalion personnel disembark to recuperate and train on the Big Island.

10 DECEMBER 1943: The tanks are offloaded at Lahaina (island of Maui), Hawaii Territory. The transported tanks are eventually assigned to the 2nd Separate Tank Company to be refurbished and used in the Marshall Islands operations.

15 FEBRUARY 1944: The battalion is disbanded. Charlie Company becomes Able Company, 2nd Tank Battalion.

APPENDIX B
TANK COMPANY ORGANIZATION AND EQUIPMENT

The official Table of Organization RD 3391(123) E-1010 for the Medium Tank Battalion and its subordinate companies was promulgated on 22 May 1943. The individual companies of the battalion were intended to be parceled out to divisions in support of the division light tank battalions. Therefore each company was to be capable of independent operation, with augmented communications and maintenance/repair capabilities.

Units often did not follow the official tables for various reasons including fluctuations in vehicles or equipment actually available, and surpluses or deficiencies in numbers of available personnel. Unit records indicate that C Company was over-strength, with a total of 157 men (plus two attached medical corpsmen) at peak strength, but eight enlisted men remained behind as a rear echelon during the Tarawa operation.

Serious shortages of the standard International 2-1/2ton M-5-6 trucks afflicted the Marine Corps through 1943 and numerous civilian model trucks were pressed into service, although there is no evidence that Charlie Company used any civilian-model trucks. Because of limited shipping space the only support vehicle actually taken to Tarawa was a single one-quarter-ton truck (jeep) fitted with a Navy TCS radio capable of communicating with the GF-RU radios in the tanks. It was never unloaded at Tarawa. In particular the absence of the company's M32B2 tank recovery vehicle was sorely felt during the post-battle salvage effort.

Units often acquired small arms that were not part of their authorized unit equipment. Photos show tank crewmen armed with the new M1 Carbine, although the official T/E specified only the M1911 pistol for tank crewmen. Some Recon Guides also reported carrying a pistol in addition to the authorized M1 Garand rifle, suggesting a number of pistols and carbines well over the official allocation. Company commander Lieutenant (later Colonel) Ed Bale has alluded to the "open checkbook" that allowed

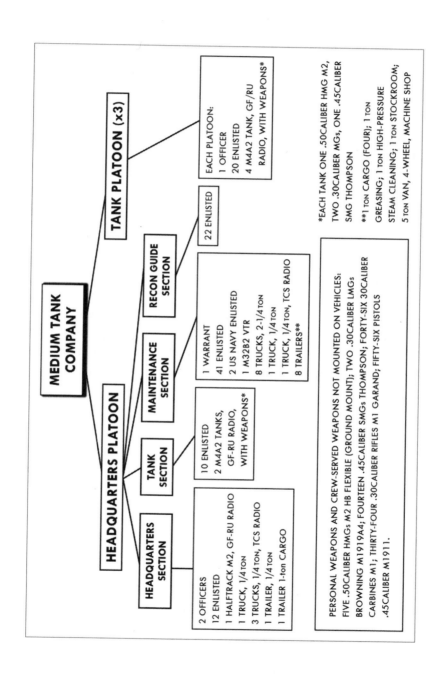

MEDIUM TANK COMPANY

HEADQUARTERS PLATOON

TANK PLATOON (x3)

HEADQUARTERS SECTION

2 OFFICERS
12 ENLISTED
1 HALFTRACK M2, GF-RU RADIO
1 TRUCK, 1/4 TON
3 TRUCKS, 1/4 TON, TCS RADIO
1 TRAILER, 1/4 TON
1 TRAILER 1-ton CARGO

TANK SECTION

10 ENLISTED
2 M4A2 TANKS, GF-RU RADIO, WITH WEAPONS*

MAINTENANCE SECTION

1 WARRANT
41 ENLISTED
2 US NAVY ENLISTED
1 M32B2 VTR
8 TRUCKS, 2-1/4 TON
1 TRUCK, 1/4 TON
1 TRUCK, 1/4 TON, TCS RADIO
8 TRAILERS**

RECON GUIDE SECTION

22 ENLISTED

EACH PLATOON:
1 OFFICER
20 ENLISTED
4 M4A2 TANK, GF/RU RADIO, WITH WEAPONS*

*EACH TANK ONE .50CALIBER HMG M2, TWO .30CALIBER MGs, ONE .45CALIBER SMG THOMPSON

**1 TON CARGO (FOUR); 1 TON GREASING; 1 TON HIGH-PRESSURE STEAM CLEANING; 1 TON STOCKROOM; 5 TON VAN, 4-WHEEL, MACHINE SHOP

PERSONAL WEAPONS AND CREW-SERVED WEAPONS NOT MOUNTED ON VEHICLES: FIVE .50CALIBER HMGs M2 HB FLEXIBLE (GROUND MOUNT); TWO .30CALIBER LMGs BROWNING M1919A4; FOURTEEN .45CALIBER SMGs THOMPSON; FORTY-SIX 30CALIBER CARBINES M1; THIRTY-FOUR .30CALIBER RIFLES M1 GARAND; FIFTY-SIX PISTOLS .45CALIBER M1911.

tank companies to acquire numerous extra tools, spare parts, and maintenance equipment. Of course no detailed accounting of any such supernumerary weapons and equipment is available for Charlie Company.

The tables also specified allocations of officer and enlisted men by rank,
and Charlie Company had 151 men for the Tarawa operation. However
the promotion system seldom kept pace with personnel demands created
by casualties and the formation of new units. As a result, many Marine
Corps units were "under led"; captain's billets were filled by lieutenants
(like Bale), and many enlisted men filled billets that called for a rank well
above their actual rank. The problem was most acute at the junior enlisted
levels. In Charlie Company only 21 of 29 sergeant's billets and 35 of 59
corporal's billets were filled, but there were 78 privates and PFCs for 44
billets. The reader should also be aware that in tank units many men in
the Maintenance and Recon Guide Sections were trained as tank crewmen;
a secondary duty for these men was to serve as a replacement pool for anticipated tank crew casualties.

As with most units, the medium tank battalion had attached Navy
medical personnel; one commissioned medical officer and nine enlisted
medical corpsmen were assigned to the battalion Headquarters and Services
Company. Corpsmen were seconded to the individual tank companies,
and Charlie Company had the typical allocation of two medical corpsmen
at Tarawa.

APPENDIX C
INSIDE THE M4A2 TANK

The following is a "guided tour" of life inside a functional M4A2 preserved at the *Musée du Général Estienne* (also called the *Musée des Blindés*) in Saumur, France.

Just mounting the tank requires good physical condition and some agility. As with all things military, there was a prescribed procedure for mounting the tank. It was one of the first things a new crewman learned, although the prescribed procedure was obviously not always observed. The preferred position for mounting was from the right front; the tank could be mounted from the left front (driver's side, to avoid passing in front of the hull machine gun mount), but this was slightly more difficult. Sure

The crewmen were taught to grasp the lifting ring with the left hand and the headlight guard with the right, and put their left foot on the drive sprocket hub. Pushing up with the left foot, the right foot went onto the fender, and from there the crewman scrambled across the slope plate using external fixtures and the main gun tube as handholds.

The driver and assistant driver could enter through their hatches on the front top of the hull. The mid-production tanks used by Charlie Company retained the small hatches of the initial production vehicles, about 12inches/30cm wide; this led to the mid-production vehicles being called the "small hatch" version.

The small hatch openings were a source of considerable concern to the crewmen. The hatches were heavy (over 44pounds/20kg) and could slow even an uninjured man trying to escape in an emergency. An additional handicap was the small hatch opening that could easily snag a belt, trapping a Marine trying to exit quickly. (Cansiere is about 71inches/182cm tall and weighs 143pounds/65kg, and it was a tight fit.)

Once inside, a man quickly found that you could not be claustrophobic and serve in a tank. In fact many infantrymen who tried to ride inside found that they preferred to take their chances outside. (Gilbert's father-in-law was trained as a radio operator and assigned to a tank, but had to be reassigned to a half-track because of claustrophobia.)

Once inside, the driver was seated to the left and the assistant driver to the right, with the massive transmission housing between them. Near each man's head was one of the ventilation exhaust fans intended to remove fumes and hot air from inside the tank. Each man sat on a metal-framed canvas seat, with minimal padding for comfort. These seats could be raised manually to allow the driver and assistant driver to operate with their heads outside the hatch openings for better vision.

The original tanks had direct vision blocks mounted in front of both positions, allowing the driver and assistant driver to see directly forward when the hatches were closed. The new hull configuration, with the direct vision blocks omitted, was designed to better resist enemy shells, not for optimum visibility. There were two periscopes each for the driver and assistant driver. The first was a fixed position in front of the hatch, looking only forward, with an arc of vision of 30 degrees to either side of the center line. This limited visibility, so the hatches incorporated a swivel periscope mount that allowed some vision to the sides. Forward visibility was limited, and there was a six foot/two meter blind spot directly in front of the tank. When moving the tank under non-combat conditions, a ground guide— a man walking in front of the tank and directing the driver with hand signals—was essential to avoid hitting obstacles.

Another problem that plagued the driver and assistant driver was that water, mud or dust often drastically reduced visibility through the periscopes.

The driver had to contend with five hand levers. On the left were the two steering brake levers; the driver steered by braking one track or the other. To their right were the two hand throttle levers that controlled the idle speed of the two diesel engines. Farthest to the right was the gear shift for the main transmission, with five forward gears and one reverse. With his feet the driver controlled the clutch pedal (on his left, as in an automobile), and the foot throttle/accelerator.

The assistant driver was charged with helping the driver identify ground hazards like holes or other obstacles. He was also responsible for operating the ball-mounted .30caliber machine gun situated directly in front of him. There was no direct sight for this machine gun, so the assistant driver had to observe where his rounds were impacting through the periscope and "walk" his fire onto the target. To his right, in the sponson overhanging the track, were machine gun ammunition and spare parts for the weapon. The barrel of the air-cooled machine gun would easily overheat during prolonged firing, so the assistant driver was equipped with an asbestos glove and several spare barrels. Combat experience led most crews to acquire as many spare barrels as possible. The machine gun could be detached from the ball mount and pulled back inside to change barrels.

To facilitate getting out of a damaged tank under fire, an escape hatch was located on the bottom of the tank just behind the assistant driver's seat. A crewman could pull a lever that disengaged locking devices and the heavy hatch would fall free under its own weight. Because of the tight space inside and the low ground clearance outside the tank, a man exiting the hatch had to go head-first, twisting his body to wriggle into the narrow space between the tank's bottom and the ground. This was taught in training, but it was slow and many men took their chances going out of a top hatch.

The three turret crewmen usually went in through the one hatch in the turret roof, although there was an opening to move between the metal cage (the turret basket) that moved with the rotating turret and the driver's/assistant driver's space.

The turret was the most spacious part of the tank, and three men worked here: the loader/radio operator (left rear), gunner (right front), and the tank commander (right rear, seated above and behind the gunner). With three men working in the small space, it was barely large enough.

The loader/radio operator had to be very agile and well organized to sort and move the rounds and empty shell casings for the main gun, replenish ammunition belts and replacement overheated barrels for the coaxial machine gun, and operate the radio. The loader had a small folding seat that attached to the turret wall, but he did much of his work standing up and trying to keep his footing inside the moving tank.

The loader's primary task was moving the heavy cannon shells located in storage spaces under the floor of the rotating turret basket, clipped to the sides of the turret basket, and in metal boxes built into the sponsons.

The loader had a periscope mounted in the turret roof at eye level, but the position on the turret roof severely restricted the field of view. This was probably the least useful of the periscopes since the loader did not have time to look outside. On the left rear of the turret at shoulder level was the pistol port, a small armored door on the side of the turret. Originally intended to allow a tank crewman to fire a pistol to eliminate enemy troops who might climb onto the tank, it was usually used to discard empty shell casings. On Tarawa infantrymen standing on the ground or crouched on the engine deck behind the turret used the pistol port to shout directions to the men inside the turret. In the turret bustle behind the loader were the radio, and sixty-four small compartments to hold extra magazines for the Thompson submachine gun.

The massive cannon breech block (which takes up almost half the space in the turret) separated the loader from the other two crewmen. The loader had to be careful to be out of the way when the gun fired, to avoid being injured or killed when the breech block recoiled into the turret interior. A single turret ventilator exhaust fan was located immediately above the breech to help suck out propellant fumes that filled the turret when the breech was opened. The fan could not pull enough air during rapid firing, so choking fumes sometimes filled the turret, and the pistol port might be opened to provide more fresh air.

The gunner sat on a seat with a back rest, the controls of the gun—a handle to rotate and elevate the gun electrically, and manual control wheels in case of a power failure—in front of him at chest level. The gunner was provided with two sights, a periscope and a telescopic sight for long-range firing, but gunners almost never used the telescope. The periscope sight was fixed, so that the gunner could only see forward and relied upon the tank commander to inform him of targets he might not see. At his feet was a panel with two buttons six to eight inches (15–20cm) apart; these fired the coaxial or the main cannon electrically. Both guns could be fired manually in case of a power failure.

The Thompson submachine gun was clipped to the turret to the right of and behind the gunner, accessible to him and the tank commander. The white-painted interior walls of the turret are cluttered with all manner of other gear; extra periscopes, flashlights, a hand held fire extinguisher (at front left), et cetera.

The tank commander sat on a folding seat that could be moved up and down, allowing him to ride either inside, or with his head and shoulders outside the hatch for better visibility. The old-style split hatch was mounted on a race ring and could be rotated 360 degrees; the tank commander could raise one half between him and the enemy, affording some minimal protection when he had to open the hatch. This was the largest hatch, about nineteen inches (60cm) in diameter, and intended for the tank commander, gunner, and radio operator/loader. As with the other hatches the two halves were heavy, about 45 pounds (20kg) each.

One half of the hatch held a 360degree rotating periscope. This periscope allowed the tank commander to see in all directions, and he had the best overall visibility. However, since it was mounted near the center of the hatch, there was a large blind area some 33 to 40 feet (10–12m) in diameter in all directions around the tank.

Starting the two engines is somewhat slow since the engines fire by compression and the ignition plugs must be pre-heated. The engine start is very loud and gives off a cloud of white smoke from the diesel fuel that is immediately sucked into the crew compartment. The smell of smoke spreads rapidly and persists despite open hatches and the ventilator fans. The temperature at Saumur was not too hot; about 81–82F (27–28C) and 86–88F (30–31C) inside the tank. However, once the engines were started the heat spread rapidly into the crew spaces. Cansiere was dressed in a tee-shirt, dungaree jacket, and jeans, but was choking from the heat and fumes only ten minutes after the engines were started.

After a while you grow accustomed to the pervasive diesel smell, and most crewmen were not aware that they and their clothing reeked of the exhaust smell. Despite the ventilator fans the air circulation was poor, and the crews must have been suffocated by propellant fumes each time the guns fired. Under very hot conditions, with the cannon firing repeatedly, some loaders in particular would lose consciousness from the effects of heat and fumes.

When the engines are running and the tank is in motion the engine sound is repetitive and tedious. The twin engines make a constant, loud, pulsing "VROOum, VROOum, VROOum" sound that you soon learn to ignore when concentrating on tasks like loading the main gun or trying to see through the small periscopes. However, a day, even a half-day, is exhausting and the noise and fumes cause fatigue and headaches. In his request to increase the number of tank personnel in the battalion, Powers stated that "Four hours of actual operation a day is the fatigue limit for a tank crew."[232]

The engine vibration is very uncomfortable even after the tank reaches cruising speed, and even maneuvering on flat ground (pavement) the tank shakes a lot. Sitting in the gunner's seat it was necessary for Cansiere to hold tightly onto the controls to keep from falling off the seat onto the floor of the turret. (The seat back on the Saumur tank was missing.) The constant shaking and impacts were brutal! The tanker's helmet was absolutely necessary to cushion blows to the head from the interior walls even on flat ground.

The intercom system in the Saumur tank was not functional, and Cansiere and the rest of the crew had to shout to communicate with each other. Even with the opening between the turret and the driver's compartment it was difficult to communicate by shouting because of the engine noise.

The armor and noise makes it impossible to hear any noises coming from outside the tank. If a man climbed onto the back of the tank and shouted into the open pistol port or hatch he could barely be heard inside. The armor also muffled the sound of the main gun being fired.

In combat, the stress level of a crewman would quickly become critical from the noise, shouting, vibration, smoke and fumes, and above all the fear of enemy action. The most frustrating feeling is being aware that something is happening outside the tank, but you cannot know what because of the noise, limited vision through the periscope, and the constant rush of tasks inside the tank.

The best way to dismount from the tank, with your legs weakened by the stress and exhaustion, is the way you came in, over the right front (the unused radio antenna mount makes an excellent step). Once on the fender you can easily jump to the ground. It is also possible to jump from the deck of the tank, slightly over six feet (about 1.8m) to the ground, and photos show that the young crewmen did this. The one way you do not want to go is down the middle of the slope plate—very slippery.

APPENDIX D
CHARLIE COMPANY
PERSONNEL AT TARAWA

The following is a compilation of known information derived primarily from official records and from Company Commander Ed Bale, but primarily from Ed Gazel, who became Company First Sergeant after Tarawa. Bale and Gazel were responsible for accounting for the dead, wounded, and missing, and remained in contact with many fellow veterans after the war. Persons having additional or corrected information are urged to contact:

Romain Cansiere, www.tanksontarawa.com, at
romain.cansiere@gmail.com, and
Jonathan Stevens, www.tarawaontheweb.org, at
jonathan.stevens@wheaton.edu

Relatives of MIAs are advised to contact the Joint POW/MIA Accounting Command (http://www.jpac.pacom.mil/), History Flight (http://historyflight.com/nw/), or the Chief Rick Stone Foundation (http://chiefrickstone.com/) for specific information.

Homer L. AKIN Jr., PFC. Serial Number 468833. Was a 2nd Platoon Tank Commander according to Ed GAZEL.

Robert C. ALLEN, PVT. Serial Number 458784. Enlisted on 5 October 1942.

Antonio ALMARAZ, CPL. Serial Number 469094. Enlisted on 6 October 1942. Was the driver of CLIPPER, 2nd Platoon.

Oral M. ANDERSON, PVT. Serial Number 468482. Enlisted on 5 October 1942.

Eugene H. ANDREWS, SGT. Serial Number 475142. Enlisted on 20 October 1942. Was part of the contingent that took part in the medium tanks fording tests at Hawke's Bay, New Zealand. Was a tank commander in the 2nd Platoon. Was wounded after his tank (CONGA?) fell into a shell hole close to the airfield on D-Day. Was replaced in the tank the next day by Donald PEARSON. Evacuated on 21 November to the USS *HAYWARD*.

John J. ARMATO, PFC. Serial Number 804250. WIA. Evacuated on 21 November. Was a tank crewman according to Ed GAZEL.

William H. ATKINSON Jr., FIRST SGT. Enlisted on 31 May 1942. Serial Number 259108.

John V. AUTENRIEB, SGT. Serial Number 411625.

Owen C. AVANT, PVT. Serial Number 474958. Enlisted on 5 October 1942 from Texas. Was part of the contingent that took part in the medium tanks fording tests at Hawke's Bay, New Zealand. MIA.

Anthony AZZARELLO, PFC. Serial Number 472280. WIA. Evacuated on 21 November to USS *HARRY LEE*.

Reed L. BAILEY, PVT. Serial Number 477776. Was a tank crewman according to Ed GAZEL.

Edward L. BAJUS, PFC. Serial Number 472325. Enlisted on 5 October 1942. Tank Commander of CHINA GAL, 1st Platoon.

Robert E. BAKER, SGT. Serial Number 462680. Was the tank commander of CLIPPER, 2nd Platoon.

Edward L. BALE Jr., 1st LIEUTENANT, Charlie Company Commander. Landed in CECILIA, Headquarters Section. Took over CHINA GAL on D+1.

Raymond A. BARKER, CPL. Serial Number 480082. Enlisted on 5 October 1942 from Chicago, Illinois. Was the driver of the tank CONDOR in the 3rd Platoon. MIA.

Harry BARTELS, PFC. Serial Number 482618. Enlisted on 5 October 1942. From Alaska, was a maintenance man according to WOOLUM.

Paul F. BEABOUT, PVT. Serial Number 475473. Was part of the contingent that took part in the medium tanks fording tests at Hawke's Bay, New Zealand. Was a tank crewman, HQ Section.

Robert L. BERGERON, PFC. Serial Number 455154. Was a tank crewman according to Ed GAZEL.

Virgil BETHURUM, PVT. Serial Number 824076. Was a tank crewman according to Ed GAZEL.

Shirley M. BROWN, SGT. Serial Number 365285. A tank mechanic and native of South Carolina. Landed on Red Beach One, in the first LCVP to leave the USS *ASHLAND*. KIA by "gun shot wounds in the left hip, left side, left shoulder."

Mervyn L. CAREY, PFC. Serial Number 802968. Was an ordnance man according to Ed Gazel.

Alfonso A. CHAVEZ, CPL. Serial Number 469055. From Los Angeles, California. Was part of the contingent that took part in the medium tanks fording tests at Hawke's Bay, New Zealand. Was the driver of CECILIA, Headquarters Section. He was married just before shipping off San Diego. There is some disagreement whether the tank CECILIA was named after his wife or daughter. He was killed on Saipan while he was a tank commander (SHIVETTS). Today, Alfonso CHAVEZ is erroneously listed as MIA since he is buried in the Los Angeles National cemetery.

Buford COLEMAN, PVT. Serial Number 449399. WIA. Evacuated on 21 November to USS *HARRY LEE*.

Hubert D. CROTTS, CPL. Serial Number 315561. Enlisted on 7 July 1941. Landed on Red Beach Three in an LCVP. On D+1, 2nd Lt. LARGEY designated CROTTS as a guide for his tank COLORADO.

Francis C. CURTIS, CPL. Serial Number 443109. Was a tank crewman according to Ed GAZEL.

Paul A. DEL BENE, SGT. Serial Number 450468. From New York. KIA on 22 November 1943.

Russell J. DENNIS, PVT. Serial Number 477780.

Warren S. DOHERTY, PFC. Serial Number 456305. Enlisted on 23 September 1942.

William C. DONALDSON, PVT. Serial Number 486589. From Kentucky. MIA.

Alphonse DUMAIS, MGY SGT. Serial Number 177214. Enlisted on 14 September 1943 from New Hampshire. Was with Ed GAZEL on Red One. Killed in the water. MIA.

William "Bill" A. DUNKEL, CPL. Serial Number 449944. Was a gunner. Landed on Red Beach Three. Became the gunner on COLORADO on D+1.

Warren E. DUPLESSIS, PFC. Serial Number 430466. Was a tank crewman according to Ed GAZEL. WIA. Evacuated on 21 November to USS *HARRY LEE*. He was a crewman in COMMANDO according to Quine.

William H. EADS Jr., CPL. Serial Number 456450. Enlisted on 1 October 1942. Was the radio operator and loader in the 2nd Platoon Leader tank, COBRA. Was wounded on D+1 when his tank was stalled into a shell hole on the reef at the junction between Red One and Two. Evacuated on 21 November to USS *MIDDLETON*.

James A. ELLIS, STAFF SGT. Serial Number 449822. Was a radio man according to Ed GAZEL.

George T. EWING, CPL. Serial Number 455931. Was a tank crewman according to Ed GAZEL. WIA. Evacuated on 21 November to USS *DOYEN*.

Herbert M. FISH, PVT. Serial Number 485854.

Robert L. FISHER, PVT. Serial Number 448377. Was the assistant driver in COLORADO, 3rd Platoon.

Harley B. FISK Jr., PFC. Serial Number 431256.

William S. FORD, CPL. Serial Number 436125. Assistant driver (in CHINA GAL?), he probably took over as a driver when JOSEFSON was wounded. Was a tank crewman according to Ed GAZEL.

Hillory H. FOWLER, PVT. Serial Number 426637.

Elmer J. FRIEDRIECHSEN, PVT. Serial Number 482933. Was on Red Beach One with Ed GAZEL. Killed on Saipan.

Herschel B. FULMER, CPL. Serial Number 438435. Enlisted on 16 August 1942. Was the radio operator and loader in CONDOR, 3rd Platoon. WIA. Evacuated on 21 November to USS *MIDDLETON*.

Sebastian B. GARDE, CPL. Serial Number 448807. Was in the first landing craft to leave the *ASHLAND*. Landed on Red Beach One. Was killed by "gunshot wounds in head and face" and buried on the island but his grave was lost. Today, he is listed as MIA.

Malcolm W. GARVOCK, CPL. Serial Number 455458. Enlisted on 17 September 1942. Was part of the contingent that took part in the medium tanks fording tests at Hawke's Bay, New Zealand. Was the gunner in CONGA(?), 2nd Platoon. Wounded after his tank fell into a shell hole close to the taxi-strip on D-Day. Was replaced by Charles MASON on D+1. Evacuated on 21 November to USS *HAYWARD*.

Edward GAZEL, SGT. Serial Number 483112. Was the Company Supply Sergeant. Landed on Red Beach One in an LCVP.

Andrew G. GEANKOPLIS, CPL. Serial Number 441262. Was a tank crewman according to Ed GAZEL. WIA. Evacuated on 21 November to *USS MIDDLETON*.

Leroy W. GLASER, PVT. Serial Number 490209. Was in the first Higgins boat to leave the *ASHLAND*. Landed on Red Beach One. WIA. Evacuated on 21 November.

George M. GLORVIGEN, CPL. Serial Number 476735. Was the Company clerk according to Ed GAZEL.

Herman "Pappy" L. GRAVES, CPL. Serial Number 488263. Was part of the contingent that took part in the medium tanks fording tests at Hawke's Bay, New Zealand. Was a tank crewman, HQ Section.

James D. GRAVES, CPL. Serial Number 475160. Was a tank crewman according to Ed GAZEL.

James R. GRAY, PVT. Serial Number 474949.

Stanley S. GRAESER, PFC. Serial Number 430453. Enlisted on 30 July 1942, from Ohio. Landed on Red Beach One with Ed Gazel. Was probably KIA on the island, but not identified and buried as "Unknown." His remains were identified in 1949 and reinterred in the National Memorial Cemetery of the Pacific in Hawaii (Punch Bowl), Section C, Site 1296.

Harry O. GREY, PVT. Serial Number 476875. From Nebraska. Was the assistant driver in CONDOR, 3rd Platoon. KIA on 20 November.

Hugh C. HAYCRAFT Jr., PLT SGT. Serial Number 364066. 2nd Platoon Sergeant. Enlisted on 26 January 1942. Was a tank crewman according to Ed GAZEL, probably the tank commander of CUDDLES, disabled ashore Red Beach Three. WIA. Evacuated on 21 November to USS *ZEILIN*.

Alfred E. HINES, CPL. Serial Number 482697.

Paul J. HOLLAND, CPL. Serial Number 447438. Was in the first Higgins boat to leave the *ASHLAND*. Landed on Red Beach One. KIA by "gunshot wounds in chest." His grave site was lost and is now listed as MIA.

Daniel G. HOLLENBECK, SGT. Serial Number 324015. Mechanic, with Ed GAZEL in the Higgins boat.

Robert J. HOPCROFT, PVT. Serial Number 455598. Was a truck driver at Pendleton.

John E. IRVINE, PVT. Serial Number 480924. Enlisted on 10 November 1942. Was a tank crewman in COUNT, 1st Platoon. Was wounded when he came out of his tank that fell into an underwater shell hole along Red Beach One. Evacuated on 21 November to USS *HARRY LEE*.

Hubert C. JOHNSON Jr., PVT. Serial Number 480926. Enlisted on 10 November 1942. From Illinois. Was a tank crewman according to Ed GAZEL. Listed as KIA on 25 November 1943.

Olaf G. JOHNSON, CPL. Serial Number 447472. Enlisted on 21 August 1942. Was a radio operator and loader in COUNT, 1st Platoon.

Vester A. JONES Jr., SGT. Serial Number 471570. Was a tank commander according to Ed GAZEL.

Eugene "Josie" M. JOSEFSON, PFC. Serial Number 480930. Enlisted on 10 November 1942. Was the driver of CHINA GAL, 1st Platoon. WIA. Evacuated on 25 November to USS *HAYWARD*.

August V. JUST, PVT. Serial Number 480931. Enlisted on 10 November 1942. Was part of the contingent that took part in the medium tanks fording tests at Hawke's Bay, New Zealand. Was a tank crewman. Was killed on Saipan.

Charles "Charlie" T. KAISER, CPL. Serial Number 481788. Was a reconnaissance guide, landed on Red Beach One. WIA according to Ed GAZEL.

Chester S. KAMINSKI, CPL. Serial Number 474481. Was a tank crewman according to Ed GAZEL.

William E. KEITH, PFC. Serial Number 480934. Enlisted on 10 November 1942. Was a tank crewman according to Ed GAZEL.

James R. KELLAR, GY SGT. Serial Number 207269. Enlisted on 29 January 1941. WIA. Evacuated on 21 November to USS *DOYEN*.

Robert "Bob" M. KELLER, SGT. Serial Number 458630. From Illinois. Was part of the contingent that took part in the medium tanks fording tests at Hawke's Bay, New Zealand. Was the original Tank Commander of CECILIA, HQ Section and became the assistant driver when Bale took over for the landing.

Orrell F. KENT, 1st LT. Was the Executive Officer at Tarawa. Was part of the contingent that took part in the medium tanks fording tests at Hawke's Bay, New Zealand. Landed on Red Beach Two and spent most of his time with Colonel Shoup according to Ed BALE. Became a company commander later in the war.

William "Scot" R. KINSMAN, PVT. Serial Number 480938. Enlisted on 10 November 1942. Was a Recon Guide for 2nd Platoon, landed on Red Beach Two.

Benedykt KOWALEWSKI, PVT. Serial Number 483109. Was a mechanic according to Ed GAZEL.

Isaac E. KRAFT, PVT. Serial Number 480944. Enlisted on 10 November 1942. Was a Recon Guide according to Ed GAZEL. Landed on Red Beach One. WIA. Evacuated on 21 November.

Ora D. LAMBERT, PFC. Serial Number 468276. Was a Recon Guide according to Ed GAZEL. Suffered heat exhaustion.

Willard J. LANDRY, SGT. Serial Number 477781. Was a tank crewman according to Ed GAZEL and Joe WOOLUM. Probably a tank commander.

Louis R. LARGEY, 2nd LT. Was the 3rd Platoon Leader. Was the Commanding Officer of CANNONBALL. Won a Silver Star for his actions on Tarawa. Was injured in training on Hawaii after Tarawa and was reassigned to selling War Bonds. Died in 1967.

Merle A. LAWLESS, PVT. Serial Number 480948. Enlisted on 10 November 1942. Remained in Marine Corps and served under Bale in 1st Tank Battalion in Korea, 1954.

Arthur J. LISIECKI, PFC. Serial Number 455266.

Franck W. LLOYD, SGT. Serial Number 270619. Was a tank commander in the 3rd Platoon according to Ed GAZEL.

Leonard A. LOVELL, CPL. Serial Number 481773.

Thomas A. LOWDER Jr., SGT. Serial Number 405961. Mechanic. Was part of the contingent that took part in the medium tanks fording tests at Hawke's Bay, New Zealand. Was in the first landing craft to leave the *ASHLAND*. Landed on Red Beach One.

Earl E. LUNDAHL, CPL. Serial Number 466442. Was a tank crewman according to Ed GAZEL. WIA. Evacuated on 21 November.

Carroll G. LUSCHE, STAFF SGT. Serial Number 278493. From Nebraska. Was in the first landing craft to leave the *ASHLAND*. He was a Company Cook and landed on Red Beach One. MIA, killed in the water on D-Day.

Donald A. MacLEAN, CPL. Serial Number 410482.

John MAEWSKY, US Navy PhM2C. Serial Number 311-71-67. Landed on Red Beach One, in the same LCVP as Ed GAZEL.

Harold C. MAGEHAN, CPL. Serial Number 447526. From Illinois. Was a Recon Guide according to Ed GAZEL and was in the first landing craft to leave the *ASHLAND*. Landed on Red Beach One. MIA, probably killed in the water on D-Day.

John "Johnny" R. MARN, SGT. Serial Number 446855. Was the original tank commander of COLORADO, 3rd Platoon. Was wounded in the evening of 20 November 1943. Was evacuated the next day. He is seen in color film footage walking alongside his tank on D DAY.

Charles "Whitey" E. MARTIN, PFC. Serial Number 490586. Was part of the contingent that took part in the medium tanks fording tests at Hawke's Bay, New Zealand. Was the gunner in CECILIA, HQ Section.

Richard C. MARXEN, PVT. Serial Number 419656. Enlisted on 6 November 1942.

Charles "Charlie" D. MASON, PVT. Serial Number 482677. Was the gunner in CLIPPER, 2nd Platoon. When CLIPPER lost one of her engines, he became a gunner in CONGA to replace Malcolm GARVOCK who was wounded.

Roger A. MASSEY, WARRANT OFFICER. Enlisted on 24 May 1937. Was the Maintenance Chief according to Ed GAZEL and Ed BALE.

Donald J. McCONVILLE, PFC. Serial Number 485202. Was a tank crewman in COUNT, 1st Platoon.

Patrick F. McGRATH, PVT. Serial Number 463712. Was a Recon Guide according to Ed GAZEL. Landed on Red Beach One.

Robert McGRATH, PFC. Serial Number 493997. Was a Recon Guide according to Ed GAZEL. Landed on Red Beach One.

Harrell "Mac" O. McNORTON Jr., CPL. Serial Number 496754. Was the original driver of COLORADO, 3rd Platoon. Was replaced by Howard RUDLOFF on D+1 when Louis LARGEY took over the tank and reorganized the crew.

Alton MERTZ, PVT. Serial Number 419702. Was a Recon Guide according to Ed GAZEL. Landed on Red Beach One. WIA. Evacuated on 21 November to USS *DOYEN*.

Dean T. MILLER, PVT. Serial Number 488621.

Claude E. MOSS Jr., CPL. Serial Number 478539. Was a radio man according to Ed GAZEL.

James W. MULLIGAN, PVT. Serial Number 440093. From New Jersey. Was in the 2nd Platoon, landed on Red Beach Two. KIA by "gun shot wounds in abdomen." His grave was lost, and he is now listed as MIA.

Ralph E. NELSON, Chief Cook. Serial Number 357742. Enlisted on 26 January 1942. Was the chief cook and landed with Ed GAZEL.

Archie W. NEWELL, PVT. Serial Number 394552. From the state of Washington. Was a Recon Guide according to Ed GAZEL, was in the first landing craft to leave the *ASHLAND*. Landed on Red Beach One. MIA, probably killed in the water on D-Day.

Howard M. OAKLEY, SGT. Serial Number 449191. Enlisted on 2 October 1942. Mechanic, landed on Red Beach One.

Clarence W. PALIN, CPL. Serial Number 447282. Enlisted on 1 October 1942. Was a Recon Guide according to Ed GAZEL. Landed on Red Beach One. WIA. Evacuated on 21 November.

Veral F. PARSONS, PVT. Serial Number 463858. Enlisted on 9 November 1942. From Kansas. Landed on Red Beach One with Ed GAZEL. KIA.

John PASTIRCAK Jr., CPL. Serial Number 448316.

Donald "Don" W. PEARSON, PFC. Serial Number 478290. Was the radio operator and loader in CLIPPER, 2nd Platoon. When CLIPPER lost one engine, he replaced Eugene ANDREWS, the tank commander of CONGA(?) on D+1, after ANDREWS was wounded.

Edward M. PETERSON, CPL. Serial Number 482681. Was the gunner in COLORADO, 3rd Platoon. Was badly wounded by grenade fragments during the first night, and replaced on the second day by DUNKEL.

Richard K. PHELPS, PVT. Serial Number 474700.

Russell I. PITTENGER, CPL. Serial Number 492253. Assistant Cook. Was in the Higgins boat with Ed GAZEL. Landed on Red Beach One.

Clifford G. QUINE, PVT. Serial Number 480975. Enlisted on 10 November 1942. Was the assistant driver of CLIPPER, 2nd Platoon.

Montesuma REED, PFC. Serial Number 499429. Enlisted on 10 November 1942. Was a tank crewman according to Ed GAZEL.

George M. REEDY, CPL. Serial Number 474561. Was a tank driver according to Ed GAZEL.

Paul L. RILES, PFC. Serial Number 477905. Was a radio man according to Ed GAZEL.

Wallace W. ROCK, CPL. Serial Number 457492. Was a radio man according to Ed GAZEL.

Earl A. ROGERS Jr., Sgt. Serial Number 411984. Was a radio man according to Ed GAZEL. WIA. Evacuated on 21 November to USS *HARRY LEE*.

Joseph A. ROJAS, CPL. Serial Number 469071. WIA. Evacuated on 21 November.

Howard E. RUDLOFF, PVT. Serial Number 489137. Enlisted on 4 November 1942. Landed on Red Beach Three in an LCVP. Was designated as replacement driver for COLORADO by LARGEY on D+1.

Charles E. RUPEL Jr., SGT. Serial Number 461507. Was an ordnance man according to Ed GAZEL and WOOLUM.

Charles E. SAUDER, PVT. Serial Number 480987. Enlisted on 10 November 1942. Was a tank crewman according Ed GAZEL.

William "Bill" F. SCHWENN, PFC. Serial Number 469341. Radio operator and loader in COLORADO, was wounded at the right hand. Replaced on D+1. Is shown in the film *With The Marines At Tarawa*, saluting the flag on 23 November during the ceremony.

Bruce J. SEWARD, PFC. Serial Number 480993. Enlisted on 10 November 1942. Was a tank crewman.

William I. SHEEDY, 1st LT. From Indiana. Was the 1st Platoon Leader and the tank commander of CHICAGO. Killed when he was outside his tank; he was found on D+2 dead, side by side with Edwin VANCIL. KIA by "gunshot wounds in abdomen."

Cecil L. SHERMAN, SGT. Serial Number 478302.

Michael "Mike" E. SHIVETTS, SGT. Serial Number 426284. Was part of the contingent that took part in the medium tank fording tests at Hawke's Bay, New Zealand. Was a radio operator and loader in CECILIA. Was lightly wounded in the duel with the Type 95 *Ha-Go*, when shrapnel went down the gun tube and came out of the breach.

Robert "Bob" F. SHOOK, SGT. Serial Number 466411. Was the tank commander of CONDOR. Was wounded in the shoulder when he exited his tank. Evacuated on 21 November to USS *ZEILIN*. Died soon after the war.

Richard "Dick" "Red" O. SLOAT, 1st LT. Was the 2nd Platoon Leader, Commanding Officer of COBRA. Was killed on Saipan.

Kenneth L. SMITH, SGT. Serial Number 406125. From Indiana. KIA on 20 November 1943.

Charles A. SOOTER, PLT SGT. Serial Number 375367. 1st Platoon Sergeant. Enlisted on 9 February 1942. Assigned as tank liaison to infantry.

Lyle D. SULLIVAN, US Navy PhM1C. Serial Number 628-04-39. Landed on Red Beach One, was in the same LCVP as Ed GAZEL.

Melvin F. SWANGO, PFC. Serial Number 468394. Was in the same LCVP as GAZEL. Landed on Red Beach One.

Jack TANCIL Jr., PFC. Serial Number 468578. Gunner in CHINA GAL, became loader when BALE took over.

James W. TOBEY, PVT. Serial Number 488633. Was a Reconnaissance Guide. Landed on Red-1.

Charles "Tommy" T. TOCCO, PVT. Serial Number 510203. Was a truck driver at Pendleton. Was a tank crewman on Tarawa according to Ed GAZEL.

Henry G. TRAUERNICHT, PVT. Serial Number 496750. Was the gunner in COBRA, 2nd Platoon.

Jack TRENT, PVT. Serial Number 490633. Was the assistant driver in COBRA, 2nd Platoon. Replaced the driver, Hester WEBB, after he was killed. Was wounded on D+1 when his tank fell into an underwater shell hole ashore Red Beach Two, close to the junction with Red Beach One. Evacuated on 21 November to USS *MIDDLETON*.

George TRINKA, PLT SGT. Serial Number 402113. 3rd Platoon Sgt, in a tank according Woolum and Gazel. Tank Commander of CHARLIE(?). WIA. Evacuated on 21 November.

Seth E. UNDERWOOD, PVT. Serial Number 483808. Was in the LCVP with Ed GAZEL. Landed on Red Beach One. WIA. Evacuated on 21 November to USS *MIDDLETON*.

John URAM, PVT. Serial Number 510182. Was a tank crewman according to Ed GAZEL.

Karl O. URLAND, PVT. Serial Number 460618.

Edwin H. VANCIL, PVT. Serial Number 482673. From the state of Washington. Was reduced from CPL to PFC and from PFC to PVT at Pendleton. Was a Recon Guide and landed on Red Beach One. Was awarded the Silver Star for using himself as a human marker. KIA by "gun shot wounds in abdomen."

John M. VANDEN BAARD, PVT. Serial Number 457506.

Ernest L. VANDENBERG, PVT. Serial Number 463643. Was a Recon Guide according to Ed GAZEL. Landed on Red Beach One.

Elbridge G. WADE, PFC. Serial Number 477861. WIA. Evacuated on 21 November.

Herbert D. WARBLE, PVT. Serial Number 480627. Enlisted on 3 November

1942. Was a tank driver according to Ed GAZEL. A gunner according to WOOLUM.

Hester S. WEBB, CPL. Serial Number 498191. From Michigan. Was the driver of COBRA, 2nd Platoon. Was killed by "gunshot wounds in neck" when his tank was stationed close to a taxi strip on D-Day evening. Was replaced on D+1 by Jack TRENT. His grave was lost and he is now reported as MIA.

Donald D. WILLEY, PVT. Serial Number 426374.

Jimmie "Willy" WILLIAMS, PFC. Serial Number 306119. Was a tank crewman in CHICAGO(?). Was the company Field Music (bugler). Was the only man in the company who had seen action before Tarawa, as a bugler on the aircraft carrier HORNET. WILLIAMS was picked up by a destroyer, which reportedly was in turn sunk. "He got sunk twice in one day." Was the bugler for the flag raising ceremony on the afternoon of D+3.

Joe D. WOOLUM, PVT. Serial Number 477082. Was the gunner in CONDOR, 3rd Platoon. Was wounded when he tried to go back to the Marines lines after his tank was disabled. Evacuated on 21 November to USS *ZEILIN*.

Earl J. ZBINDEN, PVT. Serial Number 461872. Was a member of COUNT's tank crew. WIA. Evacuated on 25 November to USS *HAYWARD*.

Asard ZEIBAK, PFC. Serial Number 490482. Was the original assistant driver on CECILIA.

Kay A. ZIRKER, SGT. Serial Number 283723. NCO in charge of the Recon Guides. Landed on Red Beach One. WIA.

HISTORICAL RESEARCH AND
PHOTOGRAPHIC ANALYSIS

For well over half a century both official and popular historians writing about the battle concentrated on different aspects. Popular histories tended to emphasize the infantry battle. Professional military historians were more interested in command relationships and the more arcane but no less significant failures in areas like doctrine and ship-to-shore logistics (the latter a continuing problem for the Marine Corps throughout the war).

The contributions of the two surviving, functional medium tanks were fully acknowledged in period assessments of the battle, and led directly to the reorganization of the divisional light tank battalions as medium tank battalions as quickly as sufficient tanks could be procured. The great strength of the new medium tank was the 75mm cannon. The half-tracked SPM—originally intended as a tank-destroyer—had an adequate 75mm cannon, but its armor was too thin. The SPMs were reassigned to the infantry regiments as mobile artillery pieces.

Within six months the light tanks were relegated to secondary roles; older M3 series light tanks were converted to Satan flamethrower tanks, while newer M5 series light tanks still in the procurement pipeline were used as escorts for the Satans. In less than a year the light tanks disappeared entirely from front-line service.

Leaders on both sides were fully aware of the contributions of the tanks. The official Marine Corps history of the Pacific War stated—rather poetically—that

Next to his rifle, the infantryman cherished the tank, which like a lumbering elephant could either strike terror into a foe or be a gentle servant to a friend. On the open field, hospital corpsmen, moving behind a tank, could get to the wounded and safely bring them off. In attack, the Marine tank-infantry team felt itself unbeatable, and the Saipan experience added confidence. The medium tank would precede the riflemen, who, in turn, protected the tank from Japanese grenades. Each half of the team needed the other.

Japanese Lieutenant General Mitsuru Ushijima, commander of the 32nd Army on Okinawa, was considerably more succinct: "The enemy's power lies in its tanks."[233]

Yet somehow in the post-war era the role of the tanks largely disappeared from popular military histories of the Pacific War; the senior author has at times been told in no uncertain terms that tanks were not used in the Pacific War because of the "jungles." More inexplicable, even professional military historians began to downplay the role of the tanks.

In more recent years there have been more efforts to resurrect and clarify the role of the tanks, notably Ken Estes's *Marines Under Armor* and Bob Neiman and Ken Estes's *Tanks On The Beaches,* but many misconceptions and myths remain common currency. The crucial role of the medium tanks on Tarawa has received some attention in recent years, but even relatively recent general histories of the battle mention the tanks only in passing.

Other works perpetuate or even create myths, such as attributing the main gun damaged by the Japanese tank to CHINA GAL. Perhaps the most ludicrous has CHINA GAL in turn ramming the Japanese tank, destroying it by spearing the enemy's turret with her damaged gun. The response of experienced tankers to this fanciful tale is best described as "incredulity." This unique achievement would be physically impossible, since the M4A2s main gun did not overhang the front of the tank's hull; the American tank would have had to move *sideways* to accomplish such a feat!

One problem that has hampered prior research is simply identifying the individual tanks. In later stages of the war, Marine Corps tanks carried distinctive tactical identification markings that allow the researcher to identify individual tanks and even units. After mid-1944, most tank units (with the exception of the 3rd Tank Battalion) used a simple system of a letter and two numbers.

The tactical markings used by Charlie Company at Tarawa were only the name selected by the crew. The tanks were assigned tactical numbers, but they were not displayed on the exterior and the names of the tanks in each platoon were not recorded. The surviving crewmen typically remembered the name of their own tank, and at best the names of a few other tanks in their platoon.

This lack of actual information has led to an enormous amount of speculation with regard to the organization of the tank company. Despite company commander Ed Bale's best efforts, numerous historians have garbled the story of the tanks, confusing one with another and placing tanks from a specific platoon on an entirely different part of the battlefield.

Some tanks can be confidently assigned to platoons based on where they were lost or disabled (three tanks from Third Platoon, their names clearly visible in photos, were destroyed within a small area).

In the final analysis we were able to associate tank names (many identified by prior researchers including Proulx, Vickers, and Jonathan Stevens) with specific platoons. A nagging question was the uncertainty as to one name, and one name was completely unknown. CHEROKEE had been reported as the name of one tank by several veterans (and by the process of elimination assigned to First Platoon), but we were never able to find definitive documentation. Fortunately, questionnaires compiled by John Oberg included one response from a crewman in this mystery tank—actually named COUNT. The tank name missing from the list was eventually identified thanks to photos supplied by Ed Gazel and a photograph found at NARA II in July 2013. The missing name was CHERRY.

An additional very fruitful line of research conducted over the past decade has been efforts to trace the course of individual tanks and to reconstruct their fates. In the heat of battle *no one* keeps a detailed track of their movements. In the aftermath of the battle and the rush to evacuate the spent troops and salvaged weapons from the island, no records were kept of the precise wreck sites. Recovery of functional and semi-functional tanks was largely conducted by the crews and the surviving members of the maintenance section. The surviving officers were absorbed by the details of locating survivors scattered among hospitals and evacuation ships, accounting for the dead and missing, compiling after-action reports, assessment of the efficacy of friendly and enemy weapons, and innumerable other administrative labors. Mapping wreck sites was simply not a priority task.

There are published examples of the detailed reconstruction of battles and tank loss sites, most notably the analysis of the final wreck or abandonment sites of the Churchill tanks, Dingo scout cars and other vehicles of the Canadian Calgary Regiment lost in the disastrous Dieppe Raid (Operation RUTTER, 14 August 1942).[234]

To our knowledge, Dino Brugioni, a retired senior photo analyst with the Central Intelligence Agency, conducted the first detailed analysis of aerial photographs taken by an observation aircraft during the course of the battle. His work was general in nature, pointing out details of Japanese defensive works, ships, LVTs, tanks, and even individual men visible in the photos.[235]

George Proulx, with a military background involving photo analysis, conducted a long-term effort to identify tanks in the aerial photos of Tarawa. In 2011, the senior author saw a presentation on the fates of the various medium tanks by Major David Vickers (USMC ret.). His work was based primarily upon analysis of the numerous photos taken by photographers on the ground. Dave later shared the preliminary results of his work with us, including a large map showing his interpretation of the final positions of wrecked or disabled tanks.

We have chosen to utilize primarily aerial photos taken during and immediately after the battle (20–24 November 1943), in conjunction with both photos taken at ground level, published and unpublished memoirs, and our own interviews with surviving Marines to reconstruct not only the locations of the wrecked tanks, but their paths during the course of battle.

The photos used are low altitude aerial obliques taken from naval aircraft that overflew the island during and immediately after the battle. The photo sorties were flown as "real time" reconnaissance missions by naval aircraft to assess the course of the battle. The available aerial photo sets consist primarily of those preserved at the Marine Corps Historical Division at Quantico Virginia, and in the National Archives II in College Park Maryland.

Some, such as those taken by an aircraft from the USS *Essex* on 24 November, were taken after many of the vehicle recovery operations were completed. There are two primary useful photo sets. The first was taken by an observation aircraft from the fleet carrier USS *Essex* on the afternoon of D-Day. This set is particularly useful because the photos are time-stamped, with a small clock-face exposed with the film that provides a precise local time for each photo. Most photos were taken from relatively high altitudes, but show the positions of tanks on the beaches and in the waters of the lagoon in the early hours of the landing.

Perhaps the most useful photo set is from a sortie flown by an OS-2U "Kingfisher" observation aircraft from the escort carrier USS *Chenango*. This set of photos was taken on the afternoon of 22 November (D+2). With the aircraft flying at recorded altitudes as low as one-hundred feet (30m), the camera captured fairly detailed images of many of the tanks.

As opposed to the more familiar vertical air photos, these aerial obliques are photos taken by an observer/cameraman leaning over the cockpit side of an aircraft. The photos were taken with hand-held cameras facing to the sides of the aircraft at various angles to the ground as the aircraft climbed, dove, turned, and banked. These missions were also typically flown in a very erratic pattern, with varying altitudes and flight paths, requiring the interpreter to first map out the sequence and viewing angles of the individual photos.

In the *Chenango* photo set, the positions of individual wrecked tanks could be determined with some confidence by correlating the tanks in the aerial photos with unique features that identify specific tanks in ground photos. For example, burned-out CANNONBALL tilted onto its side, and wrecked COMMANDO, sitting near two prominent and unusual trees with its turret traversed to the right at ninety degrees, are easily identifiable.

Only a select few of the photographs used are reproduced in this volume. Additional photos may be found at www.tanksontarawa.com, tarawa ontheweb.org, and occasionally on various other websites. Unfortunately most are reproduced at low resolution, typical of websites because of digital storage limitations.

The *Chenango* photos are particularly useful because they captured not only the positions of active and wrecked tanks at a specific moment in time (only two—perhaps three—tanks were operational at the time), but in some cases indications of the movements of the tanks through time. The medium tanks—the only heavy vehicles moving about on the island during most of the fighting—left distinctive tracks in the deep, soft sand and even on the packed sand surfaces of the airfield. This allows the photo interpreter to identify egress points through the seawall and off the beach, and sometimes to track the twists and turns as the tanks took evasive action to avoid enemy fire. The *Chenango* images are least useful by D+2, when the subsequent movement of light tanks and possibly supply amtracs obscured the medium tank tracks, particularly on the western (GREEN Beach) end of the island.

The one significant site we were not successful in locating was the position of the encounter of CECILIA and COMMANDO with the Japanese tank. That part of the island was heavily covered in vegetation, fallen trees, and wrecked enemy positions. The small Type 95 tank was apparently blown apart so that its wreckage was not identifiable amid the other debris.

Our interpretation of the tank names, platoon affiliations, paths, and actions differs significantly from previous interpretations, and we accept full responsibility for any potential errors.

NOTES

CHAPTER ONE

1 Shaw *et al, Central Pacific Drive*, p. 49.
2 For a brief history of the design see http://en.wikipedia.org/wiki/Dock_landing_ ship
3 Shaw *et al, Central Pacific Drive*, p. 48.

CHAPTER TWO

4 Millett, *Semper Fidelis, The History of the United States Marine Corps*, p. 287–290.
5 RD 3391 (32) Tank Battalion (Light) Table D80; RD 3391 (117) Special Troops Marine Division, Table E-99 (Tank Battalion Table E-80 missing from files).
6 Estes, *Marines Under Armor*, p. 39.
7 Ibid, p. 57.
8 Ibid, p. 30, 46, 54.
9 Neiman and Estes, *Tanks On The Beaches*, p. 57.
10 Estes, *Marines Under Armor*, p. 58, 62. Estes provides a lengthy summary of the new battalion's travails.
11 Bale interview by Gilbert and Cansiere, June 2013.
12 Sloat biographical notes from Zeiger, *Dick Sloat, American Hero*.
13 All Mason quotes and information are from Rhay and Collins, *Charles D. Mason Collection*.
14 http://tarawaontheweb.org/kinsman.htm
15 Gilbert, *Marine Tank Battles In The Pacific*, p. 81. Swango was almost certainly talking about the very similar four-wheeled White M3A1 Scout Car. The Corps used a few halftracks as radio vehicles, but none in the reconnaissance role.
16 Estes, *Marines Under Armor*, p. 54–56.
17 Bryk, *Edward Bale oral history interview*, p. 4. The original Defense Battalions were intended for coastal defense of naval bases. The unsuccessful defense of Wake Island made apparent the need for a maneuver element, so a tank platoon and a rifle company were added to make Composite Battalions. There were eighteen all-white defense battalions, and the 51st and 52nd Composite Defense Battalions with black enlisted personnel. Most were later converted to Anti-aircraft Artillery Battalions.
18 Powers, *Replacement of tank personnel in combat, 1 April 1943*; Schmidt, *Replacement personnel for tanks, May 1 1943*; Powers, *Replacement of tank personnel in combat, 18 June 1943*.
19 Powers, *Readiness report, 1st Corps Medium Tank Battalion, June 2 1943*; Powers,

Readiness report, 1st Corps Medium Tank Battalion, July 1 1943.

20 In modern tank units the forward air controller or artillery forward observer typically doubles as a loader. In Operation Desert Storm, Lieutenant Colonel Buster Diggs led the 3rd Tank Battalion from the loader's position of his command tank; Gilbert, *Marine Corps Tank Battles In The Middle East*, p. 42.

21 Bale, interview with Romain Cansiere and Ed Gilbert, June 2013.

22 E-mail Bale to Cansiere, 24 December 2013.

23 For a full account of the investigation see Estes, *Marines Under Armor*, p. 56–64; for an account of the episode prior to the war with Iraq see Gilbert, *Marine Corps Tank Battles In The Middle East*.

24 http://tarawaontheweb.org/kinsman.htm. The phenomenon of women joining their husbands was common. The mother of one of the authors (Gilbert) traveled from Alabama to join her husband, the author's father, in Colorado; the mother of Gilbert's wife traveled from Alabama to join her fiancé in Kentucky, where they were married.

25 The SS *John McLean* was an ED2 class Liberty ship, designed primarily to carry heavy cargo, with limited troop accommodation.

26 http://tarawaontheweb.org/kinsman.htm

27 Letter from Gazel to Cansiere, 11 February 2014.

28 http://www.pacificwrecks.com/provinces/newcaledonia_noumea_harbor.html

29 *I Corps Medium Tank Battalion War Diary, 4 October 1943.*

30 Ibid.

31 http://usstryon.wordpress.com/2012/06/; http://iancoombe.tripod.com/id50. html

32 Bale, *WW II Tank Leadership*, unpublished manuscript.

33 Bale e-mail to Ken Estes, 22 May 1999. Bale clarified to the authors that two tanks were involved in the fording test.

34 *I Corps Medium Tank Battalion War Diary*, 3 November 1943.

35 See http://en.wikipedia.org/wiki/USS_Doyen_(APA-1), and http://en.wikipedia. org/wiki/USS_Zeilin_(APA-3)

36 Bale e-mail to Ken Estes, 21 May 1999.

37 *I Corps Medium Tank Battalion War Diary*, 3 November 1943.

38 http://www.hullnumber.com/LSD-1

39 *I Corps Medium Tank Battalion War Diary*, 3 November 1943.

40 Bryk, *Edward Bale oral history interview*, p. 4.

41 Bale e-mail to Ken Estes, 22 May 1999.

42 Gilbert, *Marine Tank Battles In The Pacific*, p. 83.

CHAPTER THREE

43 Estes, *Marines Under Armor*, p. 54–56.

44 Hunnicutt, *Sherman: A History of the American Medium Tank*, p. 148–149.

45 The technical manual for the M4A2 is available on the website www.tanksontarawa.com

46 Gilbert, *Marine Tank Battles In The Pacific*, p. 313.

47 Gilbert, *Marine Tank Battles In The Pacific*, recorded numerous veterans' descriptions of the harsh conditions of life inside a tank in the Pacific Theater.

48 Estes, *Marines Under Armor*, p. 60.

49 *Marine Corps Table of Organization E-100 RD3391*, 15 April 1943. This is the T/O and T/E for the division; subordinate units are listed in subsidiary tables.

50 Shaw et al, *Central Pacific Drive*, p. 42.

51 Gilbert, *Marine Tank Battles In The Pacific*, p. 28.

52 The authors have not been able to locate period photos of the installation in a tank. For an idea of the size and complexity as installed in an aircraft, see photos in Hanz, *The B-17: Backbone of the AAF.*

53 Estes, *Marines Under Armor*, p. 64–65.

54 Gilbert, *Marine Tank Battles In The Pacific*, p. 57, 95–96.

55 For an extensive analysis of the Marine Corps' struggle to adopt suitable tanks, see Estes, *Marines Under Armor*, p. 9–42.

56 Traceability and property accountability left a great deal to be desired. In 1962–63, "The then Commandant of the Marine Corps, General Shoup . . . ask me if I [Bale] could find those tanks" to put them on display in a museum. Bale made the attempt, but to track the tanks, "We didn't have anything [serial numbers]." The search was fruitless and Bale concluded that "They probably were dumped into the water, got dumped somewhere in the ocean or cut up for scrap."

CHAPTER FOUR

57 More detailed descriptions of the uniforms can be found in Alberti and Pradier, *Uniformes et Equipement du Corps des Marines 1941–1945*; Alberti and Pradier, *USMC Uniforms and Equipment 1941–1945*; and Gilbert, *US Marine Corps Raider, 1942–1943*.

58 An alloy of 67% nickel, 30% copper and 3% iron, named for the president of the Canadian Copper Company. The bronze-colored metal resisted corrosion in graves.

59 Officer's identity discs did not have the serial number, as officers were not assigned identity numbers until after the Tarawa operation. See Chapter 11. Bale, interview with Gilbert and Cansiere, July 2013.

60 http://tarawaontheweb.org/kinsman.htm

61 Through general usage Ka-Bar has grown to be a generic term, while KA-BAR is a registered trademark of Union Cutlery.

CHAPTER FIVE

62 Second Marine Division, *Report of Galvanic Operation—LONGSUIT*, Preliminary Intelligence Report of Tarawa Operation, p. 1–16, 20 (interrogation of Shizuo Suzuki), 22 (interrogation of Zaisan Toyoyama, Korean laborer). This document provides a detailed breakdown of personnel, armaments, and organization of the defenders.

63 Joint Intelligence Center, Pacific Ocean Area, *JICPOA Translation Item #3616-A, B, C, D*. The statement "It appears . . . actual strength" is from Intelligence Section, 2nd Marine Division, *Supplement to the 'Study of the Japanese Defense of Betio Island (Tarawa Atoll)' Part I, Fortifications and Weapons*. This interpretation can be found at http://forum.axishistory.com/viewtopic.php?f=65&t=208991. We have not examined the original document.

64 Attachment to *3rd Base Force* from Oonuki statement at http://www.war44.com/war-pacific/3019-tadao-onuki-tanker-tarawa.html. Some other sources have placed the tank platoon with the *7th SNLF*. Tank conversion to recovery vehicle comment from various Bale interviews with Gilbert and Cansiere. Reference to the *Ri-Ki* from Akira Takizawa e-mail to Cansiere, 21 April 2014; see also http://www3.plala.or.jp/takihome/ri-ki.htm

65 Shaw *et al*, *Central Pacific Drive*, p. 39.

66 For comparison see www3.plala.or.jp/takihome/artillery.htm

67 See for example Gilbert, *Marine Tank Battles In The Pacific*, p. 41.

68 Wright, *A Hell Of A Way To Die*, p. 117–119.

69 Shaw *et al*, *Central Pacific Drive*, p. 48.

70 Isely and Crowl, *The U.S. Marines and Amphibious War*, p. 192–193.

71 Shaw *et al*, *Central Pacific Drive*, p. 38.

72 Ibid, p. 37.

73 For a summary of the failures of naval bombardment and the struggle to develop an amphibious tank capability, see Gilbert, *Marine Tank Battles In The Pacific*, p. 17–23.

74 Shaw *et al*, *Central Pacific Drive*, p. 39.

75 Ibid, p. 39.

CHAPTER SIX

76 All timing and other information on operations of the Transport Groups unless otherwise noted are from *Report of the Commander Transport Group to Commander Southern Attack Force, 1 December 1943*. There are temporal discrepancies between various sources, as pointed out in Shaw et al, *Central Pacific Drive*, p. 53.

77 Bale–John Oberg questionnaire, 7 November 2010; McNorton–John Oberg questionnaire, 14 December 2010; Johnson–John Oberg questionnaire, (day not specified) March 2011; Woolum–John Oberg questionnaire, 23 January 2011.

78 Commanding General Second Marine Division (Staff), *Recommendations Based on Tarawa Operation, Number 4—Tanks*, p.1.

79 Bale–John Oberg questionnaire, 7 November 2010; Quine–John Oberg questionnaire, 22 February 2011; Shivetts–John Oberg questionnaire, 8 February 2011.

80 The carefully planned operational schedule was laid out in the three-page document *Time Schedule Longsuit Operation*. All references to delays are in reference to the times set forth in this schedule.

81 Dunkel–John Oberg questionnaire, 9 November 2010; Shivetts–John Oberg questionnaire, 8 February 2011.

82 Oonuki was one of only nineteen Japanese prisoners taken on Tarawa. His experiences have been recounted in several books, and the most readily available version is at http://www.war44.com/war-pacific/3019-tadao-onuki-tanker-tarawa.html. We have not obtained the primary documents since it is not directly germane to this study, but have given this translation preference. Hoyt in *Storm Over The Gilberts*, has Oonuki sighting American amtracs and tanks on Red Beach -2 or -3, which does not appear in any other recounting. In addition Hoyt has Oonuki seeing men wading ashore from amtracs stopped at the edge of the reef as opposed to grounded boats. Hoyt's version is incompatible with Russ's version in *Tarawa: Line of Departure*. It should be noted that Oonuki's account, written much later, is very confused, placing the initial assault on 21 November, followed by a week of fighting. Oonuki was badly burned, and he and his comrades spent three weeks evading capture under horrific conditions. This accounts for his understandable confusion, but not for the varying interpretations of his memoir.

83 Shaw et al, *Central Pacific Drive*, p. 55.

84 Ibid, p. 59.

85 See Gilbert, *Marine Tank Battles In The Pacific*, p. 85–86.

86 Shoup, *Memorandum for G-3, 5th PHIBCORPS, 19 December 1943*, p. 2.

87 Bale e-mail to Ken Estes, 21 May 1999.

88 Gilbert, *Marine Tank Battles In The Pacific*, p. 86–87.

89 Bryk, *Edward Bale oral history interview*, p.4–5.

90 Zirker is not listed as a casualty. The ship's log of the *Ashland* says the LCP(R) carrying the Recon Guides returned at 1100 with one casualty aboard.

91 Unless otherwise noted Swango's comments are from an interview conducted by Gilbert, 1999. This comment from Wright, *A Hell of a Way to Die*, p. 66.

92 Wright, *A Hell of a Way to Die*, p. 67.

93 Gilbert, *Marine Tank Battles In The Pacific*, p. 88; Swango may have overestimated casualties in the immediate area as the roster does not list such a large number of casualties.

94 Silver Star citation, PVT Edwin H. Vancil.

95 Navy Cross citation, PVT James W. Tobey.

96 Gazel recalled Johnson as a tank crewman; mechanics sometimes filled a dual role, to be immediately available if a tank was damaged.

97 This and the following Kinsman passages from http://tarawaontheweb.org/kinsman.htm

98 For a pre-sinking photo of the *Saidu maru*, see http://www.wrecksite.eu/wreck.aspx?211393; for identification and discussion of the story of the Nimanoa, see shttp://disc.yourwebapps.com/discussion.cgi?disc=149620;article=12531;title=TarawaTalk

99 Bale e-mail to Ken Estes, 3 May 1999.

100 Gilbert, *Marine Tank Battles In The Pacific*, p. 89.

101 Wright, *A Hell of a Way to Die*, p. 71–72.

102 Commanding General Second Marine Division (Staff), *Recommendations Based*

on *Tarawa Operation, Number 4—Tanks*, p. 6.

103 Johnson–John Oberg questionnaire, (day not specified) March 2011.

104 Shivetts–John Oberg questionnaire, 8 February 2011.

105 Gilbert, *Marine Tank Battles In The Pacific*, p. 86.

106 Wright, *A Hell of a Way to Die*, p. 71. Intelligence maps do not show an anti-tank ditch here; it may have simply been a shelter or communications trench in the loose sand.

107 See for example Alexander, *Across The Reef*, p. 19.

108 Second Marine Division, *Report of Galvanic Operation—LONGSUIT*, Enclosure C, p. 9–11; Alexander, *Storm Landings,* p. 54.

109 Lt. Col. E.F. Carlson, USMCR, *Report of observations on Galvanic operation*, 27 December 1943, Enclosure G.

110 Johnson Richard, *Crews in 2 tanks kill 600 Japs on Tarawa*, Buffalo Courier Express, 5 December 1943.

111 Johnson–John Oberg questionnaire, (day not specified) March 2011.

112 http://www.tarawaontheweb.org/irvinejohn.htm

113 Marn–John Oberg questionnaire, 2 December 2010.

114 Isely and Crowl, *The U.S. Marines and Amphibious War*, p. 238.

CHAPTER SEVEN

115 Gilbert, *Marine Tank Battles in the Pacific*, p. 90.

116 Shaffer, *Relates Battle of Tarawa*.

117 Ibid.

118 Bryk, *Edward Bale oral history interview*, p. 6.

119 Worth McCoy's *Report of battalion commanders*, 22 December 1943 stated that both the Japanese Type 95 and CECILIA fired simultaneously, and that the round fired by CECILIA actually knocked out the *Ha-Go*. McCoy's comment was based on second-hand information, and we give more credibility to Bale's account.

120 Shivetts estimate of the time from John Oberg questionnaire, 8 February 2011.

121 Shaffer, *Relates Battle of Tarawa;* his 2nd Tank Battalion Action Report also stated that CECILIA's turret traverse mechanism was knocked out by "shell fire, known to be anti-boat gun."

122 Navy Cross citation, PVT James W. Tobey.

123 Bryk, *Edward Bale oral history interview*, p. 6.

124 There is considerable disagreement over the ultimate fate of CECILIA. Shivetts remembered that CECILIA survived the battle but Bale recalled that he waded out to sunken CECILIA to retrieve his dispatch case containing an Episcopal prayer book and a pint of Scotch. The official reports listed three tanks in operable condition after the battle, and photos show these to be COLORADO, CHINA GAL, and salvaged CHICAGO. Post-battle still photos and movie film depict efforts to salvage a tank with a damaged cannon muzzle partially buried in the sand off RED-1. The immediate post-battle account by Marine Corps

correspondent Samuel Shaffer also stated that CECILIA "... ran into a hole and was out of action for good." One other issue regarding the tanks from the Headquarters Section remains unresolved. Ground photos show the two tanks' names obscured with white paint. We first thought it was made by a censor on the photograph's negative. However, a close look at the over-painted name on CECILIA shows that it was actually applied onto the vehicle prior to the landing. CECILIA, while crossing the reef, sustained a hit on the right sponson. When the shell exploded the resulting "splash" covered a wide part of the right-front sponson armor plate and removed some paint from the name's over-coating. We thought that perhaps it was an unofficial marking made just before the landing for other tank crew to quickly identify HQ Section tanks. However, neither Shivetts nor Bale recalls such a practice.

125 Shaffer, *Relates Battle of Tarawa.*

126 Ryan, *Report of Battalion Commanders,* 22 December 1943, p. 1.

127 Ibid; COMMANDO catches fire from Commanding General Second Marine Division (Staff), *Recommendations Based on Tarawa Operation, Number 4— Tanks,* p. 3. Worth McCoy stated in his post battle report that "We did not lose a man inside the tanks."

128 Wright, *A Hell of a Way to Die,* p. 140.

129 Type 94 penetration data from McLean, *Japanese Tanks, Tactics & Antitank Weapons,* p. 135. See also comparison of the two guns at www3.plala.or.jp/tak-ihome/artillery.htm, which has more informed data on these weapons. McCoy, *Report of Battalion Commanders,* p. 1.

130 Commanding General Second Marine Division (Staff), *Recommendations Based on Tarawa Operation, Number 4—Tanks,* p. 3, 6; this tank was likely CONGA, since it appears back in action the next day.

131 Rhay and Collins, *Charles D. Mason Collection.* There are some contradictory details in Mason's interview, such as his statement that he was a crewman in CECILIA which was in the Headquarters Section on RED-1. Mason thought that they were struck by multiple eight-inch shell near the seawall; the large eight-inch guns were not positioned to fire into that zone and had already been disabled by the naval bombardment. Though it is a valuable interview, we have elected to use Mason's account judiciously, and attempted to corroborate his account with details from his surviving comrades. It is more likely that CLIPPER was disabled by a mine as recounted by Clifford Quine.

132 Problems with operating tank on one engine from Yvan Choley, personal comunication to Cansiere.

133 Brown, 2d *Tanks Still In High Demand,* p. 11.

134 Commanding General Second Marine Division (Staff), *Recommendations Based on Tarawa Operation, Number 4—Tanks,* p.3.

135 This comment by Woolum–John Oberg questionnaire, 23 January 2011.

136 Gilbert, *Marine Tank Battles In The Pacific,* see photo following p. 121.

137 Woolum—John Oberg questionnaires, 23 January 2011; see a list of C Company

personnel and their fates at http://www.tanksontarawa.com/roster-of-c-companys-personnel.html
138 Woolum–John Oberg questionnaire, 12 December 2010; Marn–John Oberg questionnaire, 2 December 2010.
139 Johnson, *600 Japanese Fall To Marine Tanks;* Largey comment from Johnson, *Crews in 2 tanks kill 600 Japs on Tarawa.*
140 Dodson Smith interview by Gilbert, 4 September 2014.
141 http://www.tarawaontheweb.org/weap22.htm
142 Damage report for USS *Independence* at http://www.history.navy.mil/library/online/wardamagereportno52.htm
143 Wright, *A Hell of a Way to Die*, p. 72.
144 Commanding General Second Marine Division (Staff), *Recommendations Based on Tarawa Operation, Number 4—Tanks*, p. 3. CHINA GAL's malfunctioning cannon from Shoup, *Memorandum for G-3, 5th PHIBCORPS, 19 December 1943*, p. 1; in context Shoup seems to be referring to a medium tank.
145 Bryk, *Edward Bale oral history interview*, p. .6–7.
146 Zurlinden, *The Attack on Tarawa*, p. 10.
147 http://tarawaontheweb.org/kinsman.htm
148 Gilbert, *Marine Tank Battles In The Pacific*, p. 93; Shaffer, *Relates Battle of Tarawa;* Shaw et al, *Central Pacific Drive*, Map III.
149 Bryk, *Edward Bale oral history interview*, p. 7.
150 Dunkel–John Oberg questionnaire, 9 November 2010.
151 Largey Silver Star citation.
152 Crotts Navy Cross citation, Spot Award 28 January 1948.
153 Wright, *A Hell of a Way to Die*, p. 79.

CHAPTER EIGHT
154 Bryk, *Edward Bale oral history interview*, p. 7.
155 Ryan reported that for at least part of the day he was supported by two functional medium tanks but in the 22 December 1943 reports of battalion commanders, Ryan reported only one tank in action on D+1; see Shaw et al, *Central Pacific Drive*, p. 75–76.
156 Bryk, *Edward Bale oral history interview*, p. 7; also Bale *Willy K's book and Two Tanks.*
157 Ed Bale interview with Gilbert and Cansiere, 31 July 2013.
158 See Gilbert, *Marine Tank Battles In The Pacific*, p. 94.
159 Second Marine Division, *Report of Galvanic Operation—LONGSUIT*, Enclosure B, p. 3; Wright, *A Hell of a Way to Die*, p. 92; Gilbert, *Marine Tank Battles In The Pacific*, p. 95; Wright, *A Hell Of A Way To Die*, p. 134; Smith quote from Shaw et al, *Central Pacific Drive*, p. 76.
160 Dunkel–John Oberg questionnaire, 9 November 2010.
161 Warth, *My Buddies Who Didn't Make It, They're The Heroes.*
162 Commanding General Second Marine Division (Staff), *Recommendations Based*

on Tarawa Operation, Number 4—Tanks, p. 5.

163 Shoup, *Memorandum for G-3, 5th PHIBCORPS, 19 December 1943,* p. 3.

164 Wright, *A Hell of a Way to Die,* p. 91.

165 See also Gilbert, *Marine Tank Battles In The Pacific,* p. 95–96.

166 Sherrod, *Tarawa: The Second Day.*

167 Second Marine Division, *Report of Galvanic Operation—LONGSUIT,* Enclosure B, p. 3; Gilbert, *Marine Tank Battles In The Pacific,* p. 96–98.

168 Bryk, *Edward Bale oral history interview,* p. 8.

CHAPTER NINE

169 Jones, *Report of Operations, Galvanic,* 6 December 1943, p. 2.

170 Bale, *Willy K's book and Two tanks.*

171 http://tarawaontheweb.org/gladson.htm

172 http://www.tarawaontheweb.org/browner.htm

173 Brown, *2d Tanks Still In High Demand,* p. 11.

174 Trey and Bale conversation, Tarawa Talk Forum, 19 December 2007. http://disc.yourwebapps.com/discussion.cgi?disc=149620;article=13207;title=TarawaTalk;pagemark=450

175 Shaw et al, *Central Pacific Drive,* p. 81–83; interview with McMillian in Gilbert, *Marine Tank Battles In The Pacific,* p. 98–99.

176 Gilbert, *Marine Tank Battles In The Pacific,* p. 99.

177 Each rifle regiment had two of these vehicles in the Weapons Company, with six more in the Special Troops anti-tank unit; Division Tables of Organization E-10 and E-99.

178 Alexander, *Across the Reef,* p 37-38.

179 Observation report by Lt. Col. C.D. Roberts, USMCR, attached to LT 2/8, 7 January 1944.

180 *Charleston Daily Mail,* Sunday, December 5, 1943, p. 6. http://newspaperarchive.com/us/west-virginia/charleston/charleston-daily-mail/1943/12-05/page-6

181 Jones, Reports of Battalion Commanders, 19 December 1943, p. 53.

182 Bale conversation with Gilbert, 11 November 2014.

183 Alexander, *Utmost Savgery,* p. 41.

184 Second Marine Division, *Report of Galvanic Operation—LONGSUIT,* Enclosure B, p. 4.

185 Johnson–John Oberg questionnaire, (day not specified) March 2011; Silver Star citation, PVT Edwin H. Vancil.

186 Shaw et al, *Central Pacific Drive,* p. 87–89.

187 Bryk, *Edward Bale oral history interview,* p. 8.

CHAPTER TEN

188 Gilbert, *Marine Tank Battles In The Pacific,* p. 103.

189 Wright, *A Hell Of A Way To Die,* p. 109–110.

190 Gilbert, *Marine Tank Battles In The Pacific*, p. 104.

191 Russ, *Line of Departure: Tarawa*, p. 171.

192 Wikipedia, *USS Liscome Bay (CVE-56)*.

193 McCoy, *Unit Report 2nd Tank Battalion, 26 November 1943*.

CHAPTER ELEVEN

194 Bale conversation with Gilbert, 11 November 2014.

195 Wright, *A Hell of a Way to Die*, p. 111.

196 Report of Japanese recovery vehicle from various conversations of Bale with Cansiere and Gilbert.

197 Bale e-mail to Ken Estes, 2 June 1999.

198 Bale, *China Gal Photo*, Friday Mar 12, 2010, http://disc.yourwebapps.com/discussion.cgi?id=149620;article=13787

199 Bale, various conversations with Gilbert. An account is also given in http://www.ibiblio.org/hyperwar/USMC/USMC-M-Tarawa/USMC-M-Tarawa-5.html

200 Stewart, *Unit Report 2nd Tank Battalion, 27 November 1943;* Stewart, *Unit Report 2nd Tank Battalion, 28 November 1943*.

201 USS *Ashland* ship's log, period 27 November–10 December 1943.

202 Bale has consistently maintained that the remaining tank is CECILIA. Organizations conducting MIA research on the island state that the tank is located off the extreme right of Red-2. This would correspond to the final loss position of COBRA. Also, a photo taken decades after the battle but before severe corrosion, show the tank's gun tube as intact

203 Shivetts–John Oberg questionnaire, 8 February 2011.

204 USS *Ashland* ship's log, period 27 November–10 December 1943.

205 Bale, conversation with Gilbert, July 2014.

206 Reed, James C., *Reports of Battalion Commander, Executive Officer G/2/2, 22 December 1943*.

207 The 2nd Tank Battalion Executive Officer, Major C. Worth McCoy, had assumed command after Lt. Col. Alexander B. Swenceski was severely wounded on 20 November. Cook had been one of the first Marine Corps tank officers, and as a major the Tank Officer of the Second Marine Brigade; Ken Estes, personal communication.

208 McCoy, *Results of inspection of six medium tanks used in Tarawa operation, 6 January 1944*.

209 Bryk, *Edward Bale oral history interview*, p.10–11.

210 McCoy, *Report of Battalion Commanders, Second Tank Battalion, 22 December 1943;* Commanding General Second Marine Division (Staff), *Recommendations Based on Tarawa Operation, Number 4—Tanks*, p. 78.

211 Woodrum, conference with LtCol. Johnson, D-3, 2d MarDiv, and Maj. McCoy, Executive Officer, 2d Tank Bn, 30 November 1943.

212 Johnson–John Oberg questionnaire, (day not specified) March 2011.

213 Zeigler Hanz, http://generouspeople.blogspot.fr/2008/11/dick-sloat-american-

hero.html; and http://generouspeople.blogspot.fr/2012/06/puyallup-high-school-baccalaureate.html

214 Gilbert, *Marine Tank Battles In The Pacific*, p. 154–155.

215 Ibid, p. 164–165.

216 Ibid, p. 315; for a biography of Buckner and another account of his death see http://en.wikipedia.org/wiki/Simon_Bolivar_Buckner,_Jr.

217 Bale, interview with Cansiere and Gilbert, June 2013.

218 See for example Burrell, *The Ghosts of Iwo Jima.*

EPILOGUE

219 Estes, *Marines Under Armor*, p. 54.

APPENDIX A

220 Ibid, p. 60 and Gazel interview.

221 Ibid, p. 64.

222 Woolum's personal notes taken during the war.

223 *First Corps Tank Battalion War Diary*, month of September 1943.

APPENDIX C

224 *Muster Roll of officers and enlisted men of the U.S. Marine Corps, Company "C" First Corps Tank Battalion, Second Marine Division* (= roster of C Co. 1st Corps Medium Tank Battalion) from 16 September to 30 September 1943 inclusive.

225 *Roster of C Company 1st Corps Medium Tank Battalion* from 1st October to 6 October 1943 inclusive.

226 Woolum's personal notes taken during the war, and *1st Corps Medium Tank Battalion War Diary*, month of October 1943.

227 *1st Corps Medium Tank Battalion War Diary*, month of October 1943.

228 *Roster of the 2nd Tank Battalion*, from 1st November to 30 November 1943 inclusive.

229 USS *Ashland* ships log, www.ussashland.org

230 *Roster of the 2nd Tank Battalion*, from 1st November to 30 November 1943 inclusive, and USS *Ashland* ships log.

231 *Roster of the 2nd Tank Battalion*, from 1st December to 31 December 1943 inclusive.

232 Powers, *Replacement of tank personnel in combat*, 1 April 1943, p. 2.

233 Shaw et al, *Central Pacific Drive*, p. 351–352; Ushijima's statement is commonly attributed, including Gilbert, *Marine Tank Battles In The Pacific*, p. 14, but the original source is obscure.

APPENDIX E

234 Cheron, Philippe, et al, *19 août 1942, 4:50 A.M., Dieppe Operation Jubilee*, p. 106–107.

235 Brugioni, *Tarawa—A New Perspective.*

REFERENCES CITED

Unless otherwise noted, all National Archives and Records Administration (NARA) documents are retained in Record Group 127, NARA II, College Park MD. Synopses for several of the reports cited under *Reports of Battalion Commanders* can be viewed at the website Tarawa on the Web, listed under Internet Sources.

Alberti, Bruno and Laurent Pradier, *Uniformes et Equipement du Corps des Marines 1941–1945*, Histoire et Collections, Paris, 2008; also available in English translation as Albertiruno and Laurent Pradier, *USMC Uniforms and Equipment 1941–1945*, Casemate Publishing, Havertown PA.

Alexander, Joseph H., *Utmost Savagery*, Naval Institute Press, Annapolis MD, 2008.

_____, *Storm Landings*, Naval Institute Press, Annapolis MD, 1997.

Anonymous, USS *Ashland* ship's log, National Archives II, Record Group 80G.

_____, *Time Schedule Longsuit Operation*.

Bale, Edward L., *WW II Tank Leadership*, unpublished manuscript dated 2001. Draft copy provided by Ken Estes.

Brown, Dave, *2d Tanks Still In High Demand*, Follow Me (Second Marine Division Newsletter), July–August–September 2012, p. 11–16.

Brugioni, Dino, *Tarawa—A New Perspective*, Leatherneck Magazine, November 1983, p. 32–39, 78.

Bryk, Clarence, *Edward Bale oral history interview OH00251*. National Museum of the Pacific War, Fredericksburg, Texas.

Burrell, Robert S., *The Ghosts of Iwo Jima*, Texas A&M University Press, 2011.

Carlson, Evans F., *Report of observations on Galvanic operation*, 27 December 1943, Enclosure G.

Cheron, Philippe, Thierry Chion, and Olivier Richard, *19 août 1942, 4:50 A.M., Dieppe Operation Jubilee: le sacrifice des canadiens*, Petit à Petit, Darnetal (FRANCE), 2002.

Commanding General Second Marine Division (Staff), *Recommendations*

Based on Tarawa Operation, Number 4—Tanks, January 2 1944. (NARA)

Estes, Kenneth W., *Marines Under Armor,* Naval Institute Press, Annapolis, 2000.

_____, *US Marine Corps Tank Crewman 1941–1945,* Osprey Publishing, Oxford UK, 2005.

Gilbert, Oscar E., *Marine Tank Battles In The Pacific,* Combined Publishing, Conshohocken PA, 2001.

_____, *Marine Corps Tank Battles In The Middle East,* Casemate Publishing, Havertown PA, 2015.

Gilbert, Ed, *US Marine Corps Raider 1942–1943,* Osprey Publishing, Oxford UK, 2012.

Hunnicutt, R. P., *Sherman: A History of the American Medium Tank,* Presidio Press, Novato CA, 1978.

Isely, Jeter A., and Philip A. Crowl, *The U.S. Marines and Amphibious War,* Princeton University Press, Princeton NJ, 1951.

Johnson, Richard W., *600 Japanese Fall To Marine Tanks,* The Chevron (San Diego area newsletter), Volume 11, Number 49, 11 December 1943, p. 10. (Note: as a "morale-building" newsletter, much of the information should be viewed critically.)

Johnston [*sic,* Johnson], Richard W., *Crews in 2 tanks kill 600 Japs on Tarawa,* Buffalo Courier-Express, 5 December 1943; available online at http://fultonhistory.com/Newspapers%2021/Buffalo%20NY%20Courier%20Express/Buffalo%20NY%20Courier%20Express%201943/Buffalo%20NY%20Courier%20Express%201943%20-%208687.pdf

Joint Intelligence Center, Pacific Ocean Area, *JICPOA Translation Item #3616-A, B, C, D—Tarawa Organization Tables & Maps included in Gilbert Area Defense Force Opord #12–43, 8 December 1943.*

Mahan, Alfred Thayer, *The Influence of Sea Power Upon History,* 1975 reprint edition, Little, Brown, and Company New York, originally published 1890.

McClendon, William A., *Recollections Of War Times: By An Old Veteran While Under Stonewall Jackson And Lieutenant General James Longstreet; How I Got In And How I Got Out,* Paragon Press, Montgomery AL, 1909. (Carmichael song lyrics)

McCoy, Charles W., *Unit Report 2nd Tank Battalion, 26 November 1943,* handwritten document 261825. (NARA)

_____, *Report of Battalion Commanders, Second Tank Battalion, 22 December 1943.* (NARA)

_____, *Results of inspection of six medium tanks used in Tarawa operation, 6 January 1944.* (NARA)

McLean, Donald B., *Japanese Tanks, Tactics, & Antitank Weapons,* Normount Technical Publications, Wickenburg AZ, 1973. (Derived from Military Intelligence Division, *Japanese Tank and Antitank Warfare,* War Department Special Series No. 34, Washington DC 1945.)

Military Intelligence Division, *Japanese Tank and Antitank Warfare,* War Department Special Series No. 34, Washington DC 1945.

Millett, Allan R., *Semper Fidelis, The History of the United States Marine Corps,* MacMillian Publishing, New York, 1980.

Moran, Jim, *U. S. Marine Corps Uniforms and Equipment in World War 2,* Windrow & Greene, London, 1992.

Neiman, Robert M, and Kenneth W. Estes, *Tanks On The Beaches,* Texas A&M University Press, College Station, 2003.

Powers, B. G., *Replacement of tank personnel in combat, 1 April 1943.* (NARA)

_____, *Readiness report, 1st Corps Medium Tank Battalion, June 2 1943.* (NARA)

_____, *Replacement of tank personnel in combat, 18 June 1943.* (NARA)

_____, *Readiness report, 1st Corps Medium Tank Battalion, July 1 1943.* (NARA)

Reed, James C. Jr., *Report of Battalion Commanders, Second Battalion, 2nd Marines, 22 December 1943.* (NARA)

Rhay, Gary and Denver Collins, *Charles D. Mason Collection,* (AC/2001/5431), Veterans History Project, American Folklife Center, Library of Congress, Washington.

Russ, Martin, *Line of Departure: Tarawa,* Doubleday, Garden City NY, 1975.

Schmidt, H., *Replacement personnel for tanks, May 1 1943.* (NARA)

Second Marine Division, *Report of Galvanic Operation—Longsuit,* Box 3, Folder 14, Archives and Special Collections, Library of the Marine Corps, Quantico.

Shaffer, Samuel, *Relates Battle of Tarawa,* Big Spring Daily Herald, 28 December 1943, available online at newspaperarchive.com/big-spring-daily-herald/1943-12-28/ (Master Technical Sergeant Shaffer was a combat correspondent on Tarawa.)

Shaw, Henry I., Bernard C. Nalty, and Edwin T. Turnbladh, *Central Pacific Drive, History of U.S. Marine Corps Operations In World War II, Volume III*, Historical Branch, G-3 Division, Headquarters U. S. Marine Corps, Washington, 1966.

Sherrod, Robert, *Tarawa: The Second Day*, Marine Corps Gazette, vol. 57, no. 11, November 1973. (Excerpted from Sherrod's book *Tarawa: The Story of a Battle*.)

Shoup, David, *Memorandum for G-3, 5th PHIBCORPS, 19 December 1943*.

Staff, *Report of the Commander Transport Group to Commander Southern Attack Force*, 1 December 1943. (NARA)

Stewart, F. P. (?), *Unit Report 2nd Tank Battalion, 27 November 1943*, handwritten document 271803. (NARA) Note: signature of reporting officer partially illegible.

_____, *Unit Report 2nd Tank Battalion, 28 November 1943*, handwritten document 281805. (NARA)

Swango, M. F., *Assault On Tarawa*, Marine Corps Gazette, vol. 79, no. 11, 1995, p. 30–33.

Warth, Gary, *My Buddies Who Didn't Make It, They're The Heroes*, North County Times (San Diego County CA), 22 November 2003. Note: The North County Times is now part of the U-T San Diego newspaper (http://www.utsandiego.com)

White, Gordon Eliot, *Tubes, Transistors, and Takeovers*, AOPA Pilot Magazine, June 1984, p. 111–114. Available online at http://www.scr-274-n.info/GWAOPA.PDF

Wright, Derrick, *A Hell Of A Way To Die*, Windrow and Greene, London, 1996.

_____, and Howard Gerrard (illustrator), *Tarawa 1943—The Turning of the Tide*, Osprey Publishing, Cambridge UK, 2012.

Zurlinden, Pete, *The Attack On Tarawa*, Marine Corps Gazette, vol. 28, no. 1, January 1944, p. 7–13.

INTERNET SOURCES

Two websites with useful information are

www.tanksontarawa.com
http://www.tarawaontheweb.org/

THE FOLLOWING MATERIALS ARE ONLY AVAILABLE ONLINE
Bale, Ed, *Willy K's book and Two tanks,* http://disc.yourwebapps.com/ Indices/149620.html; Wed Oct 8, 2008 13:53
_____,http://disc.yourwebapps.com/discussion.cgi?disc=149620;article=1 3207;title=TarawaTalk;pagemark=450
_____, *China Gal Photo,* http://disc.yourwebapps.com/Indices/149620. html, Fri Mar 12, 2010 12:48
Hanz, Michael, *SCR-AE-183,* http://aafradio.org/flightdeck/1935/SCR-AE-183.html
_____, *The B-17: Backbone of the AAF,* http://aafradio.org/flightdeck/b17. htm
Wikipedia, *http://en.wikipedia.org/wiki/USS_Liscome_Bay_(CVE-56)*
Zeiger, Hans, *Dick Sloat, American Hero,* http://generouspeople.blogspot. com/2008/11/dick-sloat-american-hero.html